The Consolation of Rhetoric
John Henry Newman and
the Realism of Personalist Thought

David M. Whalen

The Consolation of Rhetoric
John Henry Newman and
the Realism of Personalist Thought

David M. Whalen

Catholic Scholars Press
San Francisco - London
1994

Library of Congress Cataloging-in-Publication Data

Whalen, David M.
    The consolation of rhetoric: John Henry Newman and the realism of
personalist thought / David M. Whalen
        257 p.   cm.
        Includes bibliographical references and index.
        ISBN 1-883255-10-4 (cloth): $59.95--ISBN 1-883255-03-1 (pbk.): $39.95
        1. Newman, John Henry, 1801-1890. 2. Newman, John Henry, 1801-
        1890--Style. I. Title.
BX4705.N5W45   1993
282'.092--dc
                                                    93-30247
                                                    CIP

Editorial Inquiries:
International Scholars Publications
P.O.Box 2590
San Francisco, CA 94126
(4150 397-9525

To order: (800) 99-AUSTIN

For James Gerard Bloch and David Walter Bloch
Et Lux perpetua luceat eis

Table of Contents

FOREWORD by Ralph McInerny   vii

PREFACE by Dennis Quinn   ix

ACKNOWLEDGMENTS   xi

I.   NEWMAN: PHILOSOPHER OR RHETORICIAN?   1

II.   RHETORICAL KNOWLEDGE AND ARISTOTLE   17

III.   NEWMAN'S PURPOSIVE RHETORIC   31

IV.   RHETORICAL PERSONALISM   51

V.   INTELLECTUAL ANTECEDENTS:
        RHETORICAL DISCOURSE IN
        THE PATRISTIC AND MEDIEVAL ERAS   73

VI.   INTELLECTUAL ANTECEDENTS:
        RHETORICAL LOGIC AND
        DE-PERSONALIZED THOUGHT   87

VII.   INTELLECTUAL ANTECEDENTS:
        PHILOSOPHICAL ROOTS,
        MECHANISTIC BRANCHES   105

VIII.   NEWMAN'S *PHILOSOPHICAL NOTEBOOK*   129

IX.   NEWMAN'S *GRAMMAR OF ASSENT*   161

X.   THE *GRAMMAR* AND RHETORICAL KNOWLEDGE   191

XI.   NEWMAN AND RHETORICAL REALISM   205

        NOTES   227

        BIBLIOGRAPHY   247

        INDEX   251

FOREWORD

Joseph Conrad's Mister Kurtz in *Heart of Darkness* had a work to do in Africa, a chain of stations along the river leading into the heart of darkness. "Each station should be like a beacon on the road towards better things, a centre for trade of course, but also for humanizing, improving, instructing." Kurtz creates havoc instead, dehumanizing and manipulating the natives, and then falling victim to his own efforts. His life was a "mysterious arrangement of merciless logic for a futile purpose." It is fitting that T. S. Eliot took a line from this story as one of the mottos of *The Wasteland*: "Mistah Kurtz, he dead."

To recall this puts me in mind of Newman, recovering from an illness then sailing home from Sicily in the conviction that there was a work for him to do in England. "The Tamworth Reading Room" tells us what Newman thought of projects like that of the futile Kurtz, but what was the work that Newman himself had to do?

By and large, Newman was an occasional writer. Few of his books were planned just as such, though of course some were, notably *Grammar of Assent*, but most, like the magnificent *Apologia pro vita sua*, only happened, because of some contingent event to which Newman responded. There are sermons, poems, prayers, essays, and letters, amazing on the scale of his own time but all but unintelligible in the age of the telephone, evanescent E-mail and the fragile FAX, a facsimile of an original seldom seen. Is Newman's massive literary output just a hodgepodge, or is there some unifying purpose to it all, one that can help us understand the work he had to do in England?

David Whalen approaches this very broad question through a narrow door, an analysis that concentrates on Newman's most philosophical writings, the *Notebook* and the *Grammar*. He does this to question what has been made of these works. Is Newman a philosopher? And if so, is he a good or bad one? It is easy to find proponents of either answer. But is it a good question? What if it is wrong, or at least less helpful, to respond to these seemingly philosophical works as philosophical?

There have been appraisals of Newman as a Thomist, good or bad. What distinguishes the book you are about to read is that, from a Thomistic perspective, it suggests that we will catch the true meaning of Newman only if we regard him as a rhetorician. Rhetoric is not to be taken pejoratively, as in "mere rhetoric." Whalen recalls for us the nobility of this art and its range, encompassing as it can all subject matters, treating them in a distinctive way. The interpretation is Thomistic but it makes no claim that Newman was a Thomist. I think it is one of the most helpful studies of Newman to appear in a good long while. In its kindly light we discern better the nature of Newman's specific work.

The work he had to do in England turned out to have far wider relevance. The work he did in the 19th century has survived into our own and promises to go on serving readers of good will. Leo XIII, the pope who initiated the Thomistic revival with *Aeterni Patris* was also the pope who created John Henry Newman a cardinal. It is altogether fitting that an interpretation animated by a Thomistic understanding of rhetoric enables us to understand the peculiar power of this extraordinary and saintly thinker. Nor is one surprised to find several references to Newman in John Paul II's *Veritatis Splendor*. Mistah Newman, he lives.

Ralph McInerny
*Michael P. Grace Professor
of Medieval Studies
University of Notre Dame*

PREFACE

Rhetoric has fallen on hard times. One often hears statements dismissed as "just" or "only" or "mere" rhetoric, that is, words that deceive and mislead while giving the appearance of truth. Such popular disparagement arises immediately from the abuse of rhetoric in advertising, public relations, "hype," and degraded politics. These corruptions have been aggravated by a stupefying increase in the "media," and to make matters still worse, rhetoric has invaded new territory. Education, art, and theology have been rhetoricized. Even popular entertainment has become increasingly rhetorical, incessantly attempting to persuade us to adopt or oppose some social, political, or ethical "agenda." It is not surprising that a leading school of criticism has declared all human communication to be rhetorical. This elevation of one mode of discourse to totalitarian supremacy has deprived it of all credibility.

The power of the word and the dangers of its misuse have always been acknowledged. Socrates' radical critique in the *Gorgias* has seemed to many to be a complete repudiation of rhetoric, while others have concluded that Socrates meant only to discredit the Sophists who sought to dominate education in the time of Plato and Aristotle. The greatest of Roman orators, Cicero, began his defense of his art with a consideration of the dangers of eloquence. The Renaissance of the 15th and 16th centuries was as much a rebirth of Roman rhetoric as of humanistic learning.

Wherever true rhetoric has flourished, it has done so on the Aristotelian principle that the object of rhetoric is the truth. Roman Cato put the matter bluntly: *Rem tene, verba sequentur*--Seize the thing, the words will follow. Words serve the real, the *res*, the Latin root of our reality. The grasp of things even inspires the words, for the truth is itself generative of eloquence. The English poet, Ben Jonson, makes the point: "The order of God's creatures in themselves is not only admirable and glorious, but eloquent: then he who could apprehend the consequence of things in their truth, and utter his apprehensions as truly, were the best writer and speaker." This is the crux in distinguishing true eloquence from sophistry, for the object of the latter is power, not truth, and since the Renaissance, skepticism of various kinds has dominated philosophy.

A distinguished contemporary historian of philosophy towards the end of his career wrote, "All truths are humanly stated truths, and as such are neither final nor certain." It is hard to imagine that a man of such learning and intelligence could utter such an obvious and utterly self-contradictory statement, for he simultaneously asserts that what he says is certainly and finally true and that, since the truth he asserts is expressed in human language, it cannot be true.

Assertions of this kind--many of them more radical and even nihilistic denials of any reality whatever--have become modern commonplaces, especially in the academy, where skepticism has always found a home. It is not surprising then that "empowerment" has become a fashionable watchword. The old Baconian motto, "Knowledge is power" I recently found emblazoned across a poster advertising a university-sponsored public lecture. Similarly, Compton's Encyclopedia presents itself as "bringing the power of knowledge to people everywhere"; but such slogans leave unanswered the questions, Power for what? Knowledge of what? Dare anyone say power for good, knowledge of truth? Or, to go still further, dare anyone say, as did Newman, that knowledge must, above all, be sought for its own sake?

The late British philosopher C. E. M. Joad defined decadence as loss of the end or substitution of means for ends. When one has art for art's sake there is artistic decadence; when money becomes an end, there is economic decadence; power as an end brings political decadence, and pleasure as an end moral decadence.

There really is a phenomenon called *fin de siècle*. Cardinal Newman anticipated it in the 19th century and now with the *fin de millennium* in the not too rosy offing David Whalen has provided an apology for the healthy rhetoric that was Newman's most potent weapon in the wars of truth. Nothing could be more timely.

Dennis Quinn
Professor of English
University of Kansas

ACKNOWLEDGEMENTS

As this study was originally written as my doctoral dissertation in English for the University of Kansas, several people deserve thanks for their close and ready help in every stage of its development. Professors Dennis B. Quinn, Max Keith Sutton, Donald F. Warders, James K. Woelfel and Bernard A. Hirsch were an enthusiastic and most helpful committee of readers. They each made great efforts to assist the work, sometimes under extraordinary circumstances. I am also indebted to the late Professor Stephen Goldman, who, though he did not see the completion of this project, contributed much to it in his interest and expertise. The Kansas Regents, through the Pearson Scholarship, and the University of Birmingham, England, through its exchange scholarship, made possible a fruitful and delightful year of research in England. I am particularly grateful to the Fathers of the Birmingham Oratory and Gerard Tracey, Oratory Archivist, for their generous hospitality and profound knowledge of Newman and his library. Thanks are due also to Professor Charles Whitworth and the Shakespeare Institute, both of the University of Birmingham. Hester Williams deserves much credit for timely typing and running down recalcitrant bibliographic data, while Professor Janette Hodge and Simon Donoghue of Belmont Abbey College have lent me their expertise by critically reading the manuscript. Ralph McInerny, Michael P. Grace Professor of Medieval Studies at the University of Notre Dame was encouraging and generously agreed to supply the Foreword to this book. I must, in particular, give special thanks to Professors Dennis Quinn, Frank Nelick, and John Senior, teachers in the Newman tradition, who have been friends and transmitters of the larger vision out of which this work comes. I am also grateful, of course, to my long-suffering children for their patience and sacrifice. Saving the best for last, I am indebted beyond any measure to my wife, Janet. No words can do her justice for her part in this or in anything of mine.

I. Newman: Philosopher Or Rhetorician?

> *[W]hen he speaks,*
> *The air, a chartered libertine, is still,*
> *And the mute wonder lurketh in men's ears,*
> *To steal his sweet and honeyed sentences.*
> Henry V I, i.

ALL OF A PIECE

In 1842, Oxford witnessed a meeting between two men long known to be religious and educational opponents. John Henry Newman, the Tractarian, Oxford Movement leader and apologist for patristic and Catholic understandings of religious dogma, was to entertain his great adversary, Dr. Thomas Arnold of Rugby. For nearly ten years the two notables had sparred and wrestled in writing; Newman thought that Arnold's non-dogmatic moralism was unscriptural and generally unsound, while Arnold was convinced that Newman (as head of the "Oxford Malignants") was an unscrupulous provocateur, a reactionary conservative, and a dangerous manipulator of words. The occasion of their meeting was Arnold's appointment as Regius Professor of Modern History and his subsequent lectures at Oxford. Arnold was invited to Oriel's Gaudy-day dinner, and Newman was surprised to learn that as Senior Fellow, he must attend the dinner and entertain the guest. His task of entertaining Arnold was to be shared by the staunchly anti-Tractarian Oriel Provost, Edward Hawkins, and the threesome promised to be an awkward head table indeed. Newman was half amused at the prospect, aware of the tension and unease that would permeate the room. However, in the actual event, Newman's manner betrayed none of that tension. He was "simple, innocent, and modest," displaying none of the frosty or prickly reserve of the Provost.[1] The Tractarian conversed naturally and steadily; betraying no anxiety, he eased tensions and put his guest at rest largely by keeping to many "safe" subjects of interest. As people watched, no doubt with some surprise, Newman and Arnold warmed, conversed easily, and left the stiff Provost to content himself with his icy demeanor.

This is not to say that the two men became friends, nor even that there was no verbal "play" with regard to their differences. Newman's first remark to Arnold was a gentle tease, reminding the school-master that they had met once before in a divinity school disputation. The tease was in the fact that Arnold had not been able to find anyone to dispute with, and Newman had done him the favor of volunteering. But the two men did get along, even disapproving together when a third party chanced an irreverent remark.

"At last the Provost and Arnold rose up to go, and I held out my hand," recalled Newman, "which he took, and we parted."[2] Biographer Meriol Trevor recounts how Newman was later told that Arnold was surprised to find the Tractarian "not what he fancied." Somewhat embarrassed by his own impression of the meeting, Arnold would only say in reference to it that "it would not do to meet Newman often."[3] Hardly concealing her own pleasure in the incident, Trevor adds that Newman was always able to "get his professed enemies to shake hands once they had met him."[4]

Incidents like this--and Newman's biography is well-stocked with them--do more than indicate Newman's ability to be a personable and engaging companion. Rather like Samuel Johnson's character-revealing biography, the story of Newman's life consists primarily of impressions, conversations, and personalities.[5] The biographies provide anecdotes of personality reacting to personality, manner bridging difficulties, and thought overcoming prejudice. The meeting with Arnold is an example--manner and personal intimacy overcame hostility. An even larger, more general instance of the same is seen in the famous story of Newman's *Apologia*; here again, Newman exhibited a unique power of transforming controversy into a kind of consensus, primarily through the communication of his character and personality.[6] Quite simply, Newman had an unusual ability to make himself known and respected. Though he was a very private man, and in many instances a cold and unapproachable one, his acquaintances almost always had a favorable impression of him.

What is most remarkable, however, is that the impression Newman created was always the same. Whether Newman was dealing with a hostile Arnold or an amicable William Froude, a sophisticated Gladstone or an ill-educated Irish parishioner, he was always the same man. There seemed to be no Newman the scholar, Newman the dinner host, Newman the administrator, Newman the friend; he was all of a piece. The editor of Newman's Oratorian papers, Placid Murray, attests to an "intimate continuity and identity which make the Vicar of St. Mary's, the Father of the Oratory and the Cardinal of the Roman Church into one and the same man."[7] Unlike the fractured consciousnesses and personalities so appealing to twentieth-century novelists and artists, Newman seemed in many ways an uncomplicated man, a simple man.[8] It is odd, then, that the thought and writings of this man should be so varied in genre and application. Newman has been called a philosopher, a theologian, a poet, an historian, an orator and a keen spiritual writer.[9] In fact, his texts are so rich that they seem difficult to identify according to category. Though it is true that Newman's thought is highly complicated and that his copious writings did take various forms (from poetry to articles on logic), the same unity his contemporaries saw in his character can be found in the texts. The feature of mind that allowed Newman to convince staunch opponents of his personal integrity (and often of his own convictions as well) was the same feature of mind at work throughout his writings.

This study aims at identifying that feature as being primarily rhetorical in genesis and execution. I will maintain that Newman's mind was so profoundly rhetorical, that rhetorical modes of reasoning dominated his thought about virtually any subject throughout his life. Discussing Newman's place in the nineteenth century, David J. DeLaura alludes to this rhetorical feature; "Newman's role was that of the supremely adequate nineteenth-century apologist of orthodoxy in terms comprehensible to his contemporaries."[10] The fact that Newman was a masterful rhetorician is by no means unrecognized yet has been strangely unexplored, as Martin Svaglic notes in his survey of Newman's rhetorical and stylistic critics.[11] Prominent among rhetorical studies are Walter Houghton's *Art of Newman's "Apologia"* and John Holloway's *Victorian Sage*--though even these are limited to studying primarily the actual practice of Newman's rhetorical art.[12] Excluding specific criticism of the *Apologia*, Svaglic's thorough survey of rhetorical commentary and criticism totals a scant three pages, and many of these works tend to be commentaries of "warm appreciation" rather than detailed critical studies.[13] When compared to C. S. Dessain's far more compressed and highly specialized survey of "French Fantasy and German Understanding" in the same Newman study (which also runs to three pages), the pattern is clear: though many may speak of Newman as a rhetorician, few have actively considered what that means.

In fact, Newman has received far more attention as a theologian and philosopher than as a literary artist. The philosophical and theological listings in bibliographies of Newman secondary studies dwarf the listings of literary studies. Ian Ker describes the phenomenon in emphatic terms: Newman's "literary achievement is still not only underrated but also to a considerable extent unperceived."[14] In many respects this is understandable, for some of Newman's most important works (notably, the *Grammar of Assent*) discourage conventional literary study. Newman's stylistic devices as well as the specific rhetorical appeals made to his audience have received literary attention, and such studies have duly--if incompletely--revealed much about Newman the practitioner of rhetorical art. It is Newman the rhetorician in the large sense, the global, "pan-textual" and cognitive sense that has until very recently gone unexplored, perhaps because of the difficulty of looking at such "philosophical" texts as the *Grammar of Assent* in a rhetorical light. It seems difficult to see any connection between such rhetorical matters as forensic, epideictic, and deliberative discourse, pathetic, rational, and character-oriented appeals to Newman's exploration of the illative sense or his exposition of notional versus real understanding. But this is precisely what is necessary if Newman as a rhetorician is to be understood in any comprehensive, integrated fashion. If Newman was more than a man of thought who, by the by, was also quite adept at the persuasive use of language, then there must be some common ground between the St. Mary's preacher's lucent evocations of the eternal and the theorist's compelling analysis of modes of apprehension.

A proper understanding of Newman as a rhetorician is only possible if a *philosophy* of rhetoric is established that can rise above technique and trope and grasp the kinds of thought and apprehension proper to rhetorical modes of communication. The integral unity in Newman's work calls for a rhetorical study reaching beyond conventional treatments of Newman; instead, "rhetoric" must be studied in such a way as to often touch philosophical and epistemological matters. In a sense, then, a Newman "rhetorical study" must treat modes of knowledge and discourse not traditionally thought of as bearing upon rhetoric.

Until quite recently, there existed no substantial attempt at delineating the rhetorical superstructure integrating Newman's thought; rhetoric in Newman was considered a largely verbal skill, seen only in application to specific circumstances and persuasive occasions. Walter Jost's *Rhetorical Thought in John Henry Newman* (1989) is a landmark text in being the first to attempt a radically rhetorical synthesis of Newman's thought. It seeks "a comprehensive view of a complex whole," in order to integrate the various features and qualities in Newman's texts beneath a rhetorical superstructure.[15] Jost observes that "Newman's intellectual stance is thoroughly and persistently rhetorical. . . . [H]e systematically operated with rhetorical principles and methods of inquiry, argument, interpretation, and judgment. He aimed, in fact, at a rhetorical ideal of mind. . . ."[16] In many respects Jost's aims are similar to the goals of this study: to demonstrate the essentially rhetorical habit of mind[17] that consistently permeates Newman's works, and to understand that rhetorical habit as concerning the acquisition of knowledge and personal means of apprehension. As will be seen, however, there are significant differences of principle between Jost's efforts and those embodied here. Jost attempts to align Newman's epistemological writings with the twentieth-century school of "epistemic" rhetoricians represented by Kenneth Burke, Richard McKeon, George Campbell, Stanley Fish, Nicholas Lash, Chaim Perelman and Steven Toulmin. As contemporary epistemic rhetorical theorists differ on many points (most important to Jost is the opposition of Kenneth Burke's radical relativism to Richard McKeon's truth-as-intersubjectivity[18]), such an alignment is complicated and elaborate. Yet the common thread Jost follows through the various theorists concerns how the human intellect deals with an uncertain reality and the means by which certainties and "truths" are lifted out of "relative indeterminacies." As I shall show, the philosophical result is Jost's radical absorption into rhetoric of all modes of knowledge and expression. The distinct differentia among the sciences propounded by Aristotle assume a merely nominal character as the very nature of "reason" becomes equivalent to "rhetoric." The result, for the study of Newman, is to suspend his thought upon the twin horns of epistemic, moderate relativism: certainty without determinacy, truth without demonstrability.

Such an approach to Newman seems to undermine the very real epistemic force of his mind and writings. Thus, while the aim of this study is similar to Jost's, the understanding of terms as fundamental as "rhetoric" and "truth" is different, and the means used to explore Newman as a rhetorician are different as well. Here, an essentially Aristotelian/Thomistic understanding of rhetoric, philosophy, and metaphysics will be employed to delineate the rhetorical nature of Newman's thought. And as my later, more detailed exploration of Jost's text will show, the principles he seeks to locate in Newman's thought are actually incompatible with that thought.

PHILOSOPHICAL APPROPRIATION

The difficulty in focusing on Newman's intellectual principles is that they are diffuse and non-systematic in expression. Indeed, this is part of the reason for regarding Newman essentially as a rhetorician; the rhetorician, as Aristotle notes, does not necessarily argue from systematic bases.[19] It is also part of the reason for approaching rhetoric in Newman as a habit of mind rather than a systematic activity.[20] Philosophically, Newman was rather eclectic; his sympathies and affections ranged from Bacon and Locke to Aristotle and the Scottish commonsense school represented by Reid. This accounts for the difficulty in predicating of Newman a particular philosophical system, much less a method. Even in his own day, as Edward Sillem notes, "It is an undeniable fact that Newman did stand well aside, and that he intended to stand well aside and avoid playing any part in the philosophical movements during the nineteenth century. . . ."[21] "Newman belongs to no school," says J. H. Walgrave, "In the history of philosophy and theology, he appears as a great 'outsider'"[22] This is not to say that Newman lacks essential philosophical/intellectual principles, or that such principles need not be accounted for. The danger in treating such principles, however, is the temptation to shoehorn Newman into a particular philosophical school of thought.

While I will argue that, from an Aristotelian and Thomistic standpoint, Newman employs rhetorical modes of cognition, it would be wildly inaccurate to claim he was a "Thomist." Newman is no "closet" Thomist in the way that Jost's epistemic rhetorical analysis renders Newman a pre-Burke Burkean, or a pre-McKeon McKeonite; nor did Newman unconsciously stumble upon a Thomistic philosophical basis for his literary and theoretical work. No such claims to philosophical rigor can be made for Newman. And yet, philosophical renderings of Newman abound. While "Philosophers, more than any other class of persons, invariably find that their first reading of Newman is at least disconcerting," this has not prevented them from appropriating Newman's thought to some systematic school.[23] As editor of Newman's *Philosophical Notebook,* Sillem cautions against such an appropriation:

> With the best of intentions certain scholastic writers are often inclined to force Newman's ideas into the alien dimensions of their own systems, making apologies for his failure to understand their system. . . . Need we, then, be altogether surprised that some scholastic writers have concluded that Newman is, after all, neither a theologian nor a philosopher in any acceptable sense of the terms. . . .[24]

Yet, as a philosopher himself, Sillem feels the need to justify Newman on a philosophical level. While decrying attempts by scholastic philosophers to appropriate Newman, Sillem reveals a critical disregard for the intellectual integrity and potential of rhetoric. Those who regard Newman as primarily a literary (or rhetorical) author are brushed aside with scorn: "This way of dealing with Newman can now be passed by in silence."[25] Sillem ignores the possibility that Newman's universally acclaimed rhetorical skill indicates a deep and intellectually rigorous but rhetorical operation of mind upon matters of all sorts, including philosophical ones. The "respectability" of rhetoric as an intellectual discipline does not occur to Sillem (and he is merely representative of a host of philosophical and theological critics) primarily because he still conceives it as regarding merely "style." It is substance such critics are after, and substance is philosophy.

For much of this century, critical, philosophical reading of Newman has fallen into two broad but recognizable categories. First, there are those who regard Newman as "the herald of skepticism, subjectivism, relativism and sophistry."[26] Harold Weatherby--writing from a Thomistic perspective--has been highly critical of Newman in just this regard. With respect to the nineteenth-century's "subjectivism, individualism, and relativism which constitute the lineaments of modern thought," Weatherby says Newman "chose to make terms."[27] In this, "Newman's peculiar achievement may prove in the long run his peculiar failure; namely, that he did not set his face resolutely against the whole course of modern thought."[28] The other broad category includes those who, like Sillem, A.J. Boekraad, Walgrave and others, regard Newman as a proto-phenomenologist. These critics wed psychology to philosophy, and in doing so, often come teasingly close to locating Newman's thought in the rhetorical mode. According to A.J. Boekraad, Newman "carries the characteristics of phenomenology so naturally that we feel that in him it was in no way based on a programme, but was a kind of temper or principle of argumentation."[29] Nevertheless, Newman's "phenomenology" is presented by such authors as distinctly philosophical. This would seem to bear out Weatherby's assertion, for implicit in the phenomenological school is a radical interiority which isolates the intellect and "brackets" exterior reality. The radical interiority of phenomenology does indeed make it the "herald of subjectivism" and ultimately of solipsism as well. The efforts of Edmund Husserl, founder of phenomenology, to attain a reasoned basis for knowledge of truth (and even of material reality) were doomed to failure, as shown by A.D. Nuttall, precisely because of the principles of the philosophy itself.[30] If, then, Newman did establish an early form of phenomenological system, Weatherby's critique would appear to be sound. But Newman makes a problematic phenomenologist at best, for at the very heart of phenomenology proper is Husserl's denial of causation as the genuine object of philosophical study. Newman always maintained, with Aristotle, that the study of causes is the very essence of philosophy. So deep a division of principle must not be lightly brushed aside.[31]

Though the "Newman-as-skeptic" and the "Newman-as-phenomenologist" camps are opposed in method and viewpoint, they are similar in that they attempt to align Newman with particular philosophical schools. Whether radical relativist or proto-phenomenologist, Newman is deemed intellectually important because of his "philosophy." This, I suggest, is essentially a misappropriation of Newman's thought. Not only is Newman's philosophical eclecticism well documented in biography, but as Dwight Culler notes, his use of terms (even in his "technical" works) is non-systematic, inconsistent, and variable.[32] Although intellectual eclecticism was a common feature of the day, the variety of philosophical influences upon Newman is striking. He was steeped in Aristotle, the Oxford Noetics, the Platonic Church Fathers, Francis Bacon, and John Locke, and he was familiar with Paley, Reid, Perrone and St. Thomas Aquinas.[33] The biographies of Newman display him as actively assimilating the thought surrounding him, sometimes with attraction, sometimes with repulsion, but always with interest. To appropriate such a man into a philosophical school, even if it be as broad and philosophically indeterminate as phenomenology, seems fraught with danger.

RHETORICAL DISPOSITIONS

In large measure, Newman resists philosophical classification because his intellectual habits were formed primarily in reading the often brilliant but multifarious Church Fathers. Saints John Chrysostom, Athanasius, Cyril of Jerusalem, and Basil, among others, opened for Newman what he liked to call "a view." Virtually all subsequent reading was, as it were, through the spectacles of the Fathers. Indeed, more than merely formative, the Fathers were naturally congenial to Newman's temperament and inclinations. He possessed the disconcerting habit of thinking associatively about matters which a burgeoning scientific revolution normally treated mechanically. The patristic mode of discourse--speculative, wide-ranging, combining natural science, revelation, and symbolism--was also Newman's mode. Even in the catechetical lectures of Saint Cyril one finds the same combination of "information" and affective, purposive elements so frequently mixed in Newman. The lectures exhibit a blend of theological exposition, exhortation, and poetic, appreciative outburst. Audiences left such a catechetical lecture not merely informed of the doctrines of this new faith, but moved by their beauty, resolute in moral action, and aware of untold riches in further learning.

The parallel to Newman is clear. His *Discourses before Mixed Congregations* ambled freely from doctrine to observations of contemporary English psychology, from logical argumentation to poetic speculation. Even the St. Mary's sermons partook of a free and broad-ranging character reminiscent of the Fathers. Principle Shairp wrote of these sermons:

> Here was no vehemence, no declamation, no show of elaborated argument, so that one who came prepared to hear a "great intellectual effort" was almost sure to go away disappointed. . . . The look and bearing of the preacher were as of one who dwelt apart, who, though he knew his age well, did not live in it. From the seclusion of study, and abstinence, and prayer, from habitual dwelling in the unseen, he seemed to come forth that one day of the week to speak to others of the things he had seen and known. Those who never heard him might fancy that his sermons would generally be about apostolical succession or rights of the Church or against Dissenters. Nothing of the kind. You might hear him preach for weeks without an allusion to these things. . . . His power showed itself chiefly in the new and unlooked-for way in which he touched into life old truths, moral or spiritual, which all Christians acknowledge, but most have ceased to feel. . . . He laid his finger--how gently, yet how powerfully!--on some inner place in the hearer's heart, and told him things about himself he had never known till then. Subtlest truths, which it would have taken philosophers pages of circumlocution and big words to state, were dropt out by the way in a sentence or two of the most transparent Saxon. What delicacy of style, yet what calm power! how gentle, yet how strong! how simple, yet how suggestive! how homely, yet how refined! . . .[34]

This enthusiasm, it should be noted, is that of a man at sharp theological and ecclesiastical odds with Newman. He mentions the odd conjunction of opposites such as gentleness and power, knowledge of the times and retirement, philosophical truths and brief, "transparent Saxon." This distinctive combination of features is typical of Newman--one sees it everywhere: *Discourses Before Mixed Congregations, Present Position of Catholics in England, Idea of a University.* Newman freely moves from logical deduction, to historical precedent, to sympathetic appeals for broadness of comprehension.

The rhetorical utility of such movement in matter and style reveals another aspect of Newman's rhetorical habit of mind, but I mention these features here for their patristic quality. In fact, an entire study could be devoted to the highly rhetorical character of patristic theology itself. This is not to say, as does Jost, that theology *is* rhetoric,[35] or as Stanley Fish insists, that *everything* is rhetoric "all down the line."[36] Rather, the theology in much of the Fathers (as in Newman) is occasioned by a pressing controversial need such that the persuasive thrust of the discourse overwhelms the formal argumentation of theology. It is a theological rhetoric, rhetoric being the substratum upon which theology is erected, explored, and enunciated in order to advance the cause of orthodoxy in the face of a heterodox threat.[37] As Aristotle maintains in the *Rhetoric*, rhetoric is open to any class of subject with which to operate.[38]

This is in definite contrast to the theology of Aquinas. The mode of discourse in this theology (and philosophy) is highly logical, formal and deductive. The famous controversial method of the medieval schools, preserved in the scholastic, Thomistic method of presentation, is not so much rhetorical "argument" as a form for distinguishing logical errors or drawing out incipient contradictions. Though, as will be seen, the means of presentation also carries a highly verbal, personal valence, it is no secret that the arguments are dauntingly strict and often uninviting to contemporary minds. Such argument is not "argument" in the purely rhetorical sense (unless, like the epistemic rhetoricians, one equates every form of utterance with argument or persuasion). When Aristotle argues with Plato about ideal forms versus subsistent natures, he would hardly consider the argument a rhetorical one.

Likewise, the difference between the theological rhetoric of the Fathers (and Newman) and the systematic theology of the schoolmen is virtually self-evident. Newman was never attracted to the mode of argument employed by Aquinas, much as he avowed the value of the Angelic Doctor's works. Newman's sympathy and habitual mode of thought was too patristic to be "threatened" by scholasticism. As Sillem says, in the absence of actual training in Thomistic thought, Newman "consulted [the scholastics] as authorities, to be assured that what he had reasoned out for himself was in accordance with the mind of theologians whom he knew to have the approval of the Church. . . ."[39]

With regard to philosophy in general, it seems the best description of Newman is that he was a student, a *discipulus* of philosophy. This turns in large part upon a matter of definition, but it is crucial nonetheless. If "philosophy" is understood in an Aristotelian/Thomistic context as being a systematic analysis of matters according to principles and causes, specifically as regards the universals of human knowledge, then Newman is more of a student than a master. Certainly he did engage in a great deal of active philosophical speculation, much of it concerning specific themes (logic, demonstration, metaphysics) during the whole course of his life. He even set out to write a book on philosophical subjects, the closest approximation to which is his *Grammar of Assent*. But Newman never thought of himself as a philosopher, and his thought is weakest and most patchy when it is most philosophical. When writing the *Grammar*, he was extremely aware that he was approaching subjects far more "technical" than was his wont. As a safeguard he enlisted the editorial assistance of Dr. Charles Meynell, a Professor of Philosophy at Oscott, to whom Newman wrote:

> Your experienced eye will see if I have run into any language which offends against doctrinal propriety or common sense. I am not certain that you will not suddenly light on a wasp-nest, though I have no suspicion of it--but when a matter has not been one's study it is difficult to have confidence in oneself.[40]

Indeed, when it comes to metaphysics Newman openly avows: ". . . I am deeply conscious of my own ignorance on the whole matter, and it sometimes annoys me that I have ventured to write on a subject which is even accidentally connected with it."[41] Considering the breadth of Newman's reading, his ignorance may well be another man's wisdom; nevertheless, it seems justified to take him at his word, here, for Dr. Meynell found himself perplexed, confused, and largely inadequate to "censor" a text temptingly philosophical but exceedingly elusive.[42] As a close reading of the *Grammar* will show, even at his most philosophical Newman's speculation rarely exceeds a tentative, descriptive statement of things. Likewise, his independence from "schools" of thought indicates not merely a vast synthetic habit of thought, but a genuine disinclination to follow up the principles of the various schools for their own sake. He developed habits of mind and views with philosophical significance (his "Platonism"), but he was too eclectic to be framed within a specific theoretical outlook. Newman was interested in all fields of inquiry; at Oxford he studied chemistry and the new geology as well as subjects in the standard curriculum. He was willing to accept anything he recognized as true from whatever source. While it is sometimes claimed that had circumstances allowed, Newman would have worked out a formal philosophical system, it is doubtful he would have been any more systematic than interested "amateurs" like Coleridge or Sir Joshua Reynolds.

ARISTOTLE, AQUINAS, AND NEWMAN

Why or to what extent, then, is an Aristotelian and Thomistic reading of Newman valuable? What can be learned of Newman from reading him in this way? Is this not yet another attempt at casting Newman into a system not his own? The answer to these questions is crucial, but it is helpful first to note just what relation Newman had with the two philosophers whose thought informs this study. Just what role did Aristotle and Aquinas play in Newman's intellectual life? The one philosopher who unquestionably exerted the greatest influence upon Newman was the original "peripatetic" himself:

> While we are men, we cannot help, to a great extent, being Aristotelians, for the great master does but analyze the thoughts, feelings, views, and opinions of human kind. He told us the meaning of our own words and ideas, before we were born. In many subject-matters to think correctly, is to think like Aristotle, and we are his disciples whether we will or no, though we may not know it.[43]

These are the words of a mature Newman speaking before an audience of (largely) Irish Catholics perplexed by the controversial issue of religiously mixed university education. His praise of Aristotle is broad, measured, and sincere. A less measured estimation of Aristotle occurs in Newman's own Greek and Latin text of the *Nicomachean Ethics*. On the blank page facing book 10, chapter 8, where Aristotle discusses reason, the gods, happiness, and the divine happiness of the philosopher, a much younger but no less enthusiastic Newman wrote for his own eyes, "Can the finest ornaments of language produce anything so exquisitely beautiful as the chaste simplicity of Aristotle when engaged on sublime subjects! It shows that ornament of style [then, somewhat comically, Newman adds] Oh."[44] He expressed similar sentiments earlier in the text when Aristotle characterizes the bad man as "not . . . amicably disposed even to himself." Newman scribbled on the facing page, "How very beautiful is the austere simplicity yet vivid majesty of this passage."[45] Newman's remarks here are engaging, but notice how they highlight the rhetorical qualities of Aristotle's comments. Although the Victorian clearly understands the Greek's meaning, he is drawn by the "majesty," and style of "the philosopher."

Not only did Newman closely read Aristotle's *Rhetoric*, *Nicomachean Ethics*, *Poetics*, and *Posterior Analytics* as a student at Oxford, but as a tutor he taught extensively from them as well.[46] His mentor and colleague Richard Whately introduced Newman to the subtleties of logic (largely Aristotelian) which Newman so far mastered as to be called upon by Whately to assist in writing an article on logic for Coleridge's *Encyclopedia Metropolitana*. Despite famous statements in the *Grammar of Assent* as to the aridity of philosophical demonstration and the fragility of logic, it is universally understood that Aristotle's place in Newman's philosophical imagination was second to none. Sillem places Aristotle first in his list of sources for Newman, and Culler identifies entire sections of the architectonic *Idea of a University* as rooted in Aristotle's division of sciences.[47] The superabundant references to Aristotle in Newman's published works and the copious marginalia in Newman's texts of the philosopher confirm what no one familiar with early nineteenth-century Oxford would deny: Aristotle was the keystone and touchstone of formal reasoning.

While Aristotle is at the head of Sillem's list of Newman's sources, St. Thomas Aquinas is at the foot. Sillem states that this ordering is of no significance, but he does maintain that Aquinas had little influence on Newman.[48] Compared to Aristotle, certainly, Newman's exposure to and study of Aquinas was limited. This was not for want of effort on Newman's part. As his letters illustrate, Newman was more than merely "curious" about the thought of Aquinas. Aside from being naturally interested in such a notable Catholic theologian, Newman was also aware that the pagan Aristotle was most aptly supplemented in Aquinas. No one had so delicately added Christian principles to the pagan philosopher as had Aquinas, bringing to full fruition the partial vision of the Greek.

Upon his conversion to Catholicism, Newman went to Rome to pursue studies and discern his "niche" in the Roman Catholic Church. His philosophical and theoretical interests were quite strong at the time (He had just finished his *Development of Christian Doctrine*), and he desired to pursue studies in speculative theology. He was even attracted to the philosophically inclined Dominican order. Aware that his knowledge of the Church Doctor was severely limited, Newman was "particularly anxious to learn what he could from reliable authorities of the philosophy of St. Thomas, and perhaps to review his studies of Aristotle's *Metaphysics* in an atmosphere unclouded by the presence of his rationalist interpreters."[49] He was to be seriously disappointed. The combined effects of the French Revolution and Austrian interference in seminary training resulted in a sorry state of affairs in Catholic schools of philosophy and theology.[50] What learning there was consisted of scholastic "manuals" in many ways deficient, shallow, and corrupted by post-Kantian readings of Aquinas.[51] To Newman's surprise, "St. Thomas Aquinas was not read."[52] He was given token notice, venerated as a great thinker, but no actual effort was made at understanding or comprehending him. The balmy days of the "Thomistic Revival" inaugurated by Leo XIII's *Aeterni Patris*[53] were more than thirty years off, and Newman was left unsatisfied. He wrote to his fellow convert J. D. Dalgairns:

> A little talk we had yesterday with one of the Jesuit Fathers here shows we shall find little philosophy. It arose from our talking of the Greek studies of the Propaganda and asking whether the youths learned Aristotle. "O no--he said-- Aristotle is in no favor here--no, not in Rome:--not St. Thomas: . . . they are out of favor here and throughout Italy. St. Thomas was a great saint--people don't dare to speak against him, but put him aside."[54]

Newman was to find this an accurate estimation and was strongly disappointed. Though he had a complete edition of Aquinas' works even as an Oriel Fellow, he felt an introduction was needed into the thought of Aquinas--a philosophy so extensive and multi-faceted was not to be summarily apprehended. While he felt little inclination to enter into a comparatively new line of study in middle age (he was 46 years old at the time), he was eager to fill the gaps in his own learning. He threw himself into the course of studies at Rome but found them hardly advanced enough. Moreover, they never properly touched the great scholastic.

Nevertheless, it is surprising just how much of Aquinas Newman actually did read. While not a major source for Newman, the marginalia in his texts of Aquinas clearly demonstrate an active and close reading of many significant portions, particularly those relating to the nature of the Trinity, the idea of "persons," and Peter Lombard's *Sentences* (interestingly enough, Lombard and St. Bernard are the most "patristic" of medieval authors).[55] In view of Newman's "great disappointment" at finding no suitable master of Aquinas, Sillem's remark that Newman was better off without the scholastic is rather odd: "Newman was too much at home with [the Fathers] to have settled down in middle life to the disciplines and methods of the Schools; had he tried to do so, the results could well have been disappointing, if not disastrous."[56] As a later study of Newman's metaphysical speculations will show, Newman was "ripe" for a comprehensive introduction to Thomistic metaphysics and epistemology. Had an Etienne Gilson, a Jacques Maritain or especially a Josef Pieper been available to Newman in Rome, many of Newman's difficulties with Locke and other empirical philosophers would have been eliminated. Sillem underestimates Newman; where there is educated desire, surely there is at least partial aptitude. Newman certainly desired a comprehensive study of Aquinas, and his life-long sensitivity to philosophical issues suggests that an adequate presentation of the Angelic Doctor's thought would not have been lost on him. Even late in life, he hailed the Encyclical "Aeterni Patris," writing to the Pope that the medieval St. Thomas was "one" with Church Fathers St. Athanasius and St. Augustine.[57]

A thorough training in Thomistic metaphysics may have spared Newman many vexing difficulties, but his thought would ever have been most congenial to the patristic, rhetorical models it absorbed. Is it, then, unwise to study that thought from an Aristotelian and Thomistic standpoint? To return to the earlier question, what can such a study of Newman offer? There is essentially a twofold value in such a reading. First, taking Newman's focus on probable reasoning as the key, the study recognizes Newman's persistent concerns, aims, and methods as belonging to rhetoric, a thing not confined to mere artistic or stylistic persuasion but representative of a mode of cognition. Second, it discourages the misapplication of philosophical principles and terms to Newman which, because of this rhetorical mode of discourse, are difficult at best to apply. Moreover, such a reading of Newman shows that his thought depends upon the objective and the certain, the attainable truth-value of propositions arrived at by means neither demonstrative nor philosophical. Jost's study of Newman as a rhetorical thinker adequately describes Newman's methods, his use of topicality to frame questions, his technique of "concede and lead," and his emphasis on the practical, judgmental, and the personal. Many of these points will be important here as well, but with an essential corrective: a Thomistic reading of Newman, if it is sensitive to the non-systematic and personalistic use of terms and ideas, can demonstrate Newman's conception of the objective character of truths concerning matters philosophically indemonstrable. A later critique will show how Jost's approach forfeits this objective character in the attempt to radically appropriate Newman to contemporary modes of rhetorical theoretical thought.

Though Newman was no Thomist, to read him in this light allows his understanding of knowledge and truth to stand clearly in its proper relation to being, intellect and personality. It also provides for the rhetorical orientation of Newman's concepts, with "rhetoric" understood in its fullest intellectual potential of truth-finding and truth-communicating. By doing so, by fostering a proper comprehension of Newman's rhetorical habit, this study will offer a corrective to those critics who see Newman as a failed philosopher or theologian, as well as those critics who see Newman as a radically innovative, proto-twentieth-century philosopher or theologian. A moderate position between these poles, both of which (despite claims to the contrary) are essentially "appropriating," is not to be had by merely combining the two. It is to be found in the golden mean, a paradigm (as it were) outside of that defined by the two poles.

In order to obtain that mean, it will be necessary to survey the conception of rhetoric provided by Aristotle (and largely followed by Aquinas) and show in some detail how Newman's predispositions, actions, and writings consistently locate his thought in that field of rhetoric. Precedents for those predispositions will be surveyed in patristic and Medieval thought on rhetoric and education. The Renaissance, in turn, witnessed a profound shift in the idea of knowledge itself that eclipsed the cognitive value assigned to habits of mind Newman would possess. Then, in order to make sense of Newman's philosophical background, the historical survey will continue, showing the general shape and features of Europe's more strictly philosophical developments from Aquinas onwards, and how those developments influenced Newman particularly in his *Philosophical Notebook.* Ostensibly Newman's most philosophical work, the partial and unfinished *Notebook* also exhibits Newman's rhetorical habits of mind despite his attempt at strictly philosophical reasoning. This rhetoricism will finally be seen, fully fleshed out and developed, in Newman's most abstract yet most rhetorical text of all, *The Grammar of Assent.* The *Grammar* constitutes Newman's most sustained and direct attempt at countering the intellectual presuppositions of his day. It is his attempt to restore a rhetorical mode of thought to its proper grasp of truth, certainty, and knowledge. It is in *The Grammar,* finally, that his conception of the objective character of reality, the attainable nature of truth, and the "natural" or day-to-day operation of the intellect and mind will show itself to be rooted in modes of thought recognizably rhetorical in the Aristotelian/Thomist tradition.

II. Rhetorical Knowledge And Aristotle

Conceit, more rich in matter than in words,
Brags of his substance, not of ornament.
                    Romeo and Juliet III, i.

Generality And Habit

Newman's knowledge of Aristotle's treatise on rhetoric was extensive, to say the least. Not only did he study the treatise as an undergraduate at Trinity College, making a complete annotation of the text, but as an Oriel tutor he taught from another, heavily-marked edition of the *Rhetoric*.[1] His tutorial notes in the Greek text display a mind sympathetic to the matter under study, even to the point of admiration. In fact, the term "rhetoric" for Newman did not ordinarily possess the highly negative connotations usually associated with it in his own time. Carlyle, Huxley, Comte and others were openly contemptuous of rhetoric as a serious intellectual pursuit, and Jost credits this contempt for the obscurity rhetoric suffered "in the early years of the twentieth century".[2] G.K. Chesterton relates (with obvious amusement) that Huxley, when "charged with being rhetorical . . . expressed his horror of 'plastering the fair face of truth with that pestilent cosmetic, rhetoric.'" Of course, Chesterton does not neglect to observe that this was "itself about as well-plastered a piece of rhetoric as Ruskin himself could have managed."[3] Newman, in contrast, had little difficulty with the title "rhetorician," even writing to Hurrell Froude in the midst of the Oxford Movement, "You and Keble are the philosophers, and I am the rhetorician."[4]

While Newman's understanding of the term "rhetoric" was largely a product of the text that defined rhetoric for the Oxford generations of the early nineteenth century, his inherent sympathy with this mode of discourse was in part due to its breadth of application. Richard McKeon calls rhetoric a "universal art . . . applicable to all things and to no particular things. . . ."[5] Any class of subjects may be both investigated and treated from a rhetorical standpoint, whether those subjects are technical or general, the domain of the specialist or the generalist.[6] This breadth of application arises from the utility of rhetoric, from its being an art with the general end of persuasion. According to Aristotle, "Every other art can instruct or persuade about its own particular subject matter. . . . But rhetoric we look upon as the power of observing the means of persuasion on almost any subject presented to us. . . ."[7] Thus the Philosopher maintains that this art is necessarily employed by everyone in the ordinary course of life. Rhetoric is employed poorly or well (often depending upon whether one has or has not been trained in the art), but it is virtually omnipresent. And, while even technical, specialized matters may be treated rhetorically, the art normally treats its subjects in a general fashion. Aristotle warns that "people fail to notice that the more correctly they handle their particular subject the further they are getting away from pure rhetoric or dialectic."[8]

This does not mean that rhetoric is in some way an "incorrect" art. It is rather an imprecise discipline as compared, for instance, to philosophy. This issue of precision is important; for Newman it even becomes a controversy as the 19th century adopts criteria for "knowledge" which are patterned after scientific modes of precision. In a passage that could easily be Newman debating his contemporaries, Aristotle sounds an apposite warning:

> [I]t is the mark of an educated man to look for precision in each class of things just so far as the nature of the subject admits; it is evidently equally foolish to accept probable reasoning from a mathematician and to demand from a rhetorician scientific proofs.[9]

The "imprecision" and generality of application proper to rhetoric ultimately derive from its definition; rhetoric, says Aristotle, "may be defined as the faculty of observing in any given class the available means of persuasion."[10] Too often, this definition is truncated and "simplified" to something like "the art of persuasion." Such an alteration risks losing the very real nuances of Aristotle's original statement, for he highlights the fact that the art is a faculty. He does not conceive of rhetoric as an application of certain precepts for the sake of persuasion--though these precepts do exist to assist the rhetorician (and are investigated in the *Topics*). Rather, rhetoric is a faculty of mind, a feature of the intellect that is capable of seeing the various appropriate "means of persuasion" in any given case. Although this applies largely to kinds of arguments, it also includes matters of style and delivery. But as a habit of intellectual operation, it shares the features of intellect that Aristotle notes in the *Metaphysics*, *Posterior Analytics*, and *On the Soul*. It exists as a mental *habitus*, a habit or skill, which may or may not be realized in an actual rhetorical discourse.

The existence of this rhetorical faculty is important, for it lays the groundwork for a significant distinction in Newman's texts: those that are rhetorical in every respect, and those that are rhetorical primarily in the faculty they display. If, in a given person, the development of the rhetorical faculty is continuous, habitual, and pervasive, the outlook and mode of discourse employed by that person will often be recognizably rhetorical regardless of the subject at hand. This is exactly the case with Newman, and he is not entirely unique. Though Cicero fancied himself a philosopher and was quite proud of his Greek peripatetic education, his philosophical texts are noticeably ethical, occasional, and even practical in orientation; in a word, they are more rhetorical than philosophical in the intellectual faculties and arguments they employ .

The integration of faculties and sciences so essential to Aristotelian psychology is evident even regarding rhetoric. Despite the object-less utility of the faculty--it can locate arguments for anything, good or evil--Aristotle is careful to relate rhetoric to ethics.[11] Rhetoric is properly employed with an eye to genuinely ethical ends. The frequent abuse of the art does not tell against its having a proper use. "[W]e must not make people believe what is wrong," says the Philosopher.[12] Cicero, too, warns of the harm done to nations and persons when rhetoricians learn their art without regard to philosophy and ethics, the study of the true and the good.[13] Nor is this all. As the discussion of argumentation in the *Rhetoric* demonstrates, there is also great potential in the rhetorical faculty for revealing or upholding truth. Truth, for Aristotle (as for Aquinas and subsequent Thomists), is a relation--a *proper* relation of the human intellect to "the thing." It is the spark of significant contact between an objective reality and an intelligent being. As such, truth is "knowable," but as universal human experience testifies, such knowledge does not always come automatically. There are many kinds of truth which are entered into (if at all) slowly and with difficulty. Rhetoric, for all its imprecision, has a function in conveying such truths for it can enable auditors to perceive or "adequate" their intelligences to things not previously known. W. Rhys Roberts, translator of the Oxford edition of the *Rhetoric*, assigns to rhetoric the modest claim of being man's "best weapon in upholding truth and justice."[14] Beyond conveying truths, the rhetorical faculty can also perceive or discover them, as should be evident, largely by means of the same arguments the rhetor will use to enable the audience to perceive them. The rhetor is "persuaded" first, as it were. Aristotle hints at this when he speaks of the natural link between rhetoric and truth: the good and the true are "by their nature, practically always easier to prove and easier to believe in."[15] Further, in a statement suggestive of what Newman will explore as the illative sense, Aristotle affirms, "[I]t may also be noted that men have a sufficient natural instinct for what is true, and usually do arrive at the truth."[16] The intelligence is naturally equipped to grasp truths, and the rhetorical faculty itself is more than merely truth-telling; it is truth-*finding* .[17]

RHETORICAL TRUTH

The issue of truth and rhetoric is complicated because the entire process of cognition is complex and various. The traditional understanding of Aristotle normally recognizes two kinds of knowledge; there is the knowledge of first principles, and knowledge by way of syllogism. First principles are known to man but not susceptible of demonstration precisely because they are the starting points from which demonstrations follow. They are the unarguable, the indemonstrable, and usually the self-evident (*per se nota*). These principles do not exist in the mind as innate ideas or instinctual intuition; rather, they are acquired through sense perception and the cognitive faculties of memory and imagination in a synthetic and inductive process. Knowledge of first principles, then, is indemonstrable, but not innate; it arises over time through the assimilation of reality by way of the senses. Demonstration or syllogism is another means of knowledge, differing from knowledge of first principles in that it is acquired through a deductive process. Reasoning from first principles, truths already known, one proceeds deductively to the acquisition of new truths through the necessary and logical relations of the syllogistic middle term. Truths of this sort are not self-evident and in fact depend entirely upon logical necessity to guarantee their validity.

Ordinarily, Aristotle describes "knowledge" as necessary, universal, knowledge "properly so called." It is normally equated with "universals," that is, things that are such and cannot be otherwise. Propositions that articulate knowledge are of universals themselves and have a universal predicated in them. By definition they must be necessary, or else they are not "science." The emphasis is upon necessity, for Aristotle consistently equates knowledge as "science" with matters demonstrable, necessary, unvaried. Such knowledge, of course, is philosophical in its highest form, since philosophy is the study of causes in the widest sense. Though branches of science or knowledge are defined by their subject matters, within these confines the sciences are no less necessary and universal: mathematics, the science of number; physics, the science of motion. In the main, for Aristotle, truth and knowledge are described as universals that are necessary and "do not depend on our action or our volition."[18]

Rhetoric, on the other hand, is normally employed upon matters contingent (as opposed to necessary) and probable (as opposed to syllogistically demonstrated). "Probability," says Aristotle,

> is a thing that usually happens; not, however, as some definitions would suggest, anything whatever that usually happens, but only if it belongs to the class of the "contingent" or "variable". It bears the same relation to that in respect of which it is probable as the universal bears to the particular.[19]

Herein lies the difficulty as far as rhetoric and truth or knowledge is concerned, for rhetoric normally treats not what is necessary and universal, but what is generally true or probable. This would seem to divorce rhetoric from knowledge, rendering Aristotle's prior words about "truth" and rhetoric problematic. If truth (i.e. "knowledge of the truth") and science are definite or necessary, how can that which deals with things not necessary be essentially related to the acquisition of truth? In answer it should be remembered first of all that rhetoric is not confined to a particular subject. It is capable of dealing with subjects properly philosophical or necessary, for instance, but it will do so in a rhetorical fashion; its mode of argument and presentation will be rhetorical, not "scientific." More to the point, however, is the fact that the aforementioned difficulty is essentially unreal; there is in Aristotle a dual use of the term "universal," which begins to illustrate how rhetoric can indeed be a mode of knowledge. "Universal" means: (a) that which is true necessarily and always, and (b) the generically differentiating aspect of a particular thing, its "form" or essence. The second sense of the word is critical, for it demonstrates the presence of the universal in the particular. That is, the particular thing or object is not "deprived" of a universal merely for being particular.

Thus the rhetorical faculty, even when considering a matter of probability or contingency, will employ or consider a thousand particulars, each endowed, as it were, with its own universal. While this does not mean the outcome of that deliberation will be a universal in the first sense (something necessary), it does show that even probabilities are surrounded by determinate, fixed, "essential" things, all of which impinge upon the mind in its active deliberation about the contingent or probable matter. To use a material metaphor, the fabric of probability is soaked in the dye of universal or determinate things. Looking at the entire passage where the "natural instinct" for truth is mentioned, we find an interesting assessment of the rhetorical faculty's genuine power:

> The true and the approximately true are apprehended by the same faculty; it may also be noted that men have a sufficient natural instinct for what is true, and usually do arrive at the truth. Hence the man who makes a good guess at truth is likely to make a good guess at probabilities.[20]

As "approximately true' refers to probability (approximate with regard to the formal logic involved, not "quasi-true" or "sort-of-true"), we see that probability is as much of a "truth function" as non-approximate, philosophical reasoning. The intelligence is the faculty, and the work of the intellect is to know. Thus the rhetorical faculty can arrive at genuine truths because it is an intellectual faculty wherein the particulars and contingencies with which it deals are steeped in intelligible universals. One must conclude, then, that there is a kind of knowledge appropriate to the rhetorical faculty, the logical status of which may be "probable," but which in and of itself is certain and true. But if so, where is the usual Aristotelian consideration of how such knowledge is obtained? It is, as always in Aristotle, in the treatment of argumentation.

The forms of argument suited to rhetoric are those that--unlike demonstrative syllogism or incremental induction--deal with the probable and the contingent. These forms are enthymeme and example, which, as Aristotle repeatedly points out, are similar to syllogism and induction. Enthymeme is rhetorical syllogism precisely in that it treats of probability, while syllogism properly so called must be necessary. It is noteworthy that enthymeme is not merely a chain of logical middle terms from which a few links are missing. The distinctive nature of enthymeme arises out of the kind of subject matter being treated. Example, likewise, is the rhetorical counterpart of induction. Actual induction--explicit or implicit in the synthesizing faculty of memory and imagination--proceeds by way of individual phenomena and particulars coalescing into a recognizable class or causal relationships. Example is an abbreviated version of induction that provides an instance designed to illuminate whatever is being discussed.

Much of the intellectual hostility toward rhetoric in the nineteenth century was a consequence of the art being "confined" to "mere" probability. The attitude even among those who embraced Aristotle's treatise (such as the imaginative and influential Richard Whately, Newman's colleague and mentor) was that rhetoric and probability were quite all right, as far as they went, but formal logic (and later, material science) entailed truly serious learning. This dismissal of "mere" probability was to trouble Newman for most of his life, and Aristotle precedes Newman in warning against it. An argument for something cannot be refuted by the assertion that the argument is merely probable; such a refutation is valid only when the argument put forth is an attempt at necessary demonstration. The truth-value of the question at hand is left unaltered by the probability or necessity of the arguments. Whether the question is deliberative (What is the good, what is to be done?), forensic (What is the truth regarding past events or people?), or epideictic (What is the praise- or blame-worthiness of a particular circumstance or person?)--all of which are matters of probability and contingency--the truth of the conclusions is in no way diminished by the mode of the inquiry.[21] Aristotle goes so far as to say that enthymeme and example are in fact modes of *proof* despite the fact that they deal with probability.[22] Thus we approach certain truths by means that, logically speaking, are approximations. Enthymeme and example are the proper intellectual equipment for dealing with a world of contingencies, "flux," movement, all of which is, nevertheless, intelligible and real.

ELEMENTS OF RHETORIC

The extent to which Newman's intellectual predilections and inclinations are prefigured (in one form or another) in Aristotle's *Rhetoric* is quite revealing. Whether these inclinations became such as a result of Newman's study of the treatise is irrelevant. Incline he did, and there are numerous components of the rhetorical faculty and art Aristotle details which appear repeatedly in Newman's own thought. Three-fold divisions recur in the treatise, and several are of particular importance for Newman's thought. First we see that rhetorical discourse is characterized in part by its constitutive elements: speaker, subject, and person addressed. Any discourse includes these elements, of course, including physical (physics), geometrical, philosophical, or even material-scientific discourse. But as even a cursory examination of such highly subject-oriented discourse reveals, the influence of speaker and addressee is usually dwarfed by the systematic requirements of the subject. Rhetoric is unique in the high degree of influence each of these elements exerts upon its actual discourse. In fact, the aforementioned division of rhetoric into deliberative, forensic, and epideictic is determined by the various classes of possible auditors[23]. Nor does the role of the auditors end there; the state or condition of a given audience is tremendously important to the orator in deter-mining not only his diction, bearing, and tone, but even the kinds of arguments themselves. The speaker too is important in determining the variable aspects of a discourse through his own relative skill, character, and inventive power. For this reason a second three-fold division is mentioned. The rhetorician himself must have an acute and practiced ability "to reason logically, to understand human character and goodness in their various forms and to understand the emotions--that is to name them and describe them, to know their causes and the ways in which they are excited."[24] The importance of these abilities is self-evident. A genuine sympathetic ability and keen insight into human nature is as important to the rhetorician as is an understanding of valid and fallacious reasoning.

As a mode of discourse (and reasoning), rhetoric addresses and employs the entire complex unity of persons. Both of the three-fold divisions highlight the personal valence of rhetoric, but this valence is likewise apparent in the means of persuasion available to rhetoricians, notably, the "personal character of the speaker," the bringing of an audience to a proper "frame of mind," and finally the actual reasonings and proofs employed.[25] A speaker's personal character is not persuasive because it possesses an irrational influence upon an audience. Rather, as Aristotle notes, good men are quite ordinarily (and properly) believed when there is diversity of opinion upon a subject. Virtuous men normally make good choices and can discern the causes and course of affairs in human conduct. So important is the character of the speaker, that Aristotle affirms it "may almost be called the most effective means of persuasion he possesses."[26] The second means of persuasion, that which comes "through the hearers" is largely emotional. Newman will broaden the scope of this means, but Aristotle does not preclude the role of the passions in the intellect. He indicates that "Our judgments when we are pleased and friendly are not the same as when we are pained and hostile."[27] Historically, those who advocate a cool and dispassionate reasoning upon any important matter deplore the influence of the passions on the intellect. While passions can lead reasoning astray, they nevertheless have a role in reasoning when they are properly ordered to the intellect. In fact, sometimes a particular emotional response is the very sign that a thing is properly understood. The fact that people can play upon the passions in attempts to subvert proper reasoning does nothing more than highlight Aristotle's warning that rhetoric must be used for the good and the true.

The final, and less personal means of persuasion is when a truth is proved "by means of the persuasive arguments suitable to the case in question."[28] This third means is exceedingly important for it allows rhetoric its necessary breadth of argumentative strength. One may employ the strictest syllogistic reasoning in rhetorical discourse. Doing so, of course, may incline the discourse "away from pure rhetoric," but logical reasoning (even discourse specifically scientific) is available to rhetoric depending upon the requirements of the occasion and the qualifications of the audience.

Another element of the personal is introduced by Aristotle when he makes the seemingly self-evident observation that a statement "is persuasive because there is somebody whom it persuades."[29] Normally, rhetoric is not concerned with the individual person but with general classes of men and what kinds of persuasions are most effective for those classes. No art, says the philosopher, can deal with completely individual cases since the possible variations among such individuals make the generalizations necessary for an art virtually impossible. This is not to say, however, that rhetoric has no possible relation to individuals for, after all, individuals are persuaded. Rather, those aspects of individuals that are completely idiosyncratic and capricious cannot be reduced to a system or art in which one can be trained. Rhetoric can be "personal" and "general" at once. Witness, for example, the persuasive importance of something as personal as the character of the speaker. How is it that a good man is believed by virtue of his goodness? His good sense, good moral principles and conduct, and his good will communicate "character" to an audience and persuade them by a kind of living example[30]. These are all thoroughly grounded in the individual and are not qualities conveyed or analyzed systematically. The importance of such qualities is that they are fairly intangible but real and personal aspects of persuasion that bear directly upon the rhetorician's relationships to his auditors.

A PRACTICAL ART

Because rhetorical discourse is normally directed toward producing an action, it is necessary to understand its connection to what Aristotle calls practical science or knowledge. Indeed much of what Aristotle says about practical knowledge serves to clarify just how something like a rhetorical faculty can attain genuine knowledge at all. To be sure, "knowledge" usually means the apprehension by the intellect of the self-evident and the necessary, the unable-to-be-otherwise. But "knowledge" has a broader and more general sense in Aristotle when he speaks of the mind's full and complex susceptibility to an objective and intelligible reality.

"All men by nature desire to know," says the philosopher in the *Metaphysics*, and the highest order of knowledge, "wisdom," is that which deals with "first causes and the principles of things."[31] Pure knowledge, knowledge for its own sake, as it were, and unconnected to use or action is theoretical or speculative. But there is another kind of knowledge that is not for its own sake but exists for the sake of action.

> The end of the theoretic sciences is knowledge, and the subject-matters which are investigated and the truths which are sought do not depend on our action or our volition. The end of the practical sciences, on the other hand, is not merely to know, but rather to act in the light of knowledge. . . .[32]

Practical science is knowledge for the sake of something else, normally making or doing. As far as human action and production are concerned, pure speculative inquiry can be a remote "second" in utility, while the learning induced through experience can come first. "[M]en of experience [can] succeed even better than those who have theory without experience, since experience is knowledge of individuals, not of universals; and actions and productions are concerned with the individual."[33]

There is a kind of spectrum of knowledge, then, that proceeds from the particular to the general to the universal. Each is legitimate "knowledge," though that is considered highest which is strictly concerned with necessary universals. True, "universals" are behind knowledge of any sort, being "first isolated in the recognition of the one in the many of experience, [and being] thus the basis of both the skill of the artist and the knowledge of the scientist."[34] But the spectrum is one relative to intelligibility; though all knowledge begins in the senses, "The sequence from sensation to thought is a transition, as Aristotle likes to put it, from things prior and better known to us to things prior and better known in nature."[35] Newman is almost exclusively interested in the first or more immediate--"to us"-- half of that equation. Indeed, the practical sciences that deal with actions (and production), as well as contingent matters about which arguments are probable, are likewise related more to the "to us" half of the knowledge spectrum. More about the arguments later, but it is important here to see that knowledge of things prior and better known to us--such as any particular object--is actual knowledge indeed. In the *Posterior Analytics* Aristotle seems to caution those inclined to take syllogistic reasoning to an excess by noting emphatically that "there are things which are true and real [such as temporary conditions or even historical events] and yet can be

otherwise, [so] scientific knowledge clearly does not concern them. . . ."[36] He
states again in *On the Soul* that practical science as well as theoretical is directed
toward actual knowledge because for both the "soul discriminates and is cognizant
of something which *is*."[37]

Rhetoric is subsumed under practical science not only in that its end is
action --both on the part of the orator and the auditors--but also in that it is
concerned with the production of states of character. Though such concerns are
discriminations of "things that are," they are not susceptible to mathematical
precision because of their contingent character. Practical science (and by extension,
rhetoric) deals with things true and real in the realm of experience, production,
action and human character. This is precisely why rhetoric is both an art and a
faculty. The knowledge involved here, both the "discovery" of it and its
communication, will be influenced by factors it is the boast of scientific knowledge
to exclude. A proper rhetoric, such as Newman's, will "boast" of these same
factors as being wholly proper to human thought.

Learning of this practical sort is heavily influenced by experience, habit ànd
upbringing. One can be well or poorly equipped to discriminate the "things that are"
in the more immediate and action-oriented domains. Even some first principles are
acquired, says Aristotle, through "habituation"[38]--a point Newman will belabor in
his *Grammar*. Though it is Aristotle, the following passage might well have been
Newman holding forth before the attentive crowd at the University discourses or
the Cornhill Exchange audience in Birmingham:

> [W]hile we must begin with what is known, things are
> objects of knowledge in two senses--some to us, some
> without qualification. Presumably, then, we must begin with
> things known to us. Hence anyone who is to listen
> intelligently to lectures about what is noble and just and,
> generally, about subjects of political science must have been
> brought up in good habits. For the fact is the starting point,
> and if this is sufficiently plain to him, he will not at the start
> need the reason as well. . . .[39]

Right desire is also a part of man's practical reasoning, for "the good state is
truth in agreement with right desire."[40] This is why vice is capable of destroying
practical wisdom. The practical intellect's inclination toward the good is upset by a
deliberate attachment to evil, and the consequence is not merely evil action, but a
debilitating effect on the person's ability to perceive truths in the realm of character
and even production. Conversely, people can be moved to a right desire and
perception of truths that incidentally escaped them, through the rhetorical use of

remedying persuasions and truths, argument, the rhetor's goodwill and good character, and examples which are recognizable to those being persuaded. Strict philosophical argument does not have this capacity, as Aristotle notes,[41] and thus Newman's famous remark that "No man dies for a conclusion" (as opposed to a dogma) applies perhaps to many things as well as religion.

Though the art of rhetoric is a kind of practical wisdom, the truth or realities with which it deals are comprehended by a faculty Aristotle calls "understanding." In a sense, rhetoric occupies ground between practical science and understanding. Like practical science, "understanding is neither about things that are always and are unchangeable, nor about any and every one of the things that come into being, but about things which may become subjects of questioning and deliberation."[42] It differs from practical wisdom in not producing action.

> For practical wisdom issues commands, since its end is what ought to be done or not to be done; but understanding only judges. . . . Now understanding is neither the having nor the acquiring of practical wisdom; but as learning is called understanding when it means the exercise of the faculty of knowledge, so "understanding" is applicable to the exercise of the faculty of opinion for the purpose of judging of what someone else says about matters with which practical wisdom is concerned. . . .[43]

Insofar as rhetoric is meant to induce action, either the action productive of rhetorical discourse or the inducement of auditors to action, it is an art allied to practical wisdom; however, insofar as it operates upon probability, deliberating upon matters contingent (especially in "judging of what someone else says"), then it is more "understanding" than practical wisdom since no command is issued.

TRUTH VALUE

The relation of rhetoric to truth may be partially obscured in Aristotle because of the philosopher's efforts to differentiate the nature of argumentation in rhetoric and in philosophical or "necessary" science. The concentration on this distinguishing feature conveys the impression that true knowledge is confined to scientific modes of argumentation, leaving the rhetorical modes a diminished and uncertain access to truth. But this impression is an impoverished one, for it does not suggest the access to truth that rhetorical modes of argumentation have by way of the practical intellect and understanding. Nowhere does Aristotle say that arguments essentially probable and contingent are incapable of revealing the truths of propositions; quite the contrary, for he speaks of such arguments as "proof" and warns against demanding of them an alien demonstrative nature. The cause of the erroneous impression arises, however, from the fact that Aristotle is concentrating upon modes of argument--and their distinctions--rather than the objects of argument. When the objects of rhetorical argument are mentioned, they are called "true and real" and thus have an actuality all their own. Truth can be articulated in rhetorical argumentation, but it does so in forms not scientifically necessary and determined. The distinction is important, for to describe an issue as contingent, something capable of being otherwise, says absolutely nothing as to the actual "what is the fact." Caesar's crossing of the Rubicon is a fact no less factual for being contingent.

The common perception that contingent and probable matters are unreliable and that, by extension, the modes of inquiry proper to such matters are equally unreliable is largely responsible for the dubious reputation rhetoric has "enjoyed" for much of its modern history. The truth or falsity of scientific demonstration may be readily determined by examination of formal aspects of the demonstration and the individual terms. Matters not so demonstrated are infinitely more difficult and complex. They are judged true or false depending upon many obscure and intangible variables. Though this does not affect the rhetorical mode of inquiry itself, it does disturb those who demand a simple and analytical criterion for judgment. It is ironic that those who prefer such criteria give credit to the "better known by nature" category of knowledge while leaving the "better known to us"--a seemingly more immediate kind of knowledge--entirely alone. They do so by concentrating on the manner in which something is known ("how known"), rather than the object or thing ("what known").

Rhetoric as a mode of knowledge and inquiry, the mode of inquiry suitable to the probable and contingent, is fully capable of attaining truth. Nevertheless, it is likewise capable of employing the same probable and contingent arguments in support of what is not true. In this resides its well-known ease of abuse, its "danger"; the manifest *dis*service rendered by rhetoric has resulted in large-scale denial of the actual service it is capable of. Newman devoted much thought to such matters and strove to save from disregard a faculty's capacity for truth even though it argued from probability and contingency. How the validity of such arguments is discerned and how truth from falsity in such matters can be rationally determined were the subjects of his life-long study. The criteria he proposed for judgment-- reliability of testimony, character of the witness, the sense of probability uncontradicted over time--were recognizably rhetorical ones. Though Newman explained the basis for such knowledge in the *Grammar,* his sensitivity and susceptibility to the issue manifests itself throughout his works. Not only did he strive to restore the intellectual claims of the rhetorical faculty, he also employed the faculty extensively. Quite unconsciously, perhaps, Newman led a life that testified to the strength and versatility of the rhetorical mode of knowledge. It was a versatile habit, and his sensitivity to the use and personal impact of the faculty appears in his approach toward everything from the Church Fathers to educational methods. If the *Grammar* was his exposition of how the faculty worked, his life and thoughts, as we shall see, constitute the best example.

III. NEWMAN'S PURPOSIVE RHETORIC

Bulk logic with acquaintance that you have,
And practice rhetoric in your common talk.
The Taming of the Shrew I, i

A PASTORAL PURPOSE

If one of the attributes of a "Victorian sage" is the conviction that one has an overriding mission or purpose that animates all of one's actions, then Newman is certainly a sage.[1] Perhaps because of his religious labors, Newman may have been more "missionary" than his fellow sages whose concerns were more varied and diffuse. If Newman did not always know where his pursuits were going to lead him, he was certainly aware that those pursuits addressed what he considered the highest and most significant questions. He was happiest when he felt some good had been accomplished and some purpose served, such as after the publication of the *Apologia* or while tutoring as a Fellow of Oriel. He was most miserable and dejected when he felt he was not being allowed to advance religion in some way, such as occurred upon the "failure" of the Catholic University, the ending of his translation of Scripture, or the ordeal with the *Rambler*. His great practical and organizational energies were always aroused at the prospect of an impending task, and his remark at the onset of the Oxford Movement that "We have a work to do in England" is justly famous for exemplifying his energy and sense of purpose.[2]

This sense of purpose must inform any inquiry into Newman's rhetorical habit of mind, for a fundamental sense of mission motivated Newman's rhetorical approach to virtually any subject. While it is true that a "mission" or sense of purpose does not a rhetorician make, in Newman's case his sense of purpose was given form and expression in a variety of highly rhetorical ways.[3] Constitutive of this purpose is Newman's perception of the world as fallen and of man's intellect as suffering in consequence. Upon this foundation one finds the various rhetorical unfoldings of his sense of purpose. Most explicitly rhetorical is Newman's insistence that everything can have a religiously persuasive impact--from gentle-

manly conduct or liberal education to seminary formation. Then there is his
supremely important sensitivity to the workings of others' minds--a sensitivity he
put to good rhetorical use. Finally there is the rhetorical way he approached his life-
long war against Liberalism despite the fact that Liberalism had a foundation that
was philosophical. Behind each of these attitudes and ideas was Newman's conviction that he "had a work to do," a mission or purpose in which he exercised a
consistently rhetorical operation of mind.

It was not just in "projects" such as translations or book-writing that
Newman felt he was cultivating his life's work. As Placid Murray notes, the
unifying principle of that life was the all-encompassing religious purpose of a
pastor of souls:

> Right from the beginnings of his Anglican ministry,
> Newman considered the Christian priesthood above all from
> a pastoral--one might almost say, a practical--standpoint as a
> lifelong "responsibility of souls." This pastoral note is the
> great underlying bond of continuity and identity between his
> ministry before and after his conversion.[4]

Though much of his work was intellectual in character, it was always understood as
being essentially pastoral. After Anglican ordination to the diaconate, Newman
passionately scribbled in his diary ". . . 'Forever', words never to be recalled. I
have the responsibility of souls on me to the day of my death. . . ."[5] The intellectual
character of that responsibility grew in Newman's awareness during his years at
Oxford and at the onset of the Oxford Movement. Later, as a Catholic searching for
an order or congregation of priests in which to continue his work, Newman
selected the relatively "low profile" Oratorian Congregation founded in Rome by St.
Philip Neri during the sixteenth century. There were a number of factors involved
in his lighting upon the Oratory, not the least of which was his own affection and
admiration for its founder. But the primary reason was the compatibility of the
Oratorian rule with Newman's idea of a small "college" of priests engaged upon
intellectual work. His mission was to the world of thought and intellect, specifically
as regards the religious difficulties experienced by so many intellectuals of the day.[6]

A FALLEN WORLD

While this mission was an intellectual one, it was also clearly apologetic.
The enemy of the day, Liberalism, was to be met and fought in intellectual combat
similar in energy to the wrangling of the medieval schools. This combat often

addressed the very role and place of human reason in religious inquiry.[7] For most of his life, Newman was fundamentally aware that man is a fallen creature whose very reason has been clouded.[8] As a young man of somewhat evangelical bent, his idea of the Fall approached the Calvinistic doctrine of total depravity in that he thought the Fall had corrupted human nature itself. But both pastoral experience and the influence of associates soon convinced him that such a conception was reductionistic; well before leaving the Anglican Church, Newman's understanding of the Fall had become Catholic--man's nature was "wounded" but not essentially altered. Whatever theological position he happened to hold, however, he was always keenly aware that man's state suffered a lamentable disorder.

This awareness has sometimes perplexed critics who attempt a philosophical or theological reading of Newman. Harold Weatherby, in light of the Thomistic principle that "God's reason and law, the very mind of God, is manifest in the order of creation, in the body politic as well as in the cosmos," indicts Newman for failing "to see the image of God in the creation."[9] In support of this he refers to the *Apologia* where Newman meditates on the busy dissipations of a fallen man's world:

> I look out of myself into the world of man, and there I see a sight which fills me with unspeakable distress. . . . I look into this living, busy world and see no reflection of its Creator. . . . [The arguments for God's existence drawn from the world are true] but these do not warm or enlighten me; they do not take away the winter of my desolation, or make the buds unfold and the leaves grow within me, and my moral being rejoice. The sight of the world is nothing else than the prophet's scroll, full of "lamentations, and mourning, and woe."[10]

While Newman allows for the validity of philosophical proofs of God's existence, he does not allow that the fallen world necessarily strikes the imagination, "warms or enlightens" it, with the consoling vision of its Creator. He is not speaking philosophically or criticizing the theological validity of analogies of being. Though a theologian or poet might be able to watch the proceedings of the House of Commons and be transported by the vision of God therein (hardly a likely prospect), a rhetorician would not look in such places for his visions or proofs. Newman's practical orientation does not allow him the luxury of ignoring the fact that wheat is intermixed with chaff, that whatever the imprint of the Creator on the world, man has managed to obscure it wonderfully.

It is the practicality--the non-theoretical, "practical wisdom"--Newman so habitually exercised that characterizes his own perception of the fallen world. All around him was not only sickness and death, but irrationality, foolishness, uncontrolled passion, and minds seemingly impervious to reality.[11] The Fall of man did far more than allow death its entry into the world. As created by God, man possesses a nature harmonious to both the Creator and the rest of the created order. Newman well knew that man's faculties of intellect, passions and will (as well as the very body and soul of man), are not isolated aspects of human nature bound externally together like so many random volumes placed upon a shelf. His famous remark that "the whole man reasons" illustrates his conception that man's various capacities are essentially integrated. Though originally integrated, the faculties of man suffered disorder as a result of the Fall. Man was at war with himself. Intellect was clouded, the will was inclined to all manner of inordinate excesses and defects, and passions were domineering. According to St. Thomas Aquinas, "Original justice was forfeited through the sin of our first parents . . . so that all the powers of the soul are left, as it were, destitute of their proper order . . . which destitution is called a wounding of nature."[12] That wound was fourfold in effect:

> [I]n so far as the reason is deprived of its order to the true, there is the wound of ignorance; in so far as the will is deprived of its order to good, there is the wound of malice; in so far as the irascible is deprived of its order to the arduous, there is the wound of weakness; and in so far as the concupiscible is deprived of its order to the delectable, moderated by reason, there is the wound of concupiscence.[13]

Garrigou-Lagrange explains that the actual nature, powers and faculties of the soul, being spiritual, "do not admit of reduction or increase" and thus are intrinsically immune from the effects of the Fall. However, the loss of original justice acts as an obstacle to the powers of the soul, and as such the soul suffers a direct supernatural aversion to God, and an *indirect* natural aversion.[14]

This aversion to God and the disordering of the faculties that Newman witnessed all about him gave force to his sense of pastoral purpose. Though the underlying root of man's disaffection was a supernatural "dislocation," there were natural effects to be ameliorated as well as supernatural ones. The sacraments, of course, were the chief means of overcoming the supernatural and even natural effects of the Fall, but because man is an integrated being, his natural powers could also participate in alleviating the Fall's consequences. As medical arts treat the disordered body, so can rhetorical arts (as well as others) treat the disordered mind. In fact, Newman "credits" the Fall with occasioning persuasion itself. John Milton notwithstanding, there was no need for persuasion in Eden:

> Dexterity, promptness, presence of mind, sagacity, shrewdness, *powers of persuasion,* talent for business, what are these but development of intellect which our fallen state has occasioned, and probably far from the highest which our mind is capable of? And are not these and others at best only of use in remedying the effects of the fall, and, so far, indeed . . . not having a legitimate employment except in a world of sickness and infirmity?[15]

Newman's sense of purpose was thus defined by his perception of man as a fallen creature; as a priest he used the sacraments to assist in overcoming the loss of grace, but as an educator he used man's natural faculties in a rhetorical way to help overcome the disordered state of man's intellect. His highly rhetorical sensibility taught him to see in things (even in abstractions and systems of theory) their utility for effecting those interior changes of character and thought that would reintegrate man's disordered faculties. Thus his affection or disaffection for certain modes of thought (say, syllogistic reasoning) rested not upon his conception of their validity but rather upon their *usefulness* for effecting religious understanding in the nineteenth-century world. This explains why Newman's opinion of things like "sagacity" or even human reason seems to change back and forth--his "attitude" regarding a subject is determined by the particular rhetorical purpose of a given discourse. Newman's copious *opera* are crowded with examples of things praised in one place and criticized in another. While such shifts may perplex a philosopher for their seeming inconsistency, a rhetorical mind will always be free to cast matters in different lights depending upon the purpose of the discourse. Quite typically, Newman would preach (in his Anglican years) to the evangelical High Street shopkeepers of the "dangers of emotion" and turn right around and preach to the Oxford community of scholars on the "dangers of reason."[16] His frequent criticism of "reason"--too often understood (as in Weatherby) as a none-too-secret inclination toward irrationality--must be seen as a criticism of pretension or reason's weakness in a fallen state, not as a criticism of reason as such. This balance is seen even in the very sermon just mentioned:

> Now in thus speaking, let it be observed, I am not using light words of what is a great gift of God, and one distinguishing mark of man over the brutes, our reason; I have but spoken of the *particular exercises and*

> *developments*, in which it has its life in the world, as we see
> them. . . . Reason, I say, is God's gift; but so are the
> passions. . . . Since [the Fall] passion and reason have
> abandoned their due place in man's nature, which is one of
> subordination, and conspired together against the Divine
> light within him, which is his proper guide.[17]

Though Newman's understanding of metaphysics would have been en-
riched had he obtained suitable instruction in Rome, he never would have made
large-scale use of medieval argumentation in a world that conceived of such
argumentation as "chop-logic." It is not that such reasoning is invalid, but rather
that it is *ineffective* under present circumstances. This is overlooked by those who
criticize Newman for passing over systems of thought (Thomism) internally
consistent and Christian in orientation. Nor does Newman attempt to "make terms"
with systems of thought alien to Christianity, as will be seen in the study of his
Philosophical Notebook. As a rhetorician Newman was keenly aware that his
"audience"--virtually the whole of the educated Western world--was habituated to
certain (often empirical) theoretical frameworks, and thus his effort was to discover
ways of convincing the "audience" of the inadequacy of that framework. This was
not to be accomplished so much by a philosophical "head-on" collision, even were
Newman equipped to initiate one. Rather, it was to be effected by employing all the
tools of rhetoric to draw the imagination, sensibility and reason of his audience to a
vision of the complex supernatural whole he felt to be of utmost importance. He
attempted (even in his "philosophical" works) to persuade his era that there was
more in heaven and earth than was dreamed of in its philosophy.

THE GENTLEMAN RHETORICIAN

If Newman was convinced that formal reasoning alone would not suffice to
awaken a rationalistic world to the truths of religion, what would? How can the
world be aroused from a supernatural slumber? Another way of putting the question
is to ask what persuasives would be effective in drawing the imagination,
sensibility, and reason to the supernatural. One such persuasive is gentlemanliness.
The "gentleman" detailed in *The Idea of a University* is famous, of course, and
Dwight Culler notes both the clergyman's praise and dispraise of the ideal of
gentility.[18] But as regards the "use" of gentlemanliness, Newman's addresses to
his fledgling Oratorian house in England are as revealing, though less well-known,
as the University lectures. A significant target of the Tractarian Movement had been

the superficiality of Victorian religion --its willingness to disregard doctrine and consider "good manners" good religion. Now that doctrine had been "secured" so to speak, Newman felt free to shift ground, create a balance, and emphasize the role of manners in religion. He asks,

> [W]hat have gentleman-like manners and refined feelings to do with religion? . . . [I]t does not follow, because refinement is worthless without saintliness, that it is needless and useless with it. It may set off and recommend an interior holiness, just as the gift of eloquence sets off logical arguments. A bad speaker may be as firm a believer as the most accomplished of orators; yet the gift of words is necessary to be able to persuade; and so the gift of manners may be necessary to win. . . . [It is no surprise that gentlemanliness], this external polish and refinement, which is so valueless in itself morally, yet so useful as a sort of rhetoric in conduct . . . should have been one of the means by which the Oratory acted in the reformation of both clergy and laity at the time of its establishment.[19]

It had been necessary to emphasize the sovereignty of dogma and morals, as distinct from manners, in the Tractarian trenches. Through an altered purpose, the value of manners could be recovered and the rhetorical impact of such cultural "peripherals" could be explored. But the passage is also remarkable in its use of the term "eloquence." At first, Newman uses the word in typical nineteenth-century fashion; eloquence is said to "set off" logical argument, as, perhaps, spices might set off a particular food. This seems to encourage the perception that eloquence (and rhetoric itself?) is extraneous to the matter being spoken of. Though eloquence does in fact "dress" a discourse to a certain extent, it is not limited to mere window-dressing. Newman subtly but significantly broadens the power of eloquence almost immediately, as he parallels eloquence to manners. Eloquence persuades, manners win, he says, and in tying the two together or at least paralleling them, both activities emerge as means of enhancing access to the truth. In fact, in calling gentlemanliness a "rhetoric in conduct," it is clear that "manners" can be a kind of persuasion. Newman was enough of an aesthete to appreciate the gratuitous beauty inherent in refined manner, but his rhetorical sensitivity seizes upon the actual rhetorical effect of such refinement. Courtesy becomes a "rhetoric of conduct" where ordinary activities could be given their own "eloquence." Not only is such eloquence "persuasive" in that it attracts the unbeliever, but it acts as rhetorical epideictic amongst one's co-religionists. The very same "rhetoric of conduct" at work in the episode with Dr. Arnold is the kind of rhetoric Newman wants the

Oratorians to master. As the Oratorians are to pursue holiness, a rhetoric of conduct can "set off" that holiness and actually make it visible (assuming it is attained) to others. This "eloquence," then, is more than an aesthetic overcoat hurled upon the body of discourse; its power is such that, as Newman says, St. Philip Neri reformed a corrupt and decadent Rome through it.

We can see that Newman is willing to look on something as broad and pervasive as conduct as a means of persuasion. In fact, the persuasives he feels free to call upon are virtually unlimited. That is, *everything* can be looked upon from the standpoint of rhetorical utility, and what Newman exhibits by viewing things in this way may be called a "Christian utilitarianism." This "utilitarianism,"--viewing all things from the standpoint of their usefulness in achieving some end--is not utilitarianism in the conventional sense appropriate to Jeremy Bentham, John Stuart Mill, or even William James. In fact, it is not even something "new" or confined to rhetoric. Joseph Owens notes that Aristotelian metaphysics is "pursued for its own sake," while Thomistic metaphysics "is to be pursued in so far as it is helpful toward attaining that ultimate end"--which is, of course, God.[20]

Nevertheless, Newman's "Christian utilitarianism" is so rhetorical in its practical concern for finding effective means of meeting the "infidelity of the day," that his idea of a proper seminary formation takes on the same rhetorical, "utilitarian" twist. What seminarians need, according to Newman, is a liberal education such that they may be equipped to deal with the vagaries of thought in an active world:

> Young men are not looking for an encyclopedic formation, but for the capacity to judge things as they come before them--to expound and solve difficulties, to compare things one with another, to form judgements of men and events, nations and countries, to acquire a critical faculty in judging books, examining author's opinions, investigating religions and religious bodies, developing the principles of philosophy, poetry, politics. . . .[21]

All of this is essential to the formation of priests capable of acting as priests in a secular world. Everything a religious does is ultimately an act of evangelization:

> All education is a kind of preaching--all catechizing, all private conversation--all writing. In all things and at all times is a Christian minister preaching in the Scriptural sense of the word . . . and in all matters and pursuits of this world as truly, though not as directly as when engaged in religious subjects.[22]

All conversation, all intercourse is a kind of "preaching," where--whether one knows it or not--either good or harmful consequences result. Although this principle could be taken to an extreme, Newman emphasizes it to provide a counterbalance against the tendency to bracket religion and confine it to an Arnoldian "cultural utility" irrespective of its spiritual validity. His principle that all intercourse is a kind of preaching dovetails with the idea of a rhetoric of conduct--we can see Newman pulling together different strands of everyday activity and highlighting their capacities to advance religion through rhetorical means.

By looking at everything in light of its rhetorical ability to draw people toward the supernatural, Newman was not advancing or practicing some form of religious monomania. Everyone is familiar with that variety of puritan who thinks everything he does is a kind of "preaching" and who is intolerable in consequence. This is not at all what Newman meant to encourage, nor is it how he lived. His own rhetoric of conduct was far more subtle, far more roundly human than a self-conscious obsession with "winning friends and influencing people" will produce. Indeed, Newman's manner bears little resemblance to the modern and persistent notion of what proper "Victorian behavior" was. While certainly quite sensitive to social conventions and proprieties, his own manner and sociability remained thoroughly unselfconscious. Meriol Trevor relates that Newman was constantly surprising those who expected (and often desired) to find in him a stern and starched clergyman full of religious conversation. As a dinner guest, Newman was more likely to fill his lap with his host's children, play games, and tell stories than discuss religion. (In fact, Newman enjoyed the life-long distinction of being regarded the favorite visitor by many of his friends' children.) Finding the ostentatiously solemn difficult to endure, Newman almost always contrived to ruffle their feathers. While University Preacher, he upset an officious Head of House at Oxford by making shadow-rabbits on the wall after dinner and, when scolded for it, quite unashamedly fell asleep--or at least pretended to. On another occasion Newman shocked a "prim and pompous" man of staid political views (probably Berkeley of Pembroke) by suddenly turning toward him and saying "So, you wish, it seems, to change the monarchy into a republic?"[23]

The point in such incidents is not that Newman was a regular "jolly fellow" who was good with children. What is significant is that his manner had little of the solemn religiosity about it, nor was his "rhetoric of conduct" a covert intention to deceive. Rhetoric of conduct, both in Newman's exposition of it and in his actions, was a means by which something existent is made visible, is "set off." This is why

Newman was so little concerned at Oxford with building a party or browbeating newcomers with "Tractarianism." Not only did his unconcern with party-building attract more interest than party-building would have, but a great deal of Newman's popularity at Oxford rested on his lack of condescension or "donnishness," his engaging manner, sincere interest in the general welfare of students, and his animated yet serene manner of conversing. One young student, too poor to feed himself, was tactfully assisted by Newman through regular invitations to breakfast. These breakfasts gravely alarmed the student's relative, "Miss Mitford" (author of *Our Village*), who feared infection with the plague of Tractarianism. Quizzing her young relative as to the subjects of Newman's conversation, she was surprised to learn that Tractarianism never came up. The young scholar said Newman spoke of

> the classics, history, mathematics, general literature . . . and he tells me to diversify my reading, to take exercise and to get as much practical knowledge and cheerful society as I can . . . he talks to me of every sort of subject except what is called Tractarianism, and that he has never mentioned.[24]

This conversational versatility does not appear to be an isolated incidence. J. A. Froude gave Newman the highest praise for interest in science, politics, and literature, and recalled that private or sociable conversation with Newman was invariably thrilling. No one at Oxford compared to Newman, Froude said, for his non-condescending yet authoritative air, his conviviality with students, his lack of ill nature ("Not a malicious anecdote was ever heard from him"). "He was lightness itself" according to Froude, "--the lightness of elastic strength--and he was interesting because he never talked for talking's sake, but because he had something real to say."[25] The affection borne Newman by Oxford students remains remarkable for its depth even in the long history of the university. Though superiors attempted to isolate him by not assigning him students, his influence was tremendous, if unsought. A favorite saying among students at the time was "Credo in Newmannum."[26]

RHETORICAL RECEPTIVITY

The "invariable thrill" of conversation with Newman was in large part a result of his unusual faculty for sensing the thoughts and feelings of those around him. If Newman's life-long sense of mission was a pastoral/rhetorical one of restoring souls and intellects through the sacraments and discourse, then few have been so well qualified for the task. He possessed a keen sensitivity to minds that manifested itself both in his discourse and in his personal dealings with people. It was a universal sensitivity in that it allowed great insight into human practical cognition, habits of thought, character and motives, yet it did not often make him painfully or awkwardly self-conscious. The "manly" self-control Newman so admired meant more than control of the passions; it also meant one's refusal to allow self-interest and self-consciousness to render dealings with other people unnatural or awkward. Newman once wrote to Bishop Ullathorne, ". . . I cannot in conversation use smooth words, which conceal, not express my thoughts. . . ."[27] Because Newman was always sharply aware of men's attitudes and impressions, he was able to tailor conversations or discourses quite delicately to suit the people involved, though not, he avowed, at the cost of truthfulness. Even on a personal level he was generally able to discern what another's perception of him was and how that perception was generated. On the public level, it allowed him to discern what the common perception of an idea, a religious doctrine or body, or even an historical event was, and how that perception was generated.

In the main, and especially as considered from a rhetorical standpoint, Newman's sensitivity was largely his ability to cast himself wholeheartedly into a mind, an attitude, a belief not his own. When such a capacity is so deep as to be automatic, one either drowns in a flood of de-individualizing receptivity or one converts such sensitivity into action.[28] Far from being incapacitated by sensitivity, Newman was propelled into action by his motivation to use his faculties for the restoration of religious sensibilities. His ability to approximate other minds also perplexed many who mistook his lucid summaries of views he did not hold for a secret tendency toward them. Huxley asserted that a primer of infidelity could be glossed from Newman's works, to which Wilfrid Ward responds, "The skeptic's mind was vividly present to Newman's imagination. . . . He saw to the full the plausibility of the case which might have been made out against the truths he most deeply believed."[29] Newman was "quite capable," says Houghton, "of appreciating the appeal of other beliefs or the force of opposing arguments."[30] While he was unmoved by such force and plausibilities, he grasped their power and their influence on a nineteenth-century public only too ready to embrace either mechanical, scientific reasoning or emotional fundamentalism.

This "psychological insight," as Ward observes, applied to both individuals and groups; in Newman, the faculty enabled him to "size up" a body of people at a lecture or sermon, or enter into the mind of someone in private conversation.[31]

Oddly enough, the sensitivity was keen enough to actually pain Newman when dealing with individual people. He was never quite comfortable, for instance, in hearing confessions, either as an Anglican or as a Catholic. He had no doctrinal difficulty with the sacrament, nor was he afflicted with an all-too-keen English sense of privacy; he simply felt the sorrows, pains, and even temptations experienced by the persons too intensely; he "knew so much of what went on in peoples' minds, he was overwhelmingly conscious of the difficulties and dangers of dealing with them. . . ."[32] As Provost of the Oratory, Newman's responsibility for the care and even correction of those under his authority also rested heavily upon him. He had a keen faculty for discerning the source of personal faults, but the faculty caused him much pain, as the difficult episode with long-time associate and friend John Dalgairns reveals. Newman wrote to his closest Oratorian friend Ambrose St. John:

> The same clearness which makes me see other's failings makes me see my own, or at least and rather, makes me see what people think about me or may think, and in consequence, not from any supernatural feelings, but naturally, I am most keenly troubled when I feel I might on any occasion have done better.

Then, poignantly, "Sometimes for hours I have quite writhed with pain."[33] Ward notes that "Newman *saw too much* for a man of action. Difficulties were too vividly present to his mind in all his undertakings."[34]

Ward is too severe; Newman's "seeing,"--his sensitivity--was hardly incapacitating nor did it become sentimentality. Though he wept while reading Sir Walter Scott (a favorite author) and--as an elderly Cardinal--was forced by his tears to leave the Oratory schoolroom during a reading of Virgil's account of Dido and Aeneas, he was no maudlin sentimentalist. The passions did not run in a single direction, and his sympathetic capacity equally led him to admit that he "burned to have been a soldier" upon reading Wellington's dispatches. If Newman could enter into the thoughts and feelings of both groups and individuals, he was equally capable of rejecting those thoughts and qualifying those emotions. In Chesterton's memorable phrase, Newman may have been a "naked man," but he "carried a naked sword."[35] This is the man who, as a young Fellow of Oriel in charge of discipline, would cow undergraduate offenders without a word, just fixing upon them an icy stare; who alone confronted several rather large, drunken and blaspheming High Street butchers and silenced them by observing that if they knew what they were saying, they would not say it.

Like rhetoric itself, such psychological insight and sensitivity could easily be used in highly "political" ways for good or ill. It could be used to build a party of followers or bend people to one's will. But Newman did not seek influence in this way or of such a kind. Perhaps unconsciously, Newman grasped the paradox that the greatest influence is had by one who makes no deliberate effort at influence. Abstaining from such attempts at insinuation is its own greatest rhetoric, for it testifies to both the character of the "rhetor" and his confidence in the validity of what he embraces. In fact, sincerity was one of Newman's greatest tools in persuading people of his point of view. He discovered that the greatest means of allaying distrust or suspicion in a person was to become acquainted with that person. In this way, the person could see for himself and--based on experience-- make his own judgment of Newman's character. This is what occurred with the publication of *The Development of Christian Doctrine*. Many of Newman's new associates, the Catholic intellectuals, thought the book theologically questionable; the convert's response to this was to try to become acquainted with any who were suspicious. The action was largely successful. Those who questioned the book's ideas for their novelty became willing to entertain the ideas because Newman's sincerity and orthodox conception of the faith had become evident to them.[36]

SENSITIVITY AND PUBLIC RHETORIC

But what about Newman's actual public rhetoric--his oratory? Newman's success as an orator was in fact largely dependent upon this very ability to assess the mental disposition of his audience. His manner of speaking betrayed no effort at "oracular" or dramatic presentation. Religious services he conducted as an Anglican were singularly unspectacular, often disappointing to those who "came out of curiosity, expecting to see some strange and imposing figure, elaborately cere- monial, dramatically declaiming medieval doctrines."[37] His movements in services were natural, his walk very fast but smooth, his gestures minimal. The speaking voice was very distinctive but unaffected, "clear" and "of tenor pitch."[38] The sermons were read, of course, and the pitch of his voice was very steady and clear, not wavering up and down with emotional emphasis. Auditors called the voice memorable for its sweetness and simplicity, persuasive in being transparent and frank.[39] He had the unusual quality of delivering each sentence quickly, followed by a long pause.[40]

While the manner of speaking did not change with the occasion or audience, the matter of his speeches and sermons did change. Newman was fond of trying to balance his auditors' predispositions by emphasizing aspects of belief opposite to those that predominated in the audience. To the self-righteous he would preach fear of God and the inadequacy even of our best virtues; to the comfortable he would preach the sacrificial nature of faith, and the dangers of complacency; to the scrupulous he would preach the inestimable goodness of divine mercy and solicitude. The success or failure of these balancing efforts was determined largely by the acuity of Newman's sense of the particular audience. In fact, his one famous failure in oratory shows just how much his rhetorical oratory depended upon this sensitivity to the dispositions of his auditors.

Shortly after his arrival in Rome to pursue studies for the priesthood, Newman suffered a rare public humiliation. His fame having preceded him (he received a telegram from the Pope upon his conversion), he was generally well treated. Expectations can breed disaster, however, and an opportunity soon arose for a great disappointment. Upon the death in Rome of Lady Shrewsbury's Catholic niece, Newman was asked to preach the funeral sermon before a con-gregation of both Catholics and Protestants. Sensing difficulty, Newman earnestly tried to avoid the task, but he was fairly forced to take it up. Not having been long in Rome, he had little feel for the sensibilities of Italian Catholics or even the English Protestants who lived there. The result was that everyone was offended. Expected to preach conversion to the Protestants, Newman preached instead the necessity of everyone's conversion (a patristic use of the word), thus alienating some Catholics. Worse yet, he claimed that the English character was noble but deficient in that it lacked the Catholic faith. The Protestants were outraged, feeling that they had been singled out for abuse. Perhaps it was impossible to preach to a mixed congregation that largely expected a showpiece; if display is desired, a rebuke--no matter how sincere or well crafted--can only offend. Though many liked the sermon, the Protestant outcry was so intense that the occasion was considered an embarrassment. The furor even reached the ears of the Pope, who (ironically) is said to have surmised charitably that Newman "must be more of a philosopher than an orator."[41]

This occasion of rhetorical failure pained Newman a great deal, and it indicates the extent to which his sensitivity to audience fine-tuned his oratory. A successful instance of this fine-tuning was his Irish lectures on the nature and mission of the Catholic University. By taking on the founding of a university in

Ireland and having (at the bishops' request) to sell the idea to a mixed and even hostile audience, Newman was called upon to exercise rhetorical skill to the utmost. He was acutely aware of this. He had to "teach the Paddies what education was, what a university [is], and how it was their duty to have one with me for a Rector."[42] He worried that his ignorance of the audience would produce another failure, and complained that, "I have the utmost difficulty in writing for people I don't know, and I have commonly failed when I have addressed strangers."[43] He did not fail, however, and the first lecture (delivered in May of 1852) was before a crowded and largely pleased audience in Dublin. Though fearing disaster from the lecture, Newman succeeded because he knew and had a sympathetic understanding of his audience. While having little personal exposure to the Irish, he did have a very accurate and complete grasp of the issues of the controversy, of the parties and their tenets, as well as the ends desired. This knowledge, unsatisfactory as it was for Newman, was quite enough to enable him to fashion his lectures accordingly. Some of the more personal interaction Newman preferred followed the lecture, and he was delighted by what the interaction revealed. "I am amused at the great cleverness of the Irish, which far surpasses any thing I ever saw elsewhere. The very ticket takers in the room followed my arguments, and gave me analysis of the Discourse afterwards."[44] Perhaps it was this contact with the audience that led Newman to declare prior to the second lecture, "I have just discovered *how* I ought to have written my lectures, what would have been the true rhetoric and how I have plunged into a maze of metaphysics, from which I may be unable to heave myself."[45]

LIBERALISM

Newman carried his perceptivity of mental predispositions into the more intellectual realms of apologetic theory, and his fight against Liberalism, as well. Although he never called this perceptivity or its application to apologetics "rhetorical," he relied explicitly upon climbing inside the cognitive and emotive habits of an opponent. In a compact yet important passage of his *Present Position of Catholics in England*, Newman describes how he will meet Protestant arguments:

> If I select their words or their acts, I wish to throw myself into them, and determine what they mean by the light of this informing principle. And I have means of doing so which

> many others have not, having been a Protestant myself. I
> have stood their ground; and would always aim at handling
> their arguments, not as so many dead words, but as the
> words of a speaker in a particular state of mind, which must
> be experienced, or witnessed, or explored if it is to be
> understood.[46]

Though Newman was never quite a "Liberal," he employed the same strategy in confronting Liberalism as he here advocates regarding Protestantism. His "missionary campaign" against Liberalism led him into areas normally philosophical, but as "a man of action rather than a pure thinker . . . he philosophized within certain limits which were laid down for him by the exigencies of his missionary work."[47] These exigencies meant he had to confront the central tenet of Liberalism--the idea that no absolute truth was ascertainable in religious or even metaphysical matters. Newman thought this error arose because a mathematical and scientific form of reasoning was used where it did not belong. Religious Liberalism's twin brother, philosophical Liberalism, held that the only *bona fide* knowledge available to man was a kind of mathematical empiricism of strict demonstration.[48] These two Liberalisms frame much of the nineteenth-century intellectual activity and the philosophical/religious matters touched upon were many: metaphysics, epistemology, critical doubt in Descartes and Kant, the empiricism of Locke and Hume. The rhetorical atmosphere was combative and accentuated by the peculiar intensity that comes in fighting for a valid but gradually losing cause. The "response to the growing anti-religious forces constitutes a high, sometimes tragic drama of the national soul," says Richard D. Altick,[49] and Newman's role in all this was that of a great experimenter, forging and testing intellectual arguments like a smith in a weapons factory:

> From the time that I began to occupy my mind with
> theological subjects [one can almost hear "fro the tyme he
> first bigan/ To riden out. . ."] I have been troubled at the
> prospects which I considered to be before us, of an
> intellectual movement against religion, so special as to have a
> claim upon the attention of all educated Christians. . . . This
> grave apprehension led me to consider the evidences, as they
> are called, of Religion generally and the intellectual theory on
> which they are based. This I attempted with the purpose, as
> far as lay in my power, not certainly of starting doubts about
> religion, but of testing and perfecting the proofs in its
> behalf.[50]

Because the intellectual mission Newman was convinced he must pursue did not allow the luxury of "making do" with ineffective weaponry, some of his own Italian and English Catholic colleagues found themselves perplexed by his rejection of certain religious arguments. He was convinced that the Italian school of polemical argumentation, being too much influenced by the abstract rationalism of the day, mistakenly defended Christianity in an excessively demonstrative fashion. Though he did not doubt that many religious demonstrations are true and valuable, they fall short of providing any real *motivum credibile.* "'The proof of Christianity'" Newman asserts in a letter, "is just the point on which polemics and dogmatics meet on one common ground."[51] Dogmatics got the upper hand in Italian religious arguments, with the result that one's opponent was unconvinced. Newman, however, felt that there are many kinds of intellectual difficulty such arguments fail to meet and material or psychological predispositions that the same arguments fail to address. He argued that if one is to obtain the assent of an opponent, one must enter his mind and see what he sees and feel the force of arguments as he feels them. This constituted a rhetorical prerequisite that provided the necessary insight into predispositions (or character). By using the insight thus gained, one could formulate a convincing series of arguments and appeals.[52]

While Newman's psychological emphasis must have sounded quite strange in a day that considered argument demonstrative, he often used hypothetical individuals to typify the "mind" of a group or class of people. His theological notebooks provide an excellent example of this, as Newman sketches a "biography" of the skeptical mind:

> We start with what we have received as children; we accept, we prize, we defend, what we have been taught; we may see difficulties in it, which we may not be able to overcome, which may tease us, but they do not shake our confidence in it. We try how to answer the objections, which we feel, and we manage to go on without any great trouble of mind. At length as our mind grows, as our information accumulates, as we see more of the world, and exercise more freely our minds, questions occur which really require an answer, and, if we are external to the Catholic Church, begin to impair the implicit trust which we have hitherto cherished in the creed which we have received whether from our parents or on revered instruction. We gradually lose altogether that trust, which was once so simple, with or without the power of attaching ourselves to some other profession. Sometimes perhaps we think we have done so; though, generally speaking, our minds have opened far more *truly* to the hollowness of what we once believed than to the truth of anything else. However, for a time we profess some other creed, and keep steadfastly to it. But the same process recurs, the mind goes on acting, it is filled with objections it cannot answer. It sees the bottomless depth which lies before it, and is unwilling to give up what though only a

> second, it feels to be virtually a last attempt to gain a hold
> upon the truth. It attempts to modify, and patch up its theory
> as it best can; it becomes eclectic, or it tries to throw itself
> upon authority. One attempt or another it makes to retain
> itself in its position; but in proportion to the activity,
> clearness, honesty, and boldness of its intellect, it finds the
> attempt hopeless; and as time goes on it slowly and calmly is
> floated upon the bosom of an ocean without a shore, the
> dead profound of interminable, hopeless, skepticism, in
> which nothing is believed, nothing professed, nothing
> perhaps even guessed at.[53]

Such a concrete, vivid grasp of the internal processes and developments of a mind not his own--though quite common to his times--is the very ground and basis for rhetorical effectiveness. If true persuasion is to occur, one must go beyond the verbal formulations of arguments to comprehend the development of mind that generated those arguments. Thus there is an immediate and powerful rhetorical application for Newman's habitual sensitivity to others' predispositions and modes of thought.

THE PRICE OF PERCEPTION

This sensitivity was eminently useful for Newman, but it carried its own penalties. His ability to approximate habits of mind and reasoning alien to himself and his beliefs, led to a frequent misperception of Newman by his colleagues. It is paradoxical that his effectiveness in dealing with skeptics and liberals often made those who were not such rationalists fear that Newman was one himself. Even the writings of St. Thomas Aquinas have been misunderstood for the same reason. The schoolman is so exact and perceptive in his "objections" or summaries of erroneous positions, that some have concluded he favors the very arguments he refutes. By entering into the minds of opponents, by studying their positions with a comprehensiveness and clarity often exceeding their own, and, moreover, by insisting that such positions must be met and not merely ignored, Newman often upset those who shared his religious beliefs. It was feared that one who could so effectively state the opponent's point of view must have some (possibly secret or unconscious) affinity with that point of view. Likewise, to acknowledge certain strengths in the opponent's arguments and to demand that they be met made many intellectual Christians uncomfortable. It forced them out of the study and into the field of combat where arguments they were perfectly content with did not seem to be very effective. Newman's sympathetic ability was also unnerving to some of those opponents (his own brother, for instance), for they too were taken in by his ability to express their own positions with such facility; it was often thought that he was a natural skeptic who by pure force of will made himself embrace religious orthodoxy as an escape from skepticism.[54]

Such perplexity was a constant trial to Newman, for he fancied that his efforts, even his theoretical ones, concentrated on the actual processes of human thought. He did not believe his work touched upon philosophy very much, for his approach to thought was an eclectic mixture of generalities rather than universals, personal influences, and practical psychology. As Newman stated toward the end of his life, his investigations were "an attempt to test the availableness at the present time of certain conventional proofs used for polemical purposes."[55] Some critics still accuse Newman of philosophical skepticism, but his own estimation of his labors seems just: "My turn of mind has never led me towards metaphysics; rather, it has been logical, ethical, practical."[56] Indeed, this "turn of mind" is very nearly a definition of those matters most appropriate to rhetoric.

It could be asked--in the style of the chicken-and-egg dilemma--which came first; did Newman's sense of missionary purpose inspire him to develop his sensitivity or did his acute perception of people's minds sharpen his sense of purpose? Like the chicken-and-egg dilemma itself, the question hardly seems to matter. What is certain is that Newman had such a purpose and that it was expressed in rhetorical ways. Not only did he use his sensitivity to enhance his "public and private" rhetoric, but he cultivated an awareness of the influence of things not usually considered in a rhetorical context. He drew attention to the capacities of conduct and liberal education for preparing minds to receive supernatural truths and to defend them in a rationalistic world. He encouraged the development of arguments that took into account the predispositions and prejudices of opponents. He even practiced the fine art of "personal influence"--an influence based upon perception of realities, not manipulation of personality. In fact, it was largely the elimination of personal influence from so-called rational discourse or thought that he found so pernicious and artificial. In an 1873 letter to a friendly Protestant correspondent, Newman wrote:

> It seems to me to take the true and normal way of meeting
> the infidelity of the age, by referring to Our Lord's Person
> and Character as exhibited in the Gospels. Philip said to
> Nathaniel "Come and see"--that is just what the present free
> thinkers will not allow men to do. They perplex and
> bewilder them with previous questions, to hinder them from

falling under the legitimate rhetoric of His Divine Life, of
His sacred word and acts. They say "There is no truth
because there are so many opinions," or "How do you know
that the Gospels are authentic?" "How do you account for
Papias not mentioning the fourth Gospel?" or "How can you
believe that punishment is eternal?" or "Why is there no
stronger proof of the Resurrection?"[57]

The difficulty with such questions was not that they lacked answers; indeed,
Newman himself often wrangled over such matters and was well aware of what
could be answered. Rather, the difficulty was in the preemptive "poisoning of the
wells" or de-conditioning of the intellect such questions inevitably caused. They
placed a barrier that was secondary in terms of evidence or relevance into a primary
position. They placed questions dependent upon previous exposure to the Gospels
in a position antecedent to those Gospels, thus subtly changing the inquirer's
attitudes in such a way as to disable him from giving a fair reading of the texts.
"With this multitude of questions in detail," wrote Newman, "they block the way
between the soul and its Saviour, and will not let it 'Come and see.'"[58] "Come and
see" fairly summarizes both Newman's idea of the tactic religious argumentation
should take in his day and the primary value of personal influence. His sensitivity
to mental processes spurred him to embrace personal influences (whether his own
or those working in the Gospels) as an antidote to rationalism and depersonalized
thought. The next chapter will fully explore the character of the "personal" in
Newman's thought in its rhetorical significance.

IV. RHETORICAL PERSONALISM

If your love do not persuade you to come, let not my letter.
Merchant of Venice 3, ii.

PERSONS AND PERSONALISM

There is an irony about Newman's *Apologia* that demonstrates how his "personalism" was an important element of his rhetorical habit of mind. The *Apologia*, of course, is both the most famous of Newman's controversial works and the most personal of all his public texts. He conceived of the work as primarily a personal vindication and, by extension, a vindication of the priesthood. He had very little sense that the book was one of Christian apologetic; the title was quite deliberately self-referential, and he thought the defense was primarily of himself. The reception of the book pleased but surprised him. "I have sincerely tried to keep from controversy, and to occupy myself in simply defending myself, and in myself, my brethren; and, without my intending it, I have written what I hear from various quarters is found useful *controversially* [emphasis his]." Then, in a telling statement, he adds, "If I *attempted* to be controversial, I may spoil all."[1] The irony is that Newman's most effective controversial work was not broadly apologetic in intention; it was personal, almost private, and individual. He was at his best rhetorically when he was at his most personal; he addressed the argumentative standing of religious matters most capably when he addressed his own mind, circumstances, and history. The essentially rhetorical thrust of Newman's thought is the profound and instinctive personalism that characterizes every variety of his discourse. This chapter will explore that personalism and show how it is both rhetorical and cognitive in its habituation.

Even in controversy, Newman's excellence was not so much his formal reasoning as it was the personal quality of his prose or oratory. That he could command an audience is well known, but each member of the audience would feel as if he were being privately addressed. This is why Newman eschewed actual public debate; it was of little interest to him, urge him though others might. The well-known Metaphysical Society in London boasted the greatest religious and agnostic intellectuals of its day; men like Huxley, Cardinal Manning, and W. G. Ward met regularly to discuss and debate the foundations of religious belief, but Newman simply was not interested in such public jousting. This seeming paradox-- that a personalist rhetorician should avoid public debate--is quite consistent with the highly individual-directed nature of Newman's discourse. He even joked that he would consent to debate only if, as his rebuttal, he would be allowed to play the fiddle. Such debate was simply not Newman's "style," even when addressing a public audience. His "personalism" was derived from his rather automatic interest in persons, their nature, and especially their fate with regard to the soul. But in order for this insight and purpose to be viewed as the rhetorical pre-condition which animated Newman's discourse, "personalism" must be carefully defined.

The term "person" is an important one in the Christian tradition. Boethius provided the definition that was to become standard (if sometimes controversial) in medieval thought: a person is "an individual substance with a rational nature."[2] Note that the definition does not refer solely to people. While "person" might be considered identical to "man" or "human" in pre-Christian antiquity, in Christian thought such a restricted conception does not suffice. Not only is God a person, He is in fact *three*. Moreover, there are created, intelligent persons who do not possess bodies: the angels. The challenge, then, is to arrive at an understanding of the term that embraces God, man, and angels and yet speaks to an essential "whatness" of each. Boethius' definition does this, for "individual substance" speaks to the genus, while "rational nature" provides the specific difference. The strength here, then, is that both the mental capacities (whether actual or potential) naturally associated with persons as well as their individually self-subsisting quality are provided for, all the while allowing for essential differentiation in *kinds* of persons. St. Thomas Aquinas expands this definition while refuting the idea that no definition of "person" is possible since "person" is a singular thing (no singular admits of de- finition). Arguing that, in a sense, the individual can be defined through its belonging to "the genus of substance," Aquinas says:

> Further still, in a more special and perfect way, the particular
> and the individual are found in the rational substances which
> have dominion over their own actions; and which are not
> only made to act, like others; but which can act of
> themselves; for actions belong to singulars. Therefore also
> the individuals of the rational nature have a special name

even among other substances; and this name is *person* [emphasis his].[3]

By introducing the note of dominion over actions, Aquinas casts Boethius' definition in a nuanced light, a light which, while leaving the genus and difference of the definition alone, advances the idea of persons' moral or self-determinate aspect through action. Garrigou-Lagrange, in recapitulating the arguments, states that "A person is a free and intelligent subject or an individual substance with a rational nature."[4] By inserting "free," the Thomist stresses the self-determining and active quality of persons in their moral freedom. The Thomistic understanding of that freedom varies according to its agent; the freedom of action in God is generally called gratuitous, that is, free in being wholly self-willed and unconstrained. The action of angels is likewise free, though not usually called gratuitous. Though their own wills (informed by intellect) are free, they are ordered to the divine will. Man, too, possesses an independent will which, though free, is ordered to God. Thus action is moral in so far as it is ordered, and action is individual through its cause, a subsisting self.

Persons, then, are indeed rational, but their character as agents, "do-ers," necessarily involves every aspect of their being including will, passions, and in the case of man, even the body. So a person is inherently a moral being--one might even say a practical one. In man's case, there is an enormous field of action involving things of a contingent or probable nature; also, unlike angels, man does not enjoy the full and immediate grasp of things through intellectual intuition. The result of this combination is that a great deal of man's intellectual efforts treat things not necessarily "abstract" or speculative. This is largely the realm of the practical intellect, though it must be emphasized that action is mental, as well as physical.

In studying Newman, the important part of the definition of "person" is that dealing with the "rational nature." Though Newman's philosophical conception of "person" is not necessarily connected to his rhetorical personalism, he did share an interest in the idea of persons with Aquinas. One of the most heavily marked parts of Newman's *Summa Theologica* is that dealing with the three-fold personhood of the Trinity. Here we will use a Thomistic understanding of "person" because it does highlight the active, moral aspect of rational beings. As such, it intimates the integrated unity of rational beings that Newman sensed (sensed even more than theorized about)--their "wholeness" of faculties and capacities. Newman's idea of the whole man reasoning is harmonious with the Thomistic principle that does not confine "rational nature" to abstract intellectual demonstration. The active, moral

54

RHETORICAL PERSONALISM

thrust of rational natures shows that there is more than demonstrative reasoning in a rational being; there is also love (will), passion (ordered to reason), necessity for action and practical wisdom, etc. In other words, man's "rational nature" properly includes such things as affections, wrath, prudence, delight, everything proper to human beings. To be sure, there are nuances and subtleties about "person" in Aquinas that we do not treat here. In fact, the most profound part of Aquinas' "personalist" thought concerns how "rational nature" is *derived* from the ontological or metaphysical *suppositum* of selfhood and the unobjectizability of the *suppositum*.[5] But Newman--by way of a kind of connatural sympathy--treads Thomistic personal ground simply as regards the integration of rational nature, not the metaphysical conceptions of existential being and the *suppositum*.

ACTION AND PERSONAL INFLUENCE

Compared to Aquinas, Newman's personalism was far less speculative and far more practical in orientation. His personalism reveals itself in his dealings with individuals--a kind of rhetoric of conduct--and in his approach to man's intellectual development. He did not seek to establish a philosophical theory that would exalt "personhood" or make of personal consciousness the subsistence of being.[6] His interests were personal in that they considered the implications of the Fall regarding individual souls, the soul's actual working in the world, and the individual or personal means of salvation. In Newman's view, the fundamental principle of mankind's experience was the relation of each person to his Creator, and all a person's relations, interactions, and connections with other people were dependent upon that primary connection of Creator and creature. Beside this relation, man to God, all else pales in importance and priority. Yet this priority results in the paradox that ordinary experience is all the more important because of the moral character of human activity. Though one's relations with other people are secondary as compared with one's relation to God, they are primary in immediacy. The Creator can be known through creation, but one must know creation first. This is parallel, of course, to Newman's (and Aristotle's) insistence that what is philosophically secondary--the realm of practical wisdom, action, ethics--can be primary and more immediate than philosophical wisdom, even though in itself practical wisdom is not the highest order of wisdom. Therefore, depending upon the purpose one has in speaking of a thing, it may be alternately primary or secondary. This is a paradox central to the proper understanding of Newman. His "inconsistencies" are precisely of this sort, and great difficulties arise when one aspect of Newman's views are looked at to the exclusion of another. Even the percipient A. D. Nuttall has difficulties with this when he cites Newman's famous statement about the perishing of the world being preferable to a single, even venial, sin.[7] Nuttall mistakes Newman's statement for a "right-wing Christian" one that is repugnant for its unfeeling, absolutist disregard for things human; what he misses is that Newman is speaking of the world and God each considered strictly in and of itself, in which case, as Newman says, the two are "simply incommensurate." The statement is one that serves to amplify an incommensurability, *not* advocate or approve of human ruin. To interpret the statement as Nuttall does is to disregard Newman's tenet that, incommensurable though the world and God may be, it is precisely *through* the world and virtuous activity that man comes to his Creator.

Newman's regard for the immediacy of practical human action explains why he regarded "perfection" in the moral sphere as simply the performance of one's duties to the utmost of one's abilities.[8] Compared to the contemplative tradition where "perfection" is a heightened spiritual awareness and union with God (a conception Newman would not deny), Newman's conception was almost pedestrian in its practicality. True, Newman held that prayer and contemplation were part of the performance of one's duties (indeed, at the heart of them--witness his *Devotions and Meditations*) but he drew attention to what St. Therese of Lisieux would later call "the little way." Newman's emphasis on daily duties indicates his habitual sensitivity to the pragmatic ordering of one's life in all its aspects to that one relation to God. Not everyone is a mystic, a theologian, or even a religious. Many are those--whose ultimate fate and salvation is no less personally important than that of the greatest saint--who will hardly entertain a "spiritual" thought or contemplative moment in the course of their three-score and ten. Much as Newman felt he was responding to the intellectual "apostolate" so necessary in his day, it remains that a great deal of his intellectual labor aimed at defending the reasonability of faith in the uneducated, the non-intellectual. In a similar vein, his idea of "perfection" placed it within reach of the non-contemplative, non-mystical person immersed in the active life. In this regard, it is significant that Newman's Oratory was located in the heart of a poor, working-class city. Duties are universal, and perfection in the performance of them is as appropriate in the work-a-day world of a Birmingham laborer as it is behind cloister walls. When the Pope's secretary, Monsignor Talbot, invited Newman to Rome to preach Lenten sermons to an audience "more educated than could ever be the case in England," Newman declined, acerbically replying that "Birmingham people have souls."[9]

The "rhetoric of conduct" embraced by Newman both in theory and in practice was not, therefore, limited to the classes where "gentlemanliness" was at a premium. It extended in range and influence to any class of persons of whatever socio-economic background. At root, of course, this is the consequence of the very doctrines Newman was so famous for defending; "Birmingham people have souls" is as apt a summation of the doctrine of spiritual dignity as any nineteenth-century formulation. Perhaps inspired by his patristic mentors, Newman viewed religion not as an abstract series of propositions--necessary as those propositions were for clarity and comprehension. Religion was also a thing to inform and characterize routine "existence" in such a way as to frame, support, and give significance to the moral dimension of daily life. The lower classes could act upon their faith in a manner conducive to leavening the moral and spiritual liveliness of their associates, while the gentry was capable of the same thing suited to their own class. Thus a person's ordinary activities were capable of exerting an enormous influence for religious good.

Two seemingly unrelated areas demonstrate this conception of a "daily" rhetoric of conduct as applied to widely different groups. The first area, to continue the Oratorian focus, is described in Newman's addresses presented to the fledgling Oratory. These addresses were private, intimate forums in which Newman tried to present to his small assembly of recently ordained priests a sense of the value and significance of the Oratorian way of life. The talks were a unique combination of spiritual direction and counsel, Oratorian history, and practical advice for the proper conduct of community living. Newman's attraction to the Oratory of St. Philip Neri is easy to understand when the Rule of the Oratory is seen in contrast to that of conventional religious orders. Though very much like a religious order in appearance, the Oratory is an independent congregation, each house governing itself through superiors elected on a regular basis. In sharpest contrast to many religious orders, those who join an Oratory make no vows to the Oratory--they are not bound by vows but by what St. Philip called "chains of love." It is a small association of priests, rather like a family, each of whom is free to possess his own property and pursue his own interests. Pastorally, the Oratorians are directed (appropriately enough) toward preaching in urban areas as well as being con-fessors. The cement holding the community together is mutual affection, respect, and love of the Oratory itself.

Thus an Oratorian priest is tied to his congregation by love, not canonical restraints. Such a bond is benign, certainly, but all the more fragile for being unofficial, intangible, dependent upon human affections and self-restraint. For Newman, the difficulties of such a state were conquered by the very principle of the vocation: personal influence. "Obedience to the official Superior is the prominent principle of the Jesuit; personal influence is that of the Oratorian."[10] Through the influence of personal good-will and mutual accommodation, the strains of human idiosyncrasy can be overcome or at least tolerated. In principle like a family, an Oratory has no vows to "fall back upon" in times of trial or stress, but relies upon the interaction of diverse persons of mutual affection and purpose. Moreover, the leavening of personal influence acts as a constant encouragement toward spiritual progress and development. The attraction for Newman is obvious: the Oratory as described in these addresses is an example of the rhetoric of conduct applied to a small community.

In sharp contrast, Newman's *Present Position of Catholics in England* was a series of public lectures to a varied audience in response to an upsurge of anti-Catholic rioting and propaganda. These lectures were tough, ironic, often humorous, and profound in psychological insight. In analyzing the causes of anti-Catholic prejudice, Newman finds fresh indications of the place and role of a rhetoric of conduct:

> Thus Protestants judge us by their "texts"; and by "texts" I do not mean only passages from our writers, but all those samples of whatever kind, historical, ecclesiastical, biographical or political, carefully prepared, improved, and finished off by successive artists for the occasion, which they think so much more worthy of credit and reliance as to facts than us and our word, who are in the very communion to which those texts relate. Some good personal knowledge of us, and intercourse with us, not in the way of controversy or criticism, but what is prior--viz., in the way of sincere inquiry, in order to ascertain how things really lie, such knowledge and intercourse would be worth all the conclusions however elaborate and subtle, from rumors, false witnessings, suspicions, romantic scenes, morsels of history, morsels of theology, morsels of our miraculous legends, morsels of our devotional writers, morsels from our individual members, whether unlearned or intemperate, which are the "text" of the traditional Protestant view against us. This, then, is the last of the causes, which in the course of these Lectures I shall assign . . . by way of accounting for the hatred and contempt shown towards the Catholics of

England by their fellow-countrymen--viz., that the Catholics
of England, as a body, are not personally known.[11]

One reason they are not personally known, according to Newman, is that
Catholics are not in fact accorded the traditional English allowances and
considerations due to "persons". Newman informs his Corn Exchange audience of
a controversy he is engaged in with a "Mr. Seely," who accused the Birmingham
priests of dishonesty:

> He complains, that is, that I have given a *personal* turn to his
> assertion. Ah, true, I ought to have remembered that
> Catholic priests, in the judgement of a good Protestant, are
> not persons at all. I had forgotten what I have already said in
> the First of these Lectures; we are not men, we have not
> characters to lose, we have not feelings to be wounded, we
> have not friends, we have not penitents, we have not
> congregations; we have nothing personal about us, we are
> not the fellow creatures of our accusers, we are not
> gentlemen, we are not Christians, we are abstractions, we
> are shadows, we are heraldic emblazonments, we are the
> griffins and wiverns of the old family picture, we are stage
> characters with a mask and a dagger, we are mummies from
> Egypt or antediluvian ornithorhynchi, we are unresisting
> ninepins, to be set up and knocked down by every
> mischievous boy; . . . Did the figures come down from
> some old piece of tapestry, or were a lion rampant from an
> inn door suddenly to walk the streets, a Protestant would not
> be more surprised than at the notion that we have nerves,
> that we have hearts, that we have sensibilities.[12]

Catholics are not known because they are not considered persons in the sense
accorded to other Englishmen. What, then, to do? What might "solve" the problem?
The rhetorical tool Newman prescribes is the same one he looks to as the principle
of the Oratory. Personal influence is the ultimate rhetoric in this case, the argument
without proposition, the syllogism or enthymeme of conduct, the persuasion of
personal knowledge:

> Protestantism is fierce, because it does not know you;
> ignorance is its strength; error is its life. . . . Oblige men to
> know you; persuade them, importune them, shame them into
> knowing you. Make it so clear what you are, that they
> cannot affect not to see you, nor refuse to justify you. . . .
> You have but to aim at making men look steadily at you;
> when they do this, I do not say they will become Catholics,
> but they will cease to have the means of making you a by-
> word and a reproach, of inflicting on you the cross of
> unpopularity.[13]

The persuasive personalism envisioned here was much more than a
rhetorical "ploy" embraced by Newman for its polemical effectiveness. His

personalism is largely a result of his own experience, as well as his particular intellectual inclinations. He was convinced that controversies addressing "the whole man" rather than mere chains of propositional logic were more effective because these modes of controversy are what affected *him*. His educational experience and his religious sensibilities conspired to create in him a powerful bias toward the personal in every respect. Newman was himself informed and "developed" largely through modes of thought and sources of influence highly personal in character. He was best able to understand a thing, to "see" it or "really apprehend" it when it was either presented by a person or exhibited in a person.

PERSONS IN PROSE

This receptivity to learning and being "moved" to action by persons is seen in his interest in the saints, or more particularly, the literary saints' lives and autobiographies of the early Church Fathers. Not surprisingly, Newman found the typical "condition" of saints' biographies frustrating and inadequate for his own requirements and those of his times. Because these lives were highly impersonal and abstract, one did not receive the impression of a living, actual being. Intended as means of moral instruction, the saints' lives of the eighteenth and nineteenth centuries tended to be "lists" of virtues with each virtue suitably described by examples and instances. One had, as it were, an algorithm of a person, a ghost seen in outline or an anatomy of points of character. Newman was strongly dissatisfied with such "lives" and he often advocated (and assisted in) writing new editions. A living representation, one full of the personal qualities of the man or woman under study, was not simply more appealing; as an instrument of instruction, as a "rhetoric" of motivation, it was far more effective. Revealing his typical preference for the immediate and concrete, Newman writes in "The Last Years of St. Chrysostom" (published later in the *Historical Sketches*), "I am touched by my five senses, by what my eyes behold and my ears hear." Then, extending the senses by metaphor to the field of written discourse, "I gain more from the life of our Lord in the Gospels than from a treatise *de Deo*."[14]

What Newman looks for in a biography is detail and personality; details make things "real," they give fullness to an image and make the impression created lively and animate:

> [T]here is another mode of considering the Saints and their doings, which is not only valuable in itself, but increases the

> value of the teaching conveyed in the details of their history,
> and that is the view of them as living and breathing men, as
> persons and invested with personal attributes . . . such as
> belong to him and not to another.[15]

He calls this "realizing" the Saint, something that does not occur when reading a list
of abstract virtues. The Fathers of the Church, Newman's perennial favorites, are
vivid and real to Newman precisely because there is so much of their personal
attributes evident in their writings. They are "autobiography on a large scale."[16]
Even when these Fathers strive in controversy, even when they are at their most
theological, they operate in a mode uniquely personal and revealing. Newman
speaks of these writings in exactly the way this study speaks of Newman, and in so
doing he highlights the quasi-theological, highly rhetorical character of patristic
prose:

> This manifestation of themselves the ancient saints carry
> with them into other kinds of composition, where it is less to
> be expected. Instead of writing formal doctrinal treatises,
> they write controversy; . . . They mix up their own persons,
> natural and supernatural, with the didactic or polemical
> works which engaged them. Their authoritative declarations
> are written, not on stone tablets, but on what Scripture calls
> "the fleshy tables of the heart." The line of their discussion
> transverses a region rich and interesting, and opens on those
> who follow them in it a succession of instructive views as to
> the aims, the difficulties, the disappointments, under which
> they journeyed on heavenward, their care of the brethren,
> their anxieties about contemporary teachers of error. Dogma
> and proof are in them at the same time hagiography. They do
> not write a *summa theologiae*, or draw out a *catena* or pursue
> a simple thesis through the stages of a scholastic disputation.
> They wrote for the occasion, and seldom on a carefully-
> digested plan.[17]

The kind of prose the Fathers wrote struck Newman as highly
conversational.[18] Whether his own conversational prose was a deliberate imitation
of the Fathers or a natural affinity is an open question, but it is certain that he
possessed a unique ability to "talk" on paper. The most conversational of Newman's works, the *Apologia*, is famous for the intimate fashion in which, in Leanard
Deen's terms, Newman's "readers can be persuaded of his sincerity by being
brought as close as possible to reliving Newman's experience."[19] Conversation
was far more than an arid exchange of data for Newman; it was the occasion for the
intense sympathy and sensitive approximation of others' thoughts that allows one to
relive experience, see actualities, and comprehend particular anomalies which one's
own experience does not necessarily include. Not only did Newman habitually do

this himself in conversation, he could induce others to do it as well--even in his prose--thus elevating the level of communication to a high degree of intensity. Witness, for example, the often brief but energetic conversations in his novel *Callista*, or the extended conversational debate Newman writes in dialogue form in order to personalize a potentially arid topic ("Discipline and Influence"[20]).

Newman's favorite prose was always some variety of highly personal, conversational writing that brought its author vividly before the reader. Newman emphasizes that even when the Fathers write commentaries upon scripture, the personal element is intact since "A speaker and an audience are prominent throughout them."[21] The next chapter will explore the cognitive aspects of this conversational "orality" as part of a consideration of rhetorical precedents for Newman's mode of thought; here it is important to note that Newman was looking for the "whole man" both in saints' biographies and the multiform writings of the Church Fathers. His conception of a saint's biography and the value of patristic reading is grounded in the presentation of an entire person and the effective "persuasion" therein. No list of virtues will do; one must have *Chrysostom* if one is to be edified by Chrysostom. Just as one must have a personal apprehension of Christ in order for one's faith to be "realistic," so one must have examples of holiness that are filled with particular, concrete humanity in order to be effective.

PREDISPOSITIONS AND FAITH

Newman's personalism was certainly habitual--witness his preference for conversational writing and seeing personalities in biography--but his approach to intellectual questions and ecclesiastical matters was equally dominated by emphasis on persons. Despite their abstract subjects, Newman's theological notebooks on biblical inspiration and papal infallibility show how he tends toward a personal view or mode of thought upon any subject. In a matter of ecclesiastical theology, Newman uses historical fact to frame his topic and provide a concrete point of departure for a difficult subject:

> The Apostles did not reveal a set of ideas without corresponding facts. They gave the world a religion, involving social intercourse and practical duties. They said, not only that our Lord was come, but they specified who, when, and where;--not only that there were organs of His revelation, but that Peter, John, Paul were those organs. . . . All these assertions, that Peter was the vicar of Christ, that the Apostles were the organs of his revelation, that this

> gospel, this epistle, was written by St. John and St. Paul,
> were dogmatic facts and portions of the infallible teaching of
> the Church. . . . In other words, the infallibility of the
> Church not only generates and explains, but applies and
> interprets the revelation. So it did in the Apostles' days--so
> therefore it does now. Its determinations are concrete.[22]

What is known to people, even in terms of their faith, is not so much a matter of apprehension and assent to specific propositions as it is an apprehension of a Person (Christ) through the testimony of other persons. "Revelation is all about Christ the man, with His own character and individuality, not simply about moral and theological principles," says Hilary Fraser, going on to quote Newman, "'the philosopher aspires toward a divine *principle*; the Christian towards a *Divine Agent.*'"[23] This apprehension (and assent) is subsequently cast, as it were, into propositions that entail the essentials of the thing known and proffer them for others' assents, discussion, dogmatic definition, etc.:

> The Creed is for public teaching in the Church; the
> Evidences are for public disputations and lectures in the
> Schools; but the faith and reason, of which I speak, are
> subjective, private, personal, and unscientific; the mental
> acts of every Christian whatever . . . [and are] not exactly
> the same perhaps in any two. The analysis of them is not
> easy, and, though theologians do not overlook them, it is not
> perhaps rash to say that they have not satisfactorily explained
> them.[24]

The faith is subjective in that it resides in *subjects*, in persons, and is not an abstract form floating in an empty cosmos. Each person embraces it uniquely. It is not unique or subjective in being essentially different from what is known or held by other persons; it is essential to recognize that the objective character of what is known is entirely unaffected by Newman's position. He is merely pointing out the concrete fact that *persons* know, *people* have faith, and that knowledge is nonexistent outside knowing beings. The private, personal, and unique quality of knowledge is not a swamp of skepticism or solipsism; indeed, it is quite the contrary, for through it Newman reformulates what is an essential yet oft-forgotten Aristotelian and Thomistic principle: "Knowledge is according to the mode of the one who knows; for the thing known is in the knower according to the mode of the knower."[25]

Newman was well aware that to focus on "the mode of the knower" was to invite misunderstanding on both sides of the religious debate. The scientific agnostics would suspect one of attempting a sleight of hand in order to avoid their apparently rigorous and "impartial" scientific criteria for proof. The religious philosophers and theologians would, paradoxically, fear the same thing, thinking that exploration of "the mode of the knower" was somehow a disavowal of the objective and philosophically demonstrable character of the thing known. One of Newman's theological papers is typical in its attempt to preclude such mis-understanding by openly avowing that Christianity "ought to be subjected to the same rigid cross-examination" of the sciences, and asserting that "such an ordeal is actually met, undergone, and satisfied by Christianity." But he attempts to focus on a different matter:

> I am addressing myself to a question . . . viz., that the *motivum credibilitas* is personal to each individual as well as formal, public, and what may be called objective, after the manner of science. My undertaking is founded on the assumption of such individual proof and is directed to the drawing it out.
> Such individual conviction cannot rise from grounds altogether separate from the logical and formal body of evidence; it must be concurrent with and included in that moral and scientific proof. However, it is *sui generis* and varying with the individual.[26]

Aristotle would recognize at once that what Newman calls "moral proof" is in fact rhetorical proof--a phrase Newman, even had it occurred to him, would have been constrained to avoid because of the low intellectual status of rhetoric at the time. The two faculties--passions and will--not normally regarded as pertaining to the intellect or the apprehension of truth, *are* considered important by Newman. Specifically, he felt that the will had a largely unacknowledged position in the apprehension of truths, especially religious ones. While he rejected as unrealistic the assumption of some theologians that "bad-will" was the culprit for those who failed to be argued into conversion, he did acknowledge the role of the will in the intellect's estimation and evaluation of arguments. People may be sincere in their willingness to consider arguments, but that sincerity may not be sufficient to overcome an inability to apprehend the complete force of particular kinds of arguments. That is, one could conceive of oneself as being quite fair and impartial in considering arguments but be in fact wholly unprepared to give those arguments their due. It was not so much a matter of controversialists digging in their heels and refusing to assent; rather, they were habituated to certain antecedent considerations that created a skewed sense of what was probable or improbable, what was admissible and what was not, with the result that truly comprehensive judgments were impossible.

This is why Newman frequently advised religious inquirers to engage in prayer so that they might be disposed to accept the truth, to habituate themselves to religious actions so that they might more fruitfully inquire. To a skeptic such advice seems preemptive; it seems as if Newman is not trying to open the will so much as he is trying to artificially induce a religious practice. This, of course, is a perfect example of the kind of antecedent conception that makes real inquiry impossible. In fact, speaking to an audience of mixed denominations, Newman cautions against giving false assent to the Catholic faith, being forced or led by false motives to embrace the religion. First he warns against ritualism, that is, the love of ritual beauty for its own sake and not for that to which it is directed. Then he even cautions against assent to doctrines from a purely abstract sense of logical validity:

> Again, a man may say "Since this or that doctrine has so much historical evidence in its favor, I must accept it," he has no real sight or direct perception of it, but he takes up the profession of it, because he feels it would be absurd, under the conditions with which he starts, to do otherwise.[27]

The man has been argued or evidenced into the Church. What he has not done is given real assent to the doctrines he feels sufficiently proved. In a supreme paradox, he has short-circuited his will. According to the doctrine of the Fall, man's will is corrupted by being made rebellious and unruled by the rational principle, the intellect. By acting wholly out of intellectual "convictions," however, the man has *not* made his will properly subservient to the intellect. Though the will is to be subservient, it is its own faculty. What this hypothetical character has done is to actually *dissolve* his will into the intellect, a disorder as damaging as an unruly will. "He does no more than load himself with a form of words instead of contemplating, with the eye of the soul, God Himself, the source of all truth, and this doctrine as proceeding from His mouth."[28]

The idea that God is a person, is *the* Person, and as such the source as well as the object of the faith, plays a large part in Newman's economy of the transmission of faith. One must not embrace the faith until one has fully appropriated the significance of the source of the faith--a being, a person, One who speaks. There is a strongly personal, communicative, even oral aspect to Newman's conception of the origins and organs of the faith. He implicitly criticizes his own times when he says that Scripture itself is seen as a foundation, while for the Church Fathers it was an *organ*.[29] A foundation is inanimate, cold, a thing to be used and built upon; an organ, on the other hand, is living, abiding and active. What is communicated by that organ originates in a divine being and is received in persons also. It is not so much a "text" coming from the pages of a book, as a spoken word "proceeding from His mouth." This kind of knowledge, then, is personal in every sense. Its origin, recipient, means of communication, and character are personal; that is, it speaks to the whole man, intellect, passions, and will, body and soul. This is why Newman had no difficulty encouraging the passions in the "High and Dry" school of English stoic Christianity and emphasizing the intellect to evangelical shopkeepers; this is why he had no repugnance for sensible delights of every variety, from the beauty of a countryside to the taste of good wine--goods often feared by those for whom salvation was essentially a rejection of material creation.

Newman is forever trying to bring even the most abstract and general notion to a personal turn in order to more effectively communicate the origin and force of any truth. When such communication is effective, what happens is analogous to the Thomistic epistemological activity of the "agent intellect"; the truth is made one's own, is taken in, as it were, and becomes a real part of the knowing being. When that truth is communicated in turn, it carries with it the mark of the knowing being:

> [T]he truth first goes into the minds of the speakers, and is apprehended and fashioned there, and then comes out from there as, in one sense, its source and parent. The Divine Word is begotten in them, and the offspring has their features and tells of them. They are not like the dumb animal, speaking with man's voice, on which Balaam rode, a mere instrument of God's word, but they have "received an unction from the Holy One, and they know all things," and. . . while they deliver what they have received, they enforce what they feel and know.[30]

"The Gospel is a Spirit dwelling within us--we can only communicate it, while we give out our own character the while."[31]

LEARNING AND EDUCATION

In many respects, Newman's work in or about Universities was a focal point of his long career; he labored at Oxford for a good many years attempting to improve both the moral tone and the intellectual excellence of the institution, and he founded the Irish University, setting its course in his famous lectures. He always felt a special vocational call to work in education, to employ himself with the academic and moral training of young men. It is perhaps not surprising, then, that in Newman's works concerning education, his rhetorical personalism is displayed in all its features harmoniously. There one finds the yoking of intellect, passions, and will, the predominance of interest in knowledge as being a personal possession, conveyed and communicated through personal means, the primacy of orality in communication and instruction, the use or "utility" of personal influence. These various aspects come together, "concretize," as it were, in the educational treatises, displaying the essentially integrated fashion with which they were held by Newman. Again, the interest in something as apparently "abstract" as education may appear to be at odds with the clergyman's professed interest in and habit towards the moral, the practical, the particular. For Newman, however, education was particular in that it concerned individual persons and was "practical" as well-- not by way of "job training," but by equipping students to embrace their full humanity in the liberal sciences. As Culler notes (with some perplexity), the "philosophical habit" Newman praises turns out to be, for all its genuine liberality, quite practical as well.[32]

Newman's ideas about learning and education were strangely out of step for a time when even the classical education provided at the universities was something of an abstract transfer of mere data--a procedure entirely harmonious with the kind of science by which the era was increasingly fascinated. Certainly the idea of "liberal arts" had many advocates. Edward Copleston and Oxford University in general were locked in combat with the new utilitarians as represented by the *Edinburgh Review*, but such warfare was itself played out in largely abstract arguments that Newman often went beyond. Typically, Newman's own experience was formative of his educational ideas and ideals, and that experience was of "the Oriel common room, with its daily collision of mind with mind. . . ."[33] The intellectual stimulation found in the vigorous debates and discussions impressed Newman no end, and his later esteem for the medieval schools with their lively, free argumentative dialectic probably originated in this Oriel experience. As Culler observes, Newman's conception of a university received its earliest mold not so much from his Oxford undergraduate days, but from his days as a Fellow in the Oriel common room.[34]

Newman's frequent use of the phrase "mind on mind" and his constant description of the acquisition of knowledge and understanding as a kind of trial by fire underscore the complex unity of the persuasiveness of truth and the pastoral character of a teacher that abides at the heart of Newman's idea of education. While an aggressive scientism sought to minimize the element of the personal in learning,

Newman focused on truth as something loved and fought for, something objective in character, but personal in acquisition. A university is the place

> in which the intellect may safely range and speculate, sure to find its equal in some antagonist activity, and its judge in the tribunal of truth. It is a place where inquiry is pushed forward, and discoveries verified and perfected, and rashness rendered innocuous, and error exposed, by the collision of mind with mind, and knowledge with knowledge.

Then, shifting to the personal aspect of instruction, an aspect highly purposive and rhetorical in character, he continues, "It is the place where the professor becomes eloquent, and is a missionary and a preacher, displaying his science in its most complete and most winning form, pouring it forth with the zeal of enthusiasm, and lighting up his own love of it in the breasts of his hearers."[35]

Even prior to the rise of Tractarianism, Newman's pastoral conception of the role of education was well developed, and Culler points out that this pastoral character of "teacher" was directly connected to the oral/aural nature of learning and education. Newman was firm in his insistence that he was a "teacher of men" and not a "lecturer on books."[36] The distinction may seem strained and rhetorically contrived, but in actuality it strikes to the heart of Newman's personalist conception of knowledge and its communication. In his *Rise and Progress of Universities* (originally published as columns in the "Catholic University Gazette"), he addresses some fundamental university issues and reveals at once his personalist conception of education. Immediately upon propounding his definition of a university as a school for "universal knowledge," "knowledge of every kind," Newman says a university is "a place for the communication and circulation of thought, by means of personal intercourse, through a wide extent of country."[37] This formula seems dry enough until one remembers what "personal intercourse" meant for Newman in his own tutorial practices at Oxford. By "personal," he really does mean "one-on-one," a relationship between student and tutor that goes beyond lectures and becomes a kind of friendship. Even the idea of the *location* of a university was that a collected group of teachers and learners worked best because of the contact with other people.

Gaining a steady, if half-unconscious, influence in Newman's day was the idea--or perception--that knowledge was a matter of texts, of books, and the real *sedes sapientiae* were libraries. Conceptions such as these motivated the construction of the Tamworth Reading Room and the many drives to elevate the public mind through increased literacy and reading. It was perceived that knowledge and truth had a rather scientific character--that is, demonstrable, definite, removed from all accidents of time, place, and persons. Thus books were actual holding places of knowledge, storage chambers, as it were, and in order to learn one merely had to "get a book." The "book as a box of knowledge" phenomenon is hardly less pervasive today then it was in Newman's day, but Newman had exceedingly little sympathy for it. Certainly his own educational experience contradicted the idea that one could learn by simply assimilating data. Moreover, his personalist conception of language was deadly to the book-as-knowledge school.

In order for books to really "contain" knowledge, words must be absolute, entirely determinate, virtually logarithmic symbols. Though Newman acknowledged the truly symbolic character of language (beneath any flexibility or indeterminacy of words was a solid sub-stratum of concrete intelligibility), he conceived of words not so much as abstract symbols floating randomly about, but as human *acts*, *deeds*. That is, a word is a symbol, but it is a symbol acted upon, *uttered*, spoken by a rational being and thus carrying with it "the mark" of that being. Thus words and language are primarily oral, not textual, and carry with them the unique imprint of the utterer as well as the determinate meaning of the terms. This imprint was no accidental accompaniment to meaning; it was the mark of knowledge as pertains to knowing subjects, persons, whose grasp and understanding of things is figured forth not merely in abstract signification but in the particular, individual mode of knowing. It involves, again, the whole man, passions and will, body and soul, as well as intellect, and it derives its life from the active and purposive nature of utterance.[38] Thus real learning is essentially an oral/aural activity between persons, not to be supplanted or replaced by texts. Newman invokes actual practice in testimony to the primacy of personal instruction over textual instruction:

> [W]henever men are really serious about [learning], . . .
> when they aim at something precise, something refined,
> something really luminous, something really large,
> something choice, they go to another market; they avail
> themselves, in some shape or other, of the rival method, the
> ancient method, of oral instruction, of present
> communication between man and man, of teachers instead of
> learning, of the personal influence of a master, and the
> humble imitation of a disciple. . . . [T]he province and the
> inestimable benefit of the *litera scripta* [texts] is that of being
> a record of truth, and an authority of appeal, and an

> instrument of teaching in the hands of a teacher; but that, if
> we wish to become exact and fully furnished in any branch
> of knowledge which is diversified and complicated, we must
> consult the living man and listen to his living voice.[39]

Why this is so is not left to speculation:

> [N]o book can convey the special spirit and delicate
> peculiarities of its subject with that rapidity and certainty
> which attend on the sympathy of mind with mind, through
> the eyes, the look, the accent, and the manner, in casual
> expressions thrown off at the moment, and in the unstudied
> turns of familiar conversation.[40]

Knowledge is not data, it "lives in us" and one obtains it "from those in whom it lives already."[41]

Concerning education, and the personalism of learning, Newman does not distinguish secular from sacred science. Just as the faith is held *by* persons and is not an autonomous, abstract series of propositions considered in itself, secular subjects abide in knowing intelligences. This union of educational means--secular and religious--prompts Newman to call the customary mode of teaching and learning the "oral tradition," which he characterizes using religious terms even though it is applied to secular subjects. He speaks of the "preaching" and the "catechizing," of "the living voice, the breathing form, the expressive countenance."[42] Truth, of whatever variety, is itself "subtle" and "invisible"; the disciple learns of it with his whole being, "by his eyes and ears, through his affections, imagination, and reason."[43] But again, it is no mere "transfer"; the truth is made manifest to the learner by "propounding and repeating it, by questioning and re-questioning, by correcting and explaining, by progressing and then recurring to first principles. . . ."[44] Regardless of the actual origins and claims of specific sciences, the actual process of instruction in those sciences is rather rhetorical in character; there is not only an almost argumentative testing of ideas, but the full personality of both teacher and student is engaged in the acts of communication, assimilation, and eventual understanding. This is where texts fall short, and where Newman's contemporaries' emphasis on "getting up books" worked to the detriment of education; Newman quotes a scholar who bemoans the loss of personal education: "Those days never can return; for the plain reason that then men learned and taught by the living word, but now by the dead paper."[45]

As might be expected, Newman balances his championing of the educational oral tradition with a note upon its own dangers. It is necessary to see that, primarily, Newman's embrace of "oral instruction" is not purely pedagogical.

Although as a rhetorician Newman is highly sensitive to any issue of "effec-tiveness," he is not a pedagogical "oralist" from utilitarian motives; the orality comes from the very nature of human minds, learning , knowledge, and truth. Oral instruction is superior precisely because it is proper to the manner in which human beings actually do acquire knowledge and possess it. Books do not "contain" knowledge; persons know, and come to know. Thus the priority of personal instruction. This does not mean that there are no possible difficulties arising from personal instruction. In a fallen world hardly anything, no matter how natural or proper, is immune to being exaggerated or abused in some fashion. Oral, personal instruction is no different. Newman points out quite emphatically that "the speaker may suffer from the popularity of his gift, and, then, the hearer from its fascination."[46] To clarify the point, Newman quotes at length a "controversialist of the day" in recapitulation of the superiority of oral instruction:

> The type is a poor substitute for the human voice. . . . It has no variety of manner and intonation, to show by their changes how the words are to be accepted, or what comparative importance is to be attached to them. . . . Half the symbolism of a living language is lost, when it is committed to paper. . . . [The lecture] imparts to the whole teaching a human character which the printed book can never supply. The Professor is the science or subject, vitalized and humanized in the student's presence. He sees him kindle into his subject; he sees reflected and exhibited in him, his manner, and his earnestness, the general power of the science to engage, delight, and absorb a human intelligence. His sympathy and admiration attract or impel his tastes and feelings and wishes for the moment into the same currents of feeling, and his mind is naturally and rapidly and insensibly strong and attuned to the strain of truth which is offered to him.[47]

Newman does not doubt that this description is true, but he cites such influence as subject to abuse through the potential intellectual pride in the master and personal fascination in the student. At such a point, personality outstrips truth, and the entire purpose of such communication and learning--the instruction of students for the grasp of truth--is turned on its head and made a forum for mere display and cultivation of personality and "parties." Such academic manipulation Newman styles the deeds of "a set of clever charlatans, or subtle sophists, who aim at originality, show, and popularity, at the expense of truth. . . ."[48] In actual universities "Law," rule, or order can counterbalance and rein in the occasional excesses of personal influence, thus striking a balance. Newman figures forth this balance in a supernatural metaphor: ". . . the Supreme Being is both,--a living, individual Agent, as sovereign as if an Eternal Law were not; and a Rule of right and wrong, and an Order fixed and irreversible, as if He had no will, or supremacy, or characteristics of personality."[49] For Newman, in the educational framework, personal influence is the essence of learning, and Law or rule is the necessary concomitant. It is what makes personal influence properly active. In words no contemporary computer-oriented educationalist would care to hear, Newman sums up the relation of Law and influence:

> I say, then, that the personal influence of the teacher is able in some way to dispense with an academical system, but that the system cannot in any sort dispense with personal influence. With influence there is life, without it there is none; if influence is deprived of its due position, it will not by those means be got rid of, it will only break out irregularly, dangerously. An academical system without the personal influence of teachers upon pupils, is an arctic winter; it will create an ice-bound, petrified, cast-iron University, and nothing else.[50]

A mental habit displays itself both in what a person reverts to frequently and how subjects are treated. The rhetorical twist given to Newman's thought both consists of and is accentuated by his intense concentration on persons and their rationality. Of course, for Newman, rationality does not mean "rationalism." His idea of the properly rational mind includes the integrated operation of all man's faculties. He approaches matters by looking for some kind of personal access into them. That is, in persuasion Newman looks for a way of engaging an auditor through creating a personally "known" experience of whatever he is trying to explain. He tries to involve the whole man, so to speak, and not argue, simply through demonstration or abstraction. He seeks rhetorical *impact* by making whatever personal aspect a subject might have its most luminous aspect. Thus we find Newman telling Catholics to fight prejudice not by crying "Bigot!" but by making people know them; we see him initiate a religious congregation in which the principle of unity is personal influence (attachment) and the principle of spiritual growth is personal example or the exhortation of conduct; we see him regard communication in its most personal way, inclusive of voice and look. Finally, we see all these personal things always being used or considered in light of their effectiveness or utility in bringing minds to assent--be it an assent to cooperate with supernatural grace or an assent to some matter of classroom instruction. The great strength of Newman's rhetorical habit is that its personalist valence makes the rhetoric highly "rational"--that is, one can come to see truth through it. The persuasive role of rhetoric is intimately tied to moral rectitude and truth for Newman; we engage in a rhetoric of conduct in order to more effectively communicate or make truth evident. Because rhetoric encourages the use of character and personalist appeals, Newman's personalism, in conjunction with his missionary purpose and sensitivity to the mind's workings, flowered into a consistently rhetorical mode of thought. In the next chapter, a look at Newman's rhetorical ancestors, as it were, will show that he was not the first to emphasize the personalist components of thought, knowledge, and discourse.

V. Intellectual Antecedents: Rhetorical Discourse In The Patristic And Medieval Eras

> *If thou hast any sound, or use of voice,*
> *Speak to me!*
> Hamlet I, i.

Arma Virumque Cano

Newman's rhetorical personalism may have taken many of his contemporaries by surprise, but it was by no means historically unique. His personal, highly oral, and conversational approach to discourse had been thoroughly entrenched in educational practice and rhetorical theory from the post-Augustine Roman period well into the Renaissance. That such a practice and history of education had been largely forgotten by Newman's time is in part due to the limited and spotty "antiquarian" studies of his day. While nineteenth-century students learned rhetoric from Aristotle, Cicero, and post-Renaissance rhetoricians, they did not study the rhetorical practices of the patristic and medieval periods. These studies were not to develop and deepen until much later in the nineteenth and early twentieth centuries. But nineteenth-century ignorance of early Christian rhetorical practice and training was not due purely to the absence of sound historical scholarship. The century saw unprecedented growth of a conception of thought inimical to that earlier, rhetorical model. Excepting the exceptions, the idea that thought was primarily a methodical and mechanical process dominated the century. Knowledge was largely a matter of scientific trial-and-error, and any indistinct or unformulable qualities in learning and communication were either to be deplored or considered "poetry".[1] Indeed, such ideas about what constituted knowledge lie behind the vigorous debates regarding utilitarianism, educational reform, and even many social improvement schemes.

For Newman, this had the rather unfortunate result of leading some of his co-religionists to be suspicious of his intellectual inquiries. They feared that his thoughts about matters of reasoning and certainty, not to mention education, were actually anti-rational. However, despite Newman's well-known research in patristics and medieval educational practice, his own rhetorical personalism was not a product of extended antiquarian studies, though it was supported by them. His habitual method of considering questions and his own sensitivity to minds and probabilities equipped him to engage in rhetorical thought without consciously emulating the past. His defenses of this mode of thought were likewise motivated by particular circumstances rather than by a desire to inculcate a patristic or medieval method. Surrounded by what has since been called "scientism"--a sort of empirical fideism--Newman was attempting to restore the free play of the whole of man's intellect--the whole man--against the encroachments of a narrowing materialistic and an avowedly dogmatic "demonstratism." Nevertheless, there were definite historical antecedents or precedents for Newman's approach to education, religious instruction, and apologetics. In the post-Augustine period through the Middle Ages, a highly personalist educational practice and theory of rhetoric was the norm. As is well known, even the other two components of the trivium (grammar and logic) were often highly rhetorical in inclination. The very idea of knowledge--an idea constricted to either empirical experience or syllogistic reasoning in Newman's day--was nuanced and supple in the pre-Renaissance world of rhetorical education.

As Newman's patristic reading made him well aware, the early Christian Fathers, amidst persecutions and the warfare of doctrinal dispute, were sharply divided over the question of pagan letters and literature. The dispute reveals much about the patristic conception of knowledge, for the presumption behind the dispute relates directly to the subject of intellectual influence. Both pagan philosophy and literature were subject to much criticism, some criticism being quite absolute in condemnation, some of it rather more qualified and tentative. As paganism gradually lost its viability as a religious force, the debate over pagan letters cooled. Nevertheless, there was little actually said *in favor* of such letters and literature. Tertullian equated philosophy with heresy, calling philosophers the "patriarchs of heresy," and he roundly condemned the Greek philosophical schools.[2] Lactantius, Cyprian, and Justin all warned against "profane letters," and in Cyprian's case he even renounced the very use of pagan rhetoric.[3] The parade of vices attributed to the gods, the mere presence of "gods," and the dialectical potential of philosophical sharp-shooting all posed threats to a faith young, vulnerable, and recently bathed in blood by the devotees of those gods. Thus writers such as Clement of Alexandria, Synesius of Cyrene, Minucius Felix (who, paradoxically, agreed with Plato in condemning poets for "injuring the cause of truth"), and Augustine, all devoted efforts to limiting the influence of pagan letters despite the fact that many of these men were experts in those very letters.[4] The famous story about St. Jerome illustrates how strongly the Church Fathers were torn in their attraction to pagan letters: the fiery Jerome once dreamed of being propelled to heaven, where he was asked who he was. Naturally, he replied, "I am a Christian." To his confusion, the voice responded: "No, you are a Ciceronian."[5]

Though pagan letters did have defenders, most notably Augustine, Basil, and Ambrose, the Fathers' idea of *verbum* tells much about their conception of knowledge and literature. If *verbum* or *sapientia* is understood as discourse consisting entirely of unintegrated "particles" of knowledge rather divorced from persons, knowledge that is objective almost to the point of having independent existence (not *adequatio rei et intellectus* but a distinct *esse* between the thing and the intellect), then the dispute about pagan writings becomes meaningless. The Fathers were concerned that exposure to pagan literature and philosophy would encourage intellectual vices. They feared that the narrow, analytic habit of mind encouraged by dialectical controversy would lead people to approach the *Verbum* (the Word of God--not just Scripture, but Christ) in an inappropriate manner. Likewise, the habits of mind encouraged by pagan literature could lead Christians to approach sacred texts in a largely aesthetic way. These Fathers conceived of knowledge not as something summarily and mechanically attained, but something susceptible to suggestion and personal influence. Pagan writings were thought dangerous not simply on account of the multitude of gods in them--what we might call "factual error"--but on account of the influence they could exert on the imagination and intellect. Thus the patristic controversy over such literature only makes sense when the Fathers' conception of knowledge is seen to exceed the confines of philosophical demonstration.

The pagan rhetorical period known as the "Second Sophistic" (AD 50-400) roughly coincided with the Christian dispute about pagan literature, and here too we catch a glimpse of the Fathers' conception of knowledge. The Second Sophistic saw the return of an idea about rhetoric that essentially "emptied" rhetoric of any communicative substance. In so losing its claim to the communication of or even access to truth, rhetoric was thought to be essentially declamatory. "It is almost a contradiction in terms" says James J. Murphy, "to use the phrase 'sophistic rhetoric.' For sophistry--the linguistic heresy which denies communication as an end to language--is by its very definition anti-rhetorical."[6] Nevertheless, there was in this period a wide-spread emphasis on rhetoric as devoid of matter and as consisting merely of *forma*: the eloquence of words regardless of their appropriateness to any subject. It is easy to see why such a school of thought should alienate the Christian Fathers, as indeed it did, especially in view of St. Paul's preference for "wisdom" over "eloquence."[7]

The Fathers may have been divided over what to do with pagan letters, but they were entirely unanimous in their affirmation that language was to communicate, and that communication was no empty "flood" of words.[8] Augustine fully rejected the "Second Sophistic," but as Murphy reminds us, the *De doctrina christiana* warns of an opposite "heresy" as well:

> The sin of the sophist is that he denies the necessity of subject matter and believes that *forma* alone is desirable. An opposite vice, one to which historians of rhetoric have never given a name, depends upon the belief that the man possessed of truth will *ipso facto* be able to communicate it to others. It depends upon *materia* alone.[9]

The idea that rhetoric is pure *materia* is clearly anathema to those traditional aspects of rhetoric such as declamation, diction, rhythm, and even invention itself. Invention is rather superfluous if *materia* has sole dominion over communication and is already "possessed" by the rhetor. This unnamed rhetorical heresy not only does away with rhetoric just as forcefully as the sophistic heresy does, but it rests on a shallow and incomplete conception of knowledge and the intellect. The "transfer of truth"--handing it on to others like computers in interface--is a process which, in terms of actual human communication, hardly exists; such a process banishes the person and sunders the intellect from its fellow faculties. The idea of such a process also renders the intellect a purely passive faculty. In such a case, knowledge assumes the character of independent "bits" (one could even say bytes) divorced from knowing minds. One is in danger here of living in a universe of tyrannical Platonic forms that drift about and impart themselves automatically (and even arbitrarily) upon waxy, yielding, unresponsive intellects. Gone is the meeting, the embrace, as it were, of mind and thing. Such a conception of knowledge and intellect is, of course, remarkably similar to that fostered by the widespread eighteenth-century empiricism of Locke and Hume, and it held sway in England (despite the best efforts of Romantics such as Coleridge) for much of the nineteenth century. It is that against which Newman strove in trying to restore the intellectual value accorded to ordinary daily thinking, knowing, and communicating.

EDUCATION IN PRACTICE

The rhetorical features of Roman educational methods and theory (which, to varying degrees, formed the pattern for much of the education throughout Europe) display a personalist emphasis that bears a striking resemblance to Newman's educational principles. The Ciceronian rhetorical tradition was perhaps most effectively transmitted through Quintilian's *Institutio oratoria* (circa AD 92). Though this text survived for the Middle Ages only in its *textus mutilatus* form (the entire text not being recovered until 1416), it provided the educational pattern in which most Church Fathers were schooled. The preceptive *Institutio* begins a child's formal education with the *grammaticus*: one who provides instruction in literature. This instruction teaches "correctness and the interpretation of the poets" but does so through intensive exposure to literature and student commentary.[10] The presentation of materials is largely oral, as is the students' commentary. In contradistinction to the contemporary use of "grammar," the schooling provided by the *grammaticus* is not designed to be systematic or scientific. The materials employed--largely poetry--and the objectives pursued in this early stage of educational experience are very much directed toward "the whole man." Although Quintilian's object is the ideal orator, and oratory is highly "result-oriented," he implies that "*grammatica* is an art whose end is understanding (*cognitione et aestimatione rerum*) rather than result."[11] He even warns prospective *grammatici* to avoid prescriptive instruction, for such instruction belongs to later levels of rhetorical learning. The way students learn in the *Institutio* is through an interesting and highly personalist triangle. When they are actually learning to speak, they begin by reading the works of great writers. Imitation is the cornerstone, here, and the art of writing is clearly yoked to its oral counterpart, speech. Moreover, an actual teacher is necessary (rather than just texts) to conduct the students through the paths of literature. The result is a form of three-way dialogue: teacher, student, author, each of which is essential.

Preceding the *Institutio* in time but operating within the same grammatical tradition is the *Ars poetica* of Horace (23-13 BC).[12] The well-known and engaging *Ars* is highly preceptive despite the fact that "the very structure of the piece would be baffling to anyone attempting to learn an art which was new to him."[13] Its apparently random comments about poetry and its advice as to how to become a poet are extremely personal in tone and conversational in manner. Horace speaks of everything: how many actors in a drama should speak, the advisability of Greek models, the relationships between training and native genius in a great work. Throughout the *Ars*, as Murphy notes, Horace speaks in just the way Quintilian expects a *grammaticus* to speak: the conversational tone of the *Ars* is no accident.[14] We see here another instance of educational conversation between persons-- however practical and preceptive in content. Horace also makes poetic education a largely mimetic activity, where the learner is immersed in "the best that has been thought or said" in order to train the ear and form the intellect. The author, the teacher (Horace), and the student again participate in a conversation in which learning is accomplished through the personal appropriation of matter, form, and manner. Horace's charming urbanity teaches about civilized poetry as much as Homer's description of Nestor teaches about hospitality.

In this rhetorical tradition, knowledge is like virtue in being a kind of *habitus*, a learned consistency that is no less vigorous for being habitual. One is not "trained" to be a poet in the sense that one is trained to be an engineer. The intensity of memorization and exposure to poetry (and oratory) is not data transfer. Though there is much of a "mechanical" nature the student of poetry and rhetoric must learn, the emphasis in this educational method is on developing a habit of mind. One "becomes" a poet through the various influences of previous poetry, a master's own particular *habitus* of poetic appreciation, and one's own native ability. The similarity to Newman's educational ideal and method is clear. Even while Horace is laying down the poetic "law," he does so by way of a master's "influence."

There is another educational triangle in the classical (and medieval) rhetorical texts. Aside from teacher, author, and student, there is the conceptual connection between the ideas of authority, imitation, and conversation. As already seen, the exposure to the great texts of the past was regarded as the essential starting point of a formal education. The use of models in rhetorical training was extensive almost to the point of being exclusive. Because imitation was regarded as the earliest and most natural way to learn, ancient and medieval education might well be call mimetic or "poetic" education. Cicero, Quintilian, and Augustine, in good Roman fashion, recommend "the observation of good models at all levels of age and experience."[15] But the "observation" was, true to its etymology, parti- cipatory and interactive between student and text. Educational mimesis was not meant to inculcate a slavish copying of the masters, but to trigger the assimilative powers of the soul, to initiate, as Augustine notes, a cumulative comprehension of manners and matters.[16] What occurs is a conversation, as it were, between the poet (authority) and the student. The authority is such by virtue of its particular excellence, and the student *engages* the text. He is not simply "imprinted" by it. This conversation explains the "odd" fact that the vast majority of medieval texts are not original works, but commentaries. At work in a commentary is the implicit acknowledgement of an authority's authority (often considered a slavish adherence to the past during the eighteenth and nineteenth centuries) and a subsequent conversation with that authority as a "living voice."

The ancient and medieval writers did not believe that imitating and conversing with authorities was slavish, for the simple reason that the learning was predicated on influence rather than on some kind of decree. Influence is subtle and suggestive, not forceful, and writers such as Cicero, Quintilian, and Augustine affirm that such imitative learning is largely unconscious.[17] Even the heavily preceptive training in rhetoric emphasized the necessity for a broadly based, non-systematic sensitivity on the part of the rhetor. In the *Phaedrus* Plato says a rhetor must have a sound knowledge of "men's souls," while Aristotle's *Rhetorica* emphasizes a wide philosophical and psychological perceptivity on the part of a speaker.[18] Murphy notes that Plato, Aristotle, Cicero, Quintilian, and Augustine each make a plea for a kind of rhetorician whose capabilities are "more than is usually found in a single man."[19] It is interesting that Culler criticizes Newman's "gentleman" for precisely the same thing, the improbability of anyone possessing so many laudable qualities.[20]

THE VOICE OF SIGNS

Augustine's "metarhetoric"--culled from *De doctrina christiana, De magistro,* and *De catechizandis rudibus*--deals quite explicitly with the nature of learning, as the titles of the works suggest.[21] While discussing the matter of learner and master, Augustine places distinct emphasis on the "learner" side of the equation. We are here to learn, says Augustine, because we have been created with a purpose. Man exists in order to learn of God and to join God. The universe itself is a great "book" written as a vast set of signs meant to reveal their Creator. Thus everything is a sign in at least one sense, even if it is also a thing independent of its signification. The learner (and that is everyone) should acquire a knowledge of God through the correct understanding of the created universe. In fact, a correct understanding of these created "signs" contributes to sanctity: "He lives in justice and sanctity who is an unprejudiced assessor of the intrinsic value of things."[22]

Man's language also consists of signs (conventional signs) that are primarily verbal, though such visual signs as nods and gestures are part of the language as well. It is interesting to note that Augustine stresses the orality even of written language; we write because "vibrations in the air soon pass away," and so written language corresponds directly to oral or verbal language.[23] But language and communication do not connect men to each other in a symbolic, mathematical interface. Men's words do not exactly encapsulate the thoughts of the speaker, though the relation of thought to word is obviously close enough to allow for genuine communication. Words act as "prompters," that trigger or "evoke a learning response from a hearer."[24] "[E]ach man must balance the things he hears against what Augustine calls 'interior truth,' which is already resident in the person who hears the words of another."[25] This interior truth is an ability to discern truth and falsity, as well as the "intrinsic value of things." Murphy suggests that this concept of interior truth is Platonic and theological in orientation.[26] This need not be so; Aristotle speaks of man's sufficient natural capacity for truth, and there is no reason such a capacity can only grasp the supernatural. But Murphy is correct when he points out that the interior truth and the triggering effect of language "indicate a clear reliance upon an individual's powers as a private learner. . . ."[27]

Speech does not mandate learning; instruction is not a "filling up" of a student. What then of teaching? What of persuasion and the relation of master and student? Does not the idea of "evocative triggers" and the private learner's responsibility diminish the idea of a personal (or interpersonal) element in education? Not at all. For Augustine, says Murphy, the use of language is extremely important: "The proper use of conventional signs can prompt a fellow man to find his way to God, or can sidetrack him into error and disbelief. . . ." Therefore, man's use of conventional signs is "an enormous divine responsibility which God places on every man."[28] In fact, "Man is obliged to be as rhetorical as he can, in order to assist his neighbors in learning about the universe and God."[29] Thus the personal aspect of learning by no means excludes the teacher or *magister*. Quite the contrary. The well-known impact of example as an instructive device amply reinforces the importance of the teacher in the process of learning. Language is neither a strict, calculated, logarithmic exercise, nor an amorphous and unmeaning collection of signs. Though words are "triggers," they trigger precisely because they have meaning; the thought of the speaker, however, is too mysterious to be perfectly represented by words. This is how the intangibles of conversation, relationship, look, gesture, *et cetera*, may enhance or inhibit the learning taking place between a student and a teacher.

It is important to see that Augustine occupies a middle or moderate position (as will Newman) regarding language. The mysteriousness of thought does not make meaningful language an impossibility, nor does the ability of language to signify turn communication into a mere transfer of data. In fact, Augustine's personalist conception of learning shows up in *De catechizandis rudibus*, where "the interaction of speaker and hearer is *reflex*--each human being affecting the other during the rhetorical act. . . ."[30] This is exactly why the relationship between master and student is best founded on *caritas*. Where *caritas* obtains, there is a "level of communication" that one cannot be trained in, a level that allows "one human heart to speak to another heart."[31] This immediately recalls Newman's preferred mode of instruction as an Oriel tutor, his selection of the Oratorian rule where members are bound by "chains of love," and especially his Cardinalate motto *"Cor ad cor loquitur."* Clearly, Newman's emphasis on "the whole man" in communication and Augustine's interest in "the innate humanity of both speaker and listener"[32] suggest a fundamental rhetorical thrust in their approach to learning. Thus Augustine's personalism of education is quite apparent despite, or rather because of, the primacy of the individual acquisition of truth. The intellect is here a working, acting thing, not a passive recipient of data. A formal, metaphysical version of this is seen in the "agent intellect" of Aristotle and Aquinas, but even the Platonic Augustine does not leave the mind a purely passive recipient of truth.

By no means was Augustine alone in thinking of language as essentially oral or verbal. The classical and medieval traditions are consistent in regarding language as an oral manifestation of intelligence. Writing comes later in chronology and priority. Aristotle's *De Interpretatione* declares that "spoken words are symbols of mental experiences, and written words are symbols of spoken words."[33] Even the *Topica* assumes that argumentation is oral; it speaks of "hearers," "audience," and "respondent."[34] The later classical encyclopedists perpetuated this conception through their popular and influential texts. The *Institutiones grammaticae* of Priscian (AD circa 510) begins with a consideration of voice and then proceeds to letters, while the later Isidore of Seville's much reproduced *Etymologia* defines grammar as "correctness in speaking."[35] In fact, Isidore treats this speech-grammar like a geometrical principle; it is "both the origin and foundation of the liberal arts."[36] Such a broad claim for oral language is not unique to Isidore or the patristic encyclopedists. Isocrates, Cicero and Quintilian all claim for social order the basis of "speech."[37] Still later, Rabanus Maurus' (AD 776-856) *De institutione cleric-orum* yokes speaking and writing together as the subject of grammar. That Rabanus should mention writing at all is not surprising since rhetorical manuals from the fourth century AD had begun to mention writing, but he still treats language as oral and written language as derivative. Rabanus' position in history is unique, for his *De institutione* is not an encyclopedic attempt in the Boethian tradition. It does not try to transmit a coherent body of thought or theory. Instead, the text is very much a "how-to" manual. It features bits and pieces from a variety of sources selected to assist priests in the performance of their duties. Rabanus' text is quintessentially pragmatic and the first in the great medieval tradition of highly selective, pragmatic texts which make no pretense of being systematic or theoretical.[38] In short, that Rabanus should even bother to mention such theoretical points in a text meant exclusively for practical, pastoral use, indicates how fundamental the oral aspect of language was considered.

Despite the splintering of rhetoric in the Middle Ages into the *modestae* (speculative grammar or linguistics), the *ars dictaminis* (letter writing), and the *ars praedicandi* (preaching) traditions, the orality of language remained constant. The "basic medieval assumption that language is for the ear" obtained.[39] Murphy believes that the oral aspect of education in the Middle Ages was one of its most significant qualities, especially in the *disputatio*. Twelfth-century Peter Cantor of Paris assigned three duties to a teaching master, "to lecture, to preach, and to dispute," all of which are entirely oral.[40] The famous medieval disputations were oral activities all the more personalistic for being public and personally delivered. Even in non-rhetorical discourse such as theological writing, the shadow of a personalist disputation remained. "The 'Scholastic method' of Aquinas in his *Summa Theologica* is simply the classroom disputation adapted to writing. It is still the same process."[41] John of Salisbury's *Metalogicon*, in an obvious reference to a disputation technique, refers to dialectic as "carried on between two persons."[42] This personal aspect of dialectic is worth remembering. The word will later come to mean something so abstract and mechanical, that it will be virtually equivalent to "impersonal thought." Considered a discourse between persons in the Middle Ages, dialectic will later lose all sense of being discourse.

THE DIVINE ART

A few notes on the idea of preaching will illustrate some additional patristic and medieval thoughts about communication and knowledge. As regards oratory, of course, preaching is so immediately rhetorical as to constitute the absolute heart of rhetorical theory and Christian practice. But the rhetorical personalism of preaching does not begin with the Christian era, for it is deeply rooted in the Hebrew tradition. If the development of the *ars praedicandi* tradition in the Middle Ages brought to a full blossom the formal study of preaching theory and practice, the Jewish Scriptural tradition provided a unique ground for that bloom. In no ancient society but the Jewish did preaching play so prominent a part. For one thing, the Jewish liturgical rites were completely oral. The liturgy consisted of "prayer, Scriptural reading, and Scriptural discussion. All three were oral. . . ."[43] The orality of the Jewish liturgy was more than a merely verbal reading of Scripture; it was absolutely dependent upon the presence of an audience with whom discussion could take place. If no audience were present, no service could be held.[44] Also, Scripture was a record of God's direct communication with man. Not only is "[t]his purposeful corporate rhetoricality . . . not found in any other community of the ancient world," but "[t]he means of learning and the means of expressing were inextricably interwoven through the pervasive scriptural experience."[45] Thus learning was yoked to expression, which brought to the classically forensic idea of rhetoric a highly educational counterpart.

Needless to say, Christ employed the Jewish preaching tradition and taught in a highly verbal, personal, and Scriptural manner. Not only did Christ command His followers to preach, but as the Fathers were aware, He demonstrated the various means of preaching and "persuasion" through example. There was a significant shift in the idea of what preaching actually effected, however, between the established Jewish tradition and the fledgling Christian one. The word "preach" stems from the Greek for "to proclaim." It suggests the activity of bearing news, as better expressed in the Latin *evangelium*.[46] For the Christians "the news" was understood to carry a motive force, or grace, of its own. The very announcement that Christ had redeemed souls and made eternal life possible was a vehicle for grace. In part this was due to the idea (and the Jewish tradition) of "authority." If the words concerning salvation came from God, then they could be trusted, and that trust was immediately effective in bringing souls to assent. This is how the primarily non-apodeictic idea of rhetoric in the Greek and Roman periods was profoundly altered in the Christian era. As Jewish and Christian belief centered on a personal God and the Author of words, argument or preaching based upon those words was capable of more than "merely" probable truth--it was capable of a demonstrative certainty or apodeictic proof.[47]

Christian rhetoric also modified the pagan understanding of the relation between speaker and audience. Pagan rhetorical art had always striven for persuasion, but it was primarily oriented toward the speaker as a practitioner of an art. Thus rhetoric consisted of invention, arrangement, and the employment of topics to discover arguments. The audience was to be persuaded to a course of action. Christian preaching, however, existed not to persuade alone, but (like its Jewish ancestor) to teach, and ultimately to provide for the salvation of souls.[48] It is not difficult to see, then, why preaching enjoyed such an exalted place in the work of churchmen. Augustine thought preaching so important that even those who did not live as they should, but who had a gift for preaching, should preach nonetheless. Its importance did not diminish over time. Thomas Aquinas asserts that "Preaching is the noblest of all ecclesiastical functions."[49] In fact, medieval scholars thought preaching had a great dignity by virtue of its being a continuation of what the Creator did in the Garden of Eden. Fourteenth-century Robert of Basevorn expressed the common opinion that "After creating man, God preached (if we extend the word 'preaching'), saying to Adam (Gen. 2:17) 'For in what day soever thou shalt eat of it, thou shalt die the death.' This was the first persuasion of which we read in Scripture."[50]

Perhaps the most significant consequence of the Judeo-Christian appropriation of rhetoric was the subtle yet thorough development of the audience's importance in the rhetorical exchange. As noted previously, the audience of Christian preaching is not simply to be persuaded but to be brought to a state tending towards each individual's ultimate happiness. Carrying forward the Jewish liturgical tradition of learning through such discourse, Christian preaching necessarily emphasized teaching the audience. Action was still the object of this Christian-rhetorical discourse, but it was largely internal action, action of soul or assent. Consequently, what moved, informed, convinced, and edified auditors-- always a part of rhetorical art--received greater stress. Murphy maintains that the true constant of Christian preaching was the rhetorical estimation of various audiences' capacities.[51]

Gregory the Great's important *Cura Pastoralis* (AD circa 591) formalizes this recognition of audience capacity, indicating that "while the message is unitary, the hearers are diverse." This very observation is picked up by Alexander of Ashby in *On the Mode of Preaching* around 1200, and after that it is everywhere in the Middle Ages.[52] Alexander includes Gregory's entire passage on the matter, repeating:

> Therefore according to the quality of hearers ought the discourse of teachers be fashioned, so as to suit all and each in their several needs, and yet never deviate from the act of common edification. . . . Where every teacher also . . . ought to teach the hearts of his hearers out of one doctrine, but not with one and the same exhortation.[53]

Gregory also notes that the preacher should try to be loved, since a loved speaker is more willingly heard.[54] Though such concerns are heightened in the *ars praedicandi* Christian tradition, they are not wholly new. Classical rhetorical precept admonishes the rhetor to be aware of his particular audience and to employ such arguments and appeals as are effective with that audience. Likewise, the rhetor is told to obtain the favor of the auditors so that persuasion can be effective. But the Christian emphasis on actual learning is rather more educational in thrust than most classical conceptions of rhetorical art, and is a unique contribution to the classical rhetorical tradition.

The *ars praedicandi* is an excellent example of rhetorical antecedents to Newman's rhetorical personalism. The *ars praedicandi* is an amalgam of orality, sensitivity to audience, emphasis on the educational aspect of rhetorical discourse, and the personalism of discourse aimed more at the reformation of individual persons than group political action. Even Newman's "philosophical" interest in assent is foreshadowed here in the concern with the various ways people become convinced of a thing. The ancient and medieval conception of learning, knowledge, and communication, as seen in the rhetorical tradition, will be largely altered by Newman's day. Post-Cartesian philosophy will disrupt the integration of man's faculties and will render unsatisfactory the intellectual seriousness of rhetorical modes of understanding. Newman will thus be a kind of throwback, not just theologically in his interest in the Fathers, but temperamentally and intellectually as well. The terms established by post-Cartesian philosophy, terms which tend not so much to distinguish faculties but to divide them, will inhibit people's understanding of Newman as they try to systematize what is essentially a non-systematic, rhetorical habit of mind. His rhetorical habit will elude even those who attempt a

Thomistic critique of Newman, for he is too much the preacher, even in his speculative thought, to lay aside such intangibles as personal appeal, probability, and even poetic comprehension, to engage the strictures of such a system.

VI. INTELLECTUAL ANTECEDENTS: RHETORICAL LOGIC AND DE-PERSONALIZED THOUGHT

> *When thou clovest thy crown i' the middle and gavest away both*
> *parts, thou borest thine ass on thy back o'er the dirt.*
> King Lear I, iv.

PETER OF SPAIN AND AGRICOLA

At the end of the Middle Ages, a profound shift occurred in the conceptions of knowledge and communication that set the stage for the conceptions prevailing in Newman's day. The history of that change is very much like a story, despite the philosophical nature of the subject. The shift is in good part traceable to specific people and specific texts, and its over-all effect was to depersonalize and simplify ideas about man's intellectual faculties. As regards Newman, the ultimate consequence of this was to cast him "out of his age" in making his thought something of a throwback to earlier, more integrated ideas about knowledge. Walter J. Ong analyzes this shift in *Ramus, Method, and the Decay of Dialogue* (1958, 1983), and the "archeology of thought" explored here draws largely upon his analysis.[1]

The hinge upon which this shift of consciousness turned was the well-known logician and philosopher at Paris, Peter Ramus (1515-1572). Though his importance in the history of rhetoric is well known to scholars, his influence on Western thought far exceeds his standing as a philosopher. In his day and for some time after, his books poured from Europe's many creaking presses and were used as fundamental texts in rhetoric and logic. No hinge is without a forge, however, and a number of intellectual and historical features of the Middle Ages coalesced to prepare the ground for Ramus' dramatic influence upon Western thought. Ironically, Ramus would probably be disturbed at the suggestion that his intellectual antecedents were primarily medieval. French Renaissance humanist as he was, he held himself aloof from medieval sources and consistently cited only classical originals for his work. He felt quite strongly, as did many humanists (Thomas More, Erasmus), that the learning of the Middle Ages was encumbered by impossible complexity and logical subtlety. This perception is itself burdened by countless paradoxes. One such paradox is that a major precursor to Ramist rhetorico-logic was a medieval text expressly denounced by Ramus: Peter of Spain's *Summulae logicales.*

"Peter of Spain is probably the most important of all scholastics and his *Summulae logicales* the most widely read of all scholastic works."[2] Though the term "scholastic" is now usually associated with theologians such as Thomas Aquinas and Albertus Magnus, regarding the education as practiced in the schools, Peter of Spain's text was far more widespread (and even influential) than the works of these two Doctors. The typical medieval university curriculum consisted of four branches: first, the arts courses of grammar, logic, and rhetoric, followed by the quadrivium. Then, those pursuing further studies entered one of three advanced schools: the theological school, medical school, or law school. These latter three branches were all much smaller than the arts curriculum. They had far fewer students and were less influential in many ways than the large arts schools. Interestingly, the theology schools actually exerted the very least influence upon what was taught and read in the arts courses. Thus, "St. Thomas Aquinas or . . . St. Bonaventure were theologians, members of an important but relatively small higher faculty, and quite unknown to the general mass of students of the scholastic philosophy in the arts course."[3]

The scholastic philosophy and logic of the Middle Ages was not, then, the largely metaphysical philosophy of Aquinas but a rigorously logical philosophy that elaborately worked out the principles of logic in the *Organon.* It was this elaboration that the humanists rejected, and when they speak "against scholastics, there is no name they cite with such regularity and cold fury as that of Peter of Spain."[4] Thomas More, for instance, writes that Peter of Spain's *Little Logicals* (*Summulae logicales*) is called such "because it has very little logic in it, [and] is a precious piece of work to see, . . . with its little rules, not only clumsy but even false. . . ."[5]

The primary logical contribution of the *Summulae logicales* was the unfolding of suppositions (what is now called quantification), which is the application of quantities to syllogistic argument. However, the importance of the work as regards Ramus (and, ultimately, Newman's defense of probabilistic knowledge) is in its subtle but far-reaching confusion of probable and scientific argumentation. The confusion begins with the absolute equation of logic and dialectic. Peter of Spain defines his subject thus: "Dialectic is the art of arts and the science of sciences, possessing the way to the principles of all curriculum subjects."[6] "There is no definition or mention of logic apart from this dialectic, except in the title *Summulae logicales* itself, so that the impression is left that dialectic and logic are one and the same thing."[7] Impression is hardly the word; there is only one logic, in the *Summulae*, and it is called dialectic. This is in contrast to the Aristotelian and Thomistic understanding that there are different kinds of logic, each appropriate to a particular science and mode of discourse. First, there is logic properly so-called, a logic of absolute demonstration; then, in the order of probability, there is dialectical logic that argues to truths but does so using probabilities; then rhetorical logic which also employs (by definition) the probable but does so with an eye to action of some sort; then poetic logic which is a logic "as-if," and lastly sophistic or false logic. As Ong notes, "these lucubrations of Aquinas the theologian were hardly viable in the world where scholastic philosophy was taught."[8] That philosophy recognized only one logic: Peter of Spain's dialectic.

This is the source of the confusion in the *Summulae* between scientific and probable argumentation, because the equation of logic and dialectic confuses the distinction between formal logic and dialectic which argues from probable premises. Peter of Spain reinforces his logic-lumping, stating immediately after his definition of dialectic that "dialectic alone disputes with probability concerning the principles of all other arts, and thus dialectic must be the first science to be acquired."[9] Not only does the fact that this "art of arts" is to be learned prior to any other subject heighten the "impression" that logic properly so-called is the matter of instruction, but Aristotle would be quite wary of the philosophical conjunction of "probability" and "principle" seen here.

Aggravating this confusion is the appearance in the *Summulae* of "loci" or topics. Aristotle distinguishes topics by saying that they are tools or "places" where probable arguments can be found or constructed. Topics are inventional faculties designed to guide thought about a probable or contingent matter in such a way as to allow the "inventor" to invent--come into--a potentially useful argument. "Loci" or topics thus apply to rhetorical thought and discourse, though a somewhat altered use of them may be employed in dialectic. They have nothing at all to do with logic properly so-called, or scientific demonstration. In the *Summulae*, however, they have a prominent position. Thus, generations of medieval students felt they were being taught formal "logic" from this text, when in fact they were mastering a mixed bag of formal, dialectical and rhetorical "logics." At Paris, for example, fully one year of the three year's philosophy course was devoted to the *Summulae*. In so dominating the medieval educational world, then, Peter of Spain's text prepared the ground well for additional confusions, blendings, and other mixtures of logical matters best kept distinct.

This blurring of distinctions in the *Summulae* does not mean that the formal quality of medieval logic was utterly lost. Though "foreign matter" had been introduced into logic, the exposure to Aristotle's own texts as well as the emphasis on formal logic in quantitative or suppositional terms preserved an essentially Aristotelian logic. Paradoxically, it was not those confusions of dialectic and scientific logic (or probable and demonstrative reasoning) which the humanists were so vociferously to denounce. Though they normally advocated classicism over medieval "accretions," the Renaissance humanists who denounced Peter of Spain did so largely on account of his quantifications--a feature of logic resurrected in contemporary, post-Boolean logic. They did not point out his "un-Aristotelianism." Indeed Ramus, the arch-humanist of the logicians, was to openly denounce Aristotle himself. Nevertheless, Peter of Spain provided the humanist logicians with their starting point. In glossing over the varieties of logic and introducing topical considerations into supposedly formal logic, the way was paved for the important humanist and logical revisionist: Rudolph Agricola.

Agricola (1444-1485), a working "scholar" who dabbled in virtually every thriving art of fifteenth-century Italy, "shuttled back and forth through the Rhine Valley and over the Alps, transplanting Italian humanism into Northern Europe."[10] He obtained a Master of Arts in Louvain, studied law at Pavia and devoted himself to art and letters through the study of the classics. His next important work--virtually his only important one--was the *Dialectical Invention*, a text in three volumes that did not become widespread until after his death. He was a thorough humanist; he adulated the classics and disdained medieval sources. On one occasion, for example, he cites the fourth-century Aristotelian commentator Themistius as one of his sources; he does not mention that this commentator's work was known only through Boethius--a great favorite during the Middle Ages.

The influence of Agricola on logic was as great in the Renaissance as Peter of Spain's was in the Middle Ages. His logic "became for generations after him, in the absolute sense, logic unqualified."[11] Ong testifies that Agricola effected the turn from an Aristotelian to a Ciceronian logic, and that this accounts for the shift in theological technique from Thomas Aquinas to Renaissance theologians such as Melchior Cano, Francis Suarez, Robert Bellarmine, Melanchthon, and others.[12]

Agricola's work on dialectic further blurred distinctions Aristotle or Aquinas would be at pains to maintain. Dialectic is used in a "large, loose and practically undefinable sense to cover the whole of discourse."[13] This is of critical importance. Agricola's dialectic is, like Peter of Spain's conjunction of discourse and logic, equated with discourse itself. Discourse is seen as one. Dialectic is defined as the "faculty of discoursing" and includes everything from the passions to the reasoning powers.[14] At first this may appear to be an integration of faculties harmonious with "the whole man" approach to thought. Ramus' development of this merging of discourse will show just how far that appearance is from the truth.

An equally profound movement in logical theory involves Agricola's use of the "loci" or topics introduced into logic by Peter of Spain. Agricola had already merged dialectic with "discourse" itself, and likewise perpetuated the *Summulae's* confusion of probable and scientific demonstration. He goes further, though, and executes a "fiat" of great consequence and startling simplicity. Dialectic and rhetoric, joined in a common use of probability, are utterly divorced by Agricola through his complete denial of topics to rhetoric and their entire appropriation to dialectic. Topics and topical invention itself belong entirely to dialectic. There is no such beast as rhetorical topical invention. The only invention available to rhetoric is the dubious one of *elocutio*. Agricola is both definite and determined about this:

> [H]e insists that no one before himself [not Aristotle, not Cicero, not Quintilian, certainly not Boethius] had ever properly related invention to ornate or striking expression. . . . The divorce of rhetoric from dialectic implies at the same time a union of invention and striking expression in any given text. . . .[15]

By limiting topics to dialectic, and by making dialectic a "super-discourse" to begin with, Agricola abandons rhetoric to sheer ornamentation. Moreover, he (and later, Ramus) complete what the medieval arts curriculum began. That curriculum had never properly distinguished strictly logical demonstration (logic properly so-called) and probable argumentation; they were both learned at once. The meager remaining distinction is wiped out by Agricola and Ramus who level all kinds of knowing or discourse to one rather probable variety. Here again is a paradox; though abandoning rhetoric to mere ornament, these logicians in effect rendered *all* discourse rhetorical by a combined "merge-and-elevate" strategy. They fused all logic and discourse into dialectic, then turned purely probable reasoning into logic per se (through the wholesale importation of the topics); thus logic is turned into a highly refined rhetoric.[16] Ong sums it up in this fashion:

> The distinction between a dialectic of probabilities and
> scientific demonstration, uncertain enough in the central
> medieval tradition, is deliberately eliminated. Either the
> scholastic disputation striving for scientific certitude
> (although often falling far short of it) is assimilated to other
> less scientific forms of discourse (Agricola's sympathies
> favor this) or all discourse can be assimilated to scientific,
> and the poem made as "logical" as the mathematical treatise
> (Ramus' [sic] will advance this view explicitly).[17]

It is not difficult to see the historical consequences of this. Ramus' view will "win
out" (although the epistemic rhetoricians of this century, including Walter Jost,
incline toward a more Agricolan formula), and the ages of science and discovery
will readily follow the mathematical, diagrammatic model of discourse Ramus
advances. It is this model that Newman will reject.

THE CALL OF KNOWLEDGE

Ong's central "anthropological" observation is that a change of consciousness
occurred in the Renaissance that profoundly altered the way people think about
knowledge and discourse. Though there are specific "players" such as Agricola and
Ramus, the change is not confined to "this text" or "that author." Ong demonstrates
at great length the cultural build up of pressures, some pedagogical, some tech-
nological, that cooperated with logical confusions to effect the alteration. We have
seen how topics entered the logical tradition and were made dialectically sovereign
by Agricola. What the topics *displaced* in logic is perhaps more significant to the
change of conception or consciousness Ong is analyzing. Aristotle's essential
logical tool in terms of classification is not topical but categorical. The categories are
the fundamental component of Aristotle's logic, and it is from the categories that
such essential logical conceptions as the predicables (genus, species, specific
difference, property, accident) are derived. Agricola's topics replaced (or more
accurately, subsumed) these categories:

> The *Categories* or *Predicaments* of Aristotle are not a
> classification of things, nor of being-in-general, nor are they
> a classification of the whole range of human concepts as
> such. Neither are they categories in the modern sense of a
> system of classes into which items are "put." As their name
> indicates and a recent study confirms, they are types of
> predicates conceived of more or less as "accusations" (or
> "outcries" in the market place or assembly, *categoriae*,
> transformed into Latin as *praedicamenta*, things spoken out)

which can be brought against a subject or "prime substance."
They are a generic list of the kind of things one attributes or
urges against a subject (of an enunciation) by *saying*
something of a subject. . . . This attribution is effected by a
statement, an assertion, a proposition, which expresses a
judgment or decision regarding the validity of the attribution,
or the justness of the "accusation". . . .[18]

The classical definition of a predicable as a thing *said* of another thing, underscores
the verbal, oral/aural aspect of this fundamental logical apparatus. Indeed all
intellectual or cognitive activity is referred to in analogies of sense:

It is a commonplace that, because of the derivative character
of our knowledge through the senses, all intellectual
cognition must be treated by analogy with sensory cognition.
. . . Thus, description of mental activity in terms of
"composition" (putting together), or "implication" (folding
up, or folding back upon), or "definition" (setting bounds or
limits), or "division," or even description (drawing a line
around or sketching) all exploit, more or less evidently, an
analogy between the field of intellectual activity and a field
which involves local motion and is sensorily apprehended in
terms of sight.[19]

It is an interesting intellectual game to watch for the sensory analogies of
individual terms employed in everyone's language. But as noted, *visual* analogies
are preeminent in cognitive terminology, and justly so. The visual sense is the most
static and fixed, the least dependent upon time and contact, and the most integrative
of all the senses. "A drift toward the visual," says Ong, "is inseparable from any
economy of explanation. . . . We are today more than ever witnesses of attempts to
reduce everything supplied by the other senses--sounds, smells, tastes, pressures--
to charts and tables which can be visually assimilated."[20] Ong mentions that the
reverse procedure--representing visual matters through other sensory means--
almost never happens. Even metaphysics, despite its high degree of abstraction,
relies heavily on visual analogy to explain its concepts.[21] Nevertheless, inseparably
united to the very idea of the categories is a profoundly oral/aural analogy; these
basic building blocks of Aristotelian logic (the categories) are the link between
reasoning and communication, thinking and speaking about things:

[T]he categories are at root (although not always explicitly)
conceived of as parts of enunciations. Human knowledge for
Aristotle exists in the full sense only in the enunciation,
either interior or exteriorized in language; the *saying* of
something about something, the *uttering* of a statement, the
expression of a *judgment* (ultimately a declaring a "yes" or a
"no"), or, in what from the point of view of grammar is a
sentence, a union of subject and predicate (*praedicatum* = the

thing *said*). . . . The enunciation alone makes "complete" sense. But the enunciation cannot be conceived of solely in terms of visual analogies; these must be complemented with the aural if we are to form a concept at all adequate to the elemental cognitive process.[22]

The relation between knowledge and enunciation (either internal or external) is so fundamental that a danger exists in excessively visualizing cognition and knowledge. Though the visual has a natural priority in the analogies used to express cognitive processes, that priority can become a kind of tyranny in which something small but essential--oral/aural components of cognition--becomes lost:

There are difficulties, however, in the tendency to reduce other sensory knowledge to visual terms. An oscillograph of a sound gives everything about the sound--except the sound itself. This is the price of becoming more "abstract," or explanatory. The description of a word (*verbum*, or *vox*) as a sign (*signum*) suffers from the same disability insofar as the notion of sign is based on a visual analogy. A word is more than a sign of some*thing*, even of an intelligible something such as a concept. It is a cry, a voice, something which comes from the interior of a person, who as a *person* can never be "explained," and which somehow manifests this interior. Human cognitive processes and intellectual activity can thus never be adequately grasped for what they are unless they are thought of not only in terms of knowledge-by-sight but also in terms of this knowledge-by-sound and the aspects of this knowledge-by-sound which do not reduce to visual analogies. These aspects are much more evident in the enunciation than anywhere else--which is to be expected, since this is the central act of intellection which has "complete sense." Thus it is that the enunciation is intransigent in the face of all attempts to conceive of it in terms of visual analogies alone. It can be conceived of as a "judgment," a judicial act, a saying yes or no--but there is no adequate visualist equivalent of this act. It can be conceived of as an "enunciation"--a speaking out. It can be conceived of as the coupling of two concepts, but of what kind of concepts, for conjunctions and prepositions couple concepts? It is a coupling of subject and predicate--and this last term conceals an auditory analogy again; *praedicatum* is the thing cried out or *said*.[23]

The importance of these observations can hardly be overestimated. Though it is unlikely that Ong had Newman in mind when writing the text on Ramus, one can almost hear Newman's observations about teaching and learning in the passages just read. Knowledge is most complete when it involves "the whole man," when the personhood of the knower is most fully engaged in the thing known. This occurs when a full interior assent (declaring a "yes" or a "no") occurs, the fruition of which is utterance. But utterance is no by-product of knowledge; rather it is its most natural state. It is such because an utterance, as Newman notes, is an act, a deed; it necessarily involves aspects of the knowing being which are not reducible to formula or even syllogism. Just as one cannot truly learn of a thing (in Newman's view) from a text but must have a "living voice" as well, so one cannot be said to teach unless the full personal being of the teacher is engaged, and this is a strongly oral/aural engagement. In such a circumstance, a professor is exactly that-- one who professes, who utters, who *enacts* knowledge, as it were, through the judgmental activity of intellect and the radical freedom of the will to act--in this case to act in utterance. Thus the *voice* or cry of which Ong speaks does indeed reflect the personal origin of the thing said for such an "enunciation" is a coalescing or "concretization" of cognitive processes that are proper to human beings.

The qualities of cognition and the analogies of sense described by Ong display in miniature Newman's instinctive grasp of the personal element of thought and knowledge. There is the importance of the "one-who-utters" in the formation of intellects and the communication of truth; there is the perception that, beyond mere pedagogical effectiveness, the living voice is an essential component of epistemolgical or cognitive processes; there is even the sense of the *will's* role in thought. Ong's approach is more philosophical than Newman's almost conversational comments upon learning, but the thrust is the same. Indeed the comparison of Ong to Newman is a ready-to-hand example of the difference in modes of discourse. Continuing in the philosophical vein, however, Ong highlights the epistemological relevancy of assertion, noting that it is an act

> which establishes contact between the outer world of reality and the inner world of the person (however one may ultimately explain these two worlds), and the categories or predicaments which enter into this act are denizens of the bridge between the mind and things.[24]

Returning to history, he adds, "This is why, much to Ramus' chagrin, Aristotle discusses predication and categories not only in his logical treatises but also in his *Metaphysics*."[25] The chagrin was a gift from Agricola, who made the categories problematic by "substituting for the categories as a classificatory apparatus at the center of philosophical studies the topics or loci as "places" (also called common-places)."[26] The analogy is visual, and thus the discourse to which it is directed "is conceived of as the sort of thing that can be moved into and out of the 'places.' And the oral-auditory is liquidated in favor of the visual."[27]

RHETORICAL CONSEQUENCES, HABITS OF THOUGHT

Eliminating the categories and replacing them with topics has two concurrent and related consequences. The first is to magnify the "rhetorization" of philosophical discourse, and the second is to encourage mechanistic thinking. Though the relation between these consequences may seem paradoxical, it is not difficult to account for. Amplification (or more correctly, importation) of the topics into logic and "philosophical" discourse not only liquidates whatever personalist and verbal characteristics logic may have, but it orients that logic to what are properly rhetorical kinds of argumentation. The traditional logic, based on categories, centered on three divisions of its material: simple terms, propositions, and argumentation. The Agricola-Ramus topical logic jettisoned this orientation and instead focused upon invention and *dispositio*--the traditional, rhetorical counterpart to the more philosophical dialectic.[28] As a result, their logic or dialectic was "rhetoricized," weakening and destabilizing the unique cognitive claims of each mode of discourse. The paradox, of course, is that while rhetoricizing dialectic, Ramus and Agricola actually *deflate* rhetoric itself, leaving it only ornamentation and evacuating it of its own intellectual rigor. One is left with an enervated rhetoric as a direct result of rhetoricizing the non-rhetorical.

Moreover, and more critical for the history of Western thought, the very idea of reasoning becomes swamped by visual analogies of abstractions. Topical conceptions are visual because of the spatial aspect inherent in the idea of a place, *loci*, or seat. Reasoning becomes the mental activity of resorting to particular locations, extracting from those locations an "argument," and then casting that argument in an intelligible order. The entire activity very much resembles a re-arrangement of cognitive furniture, a simple moving of "parts" to effect "reason." Needless to say, this conception of reason has fascinating consequences as far as the habit of thought it encourages. Thought itself becomes a matter of "content." Like the stores of a warehouse, one's mind is "filled" with content, and one's reasonings are a shifting about of those contents. Newman will revolt against this, of course, claiming for reasoning an unformulable quality not reducible to mere "arranged content." He will do so while protesting that the personal aspects of different kinds of reasoning should not be confused, thus instinctively sensing the confusion in Agricola and Ramus. This confusion was largely diffused throughout the West by means of Ramus' popular texts, and it was codified in the works of idealist and empiricist philosophers. The conceptions of reasoning encouraged by Ramus *et alii* enhance mechanistic approaches to thought:

> [T]he mind trained in place logic habitually "locates" things or ideas indifferently one inside the other. We are confronted with our own present-day habits of thought; for we ourselves think of books as "containing" chapters and paragraphs, paragraphs as "containing" sentences, sentences as "containing" words, words as "containing" ideas, and finally ideas as "containing" truth. Here the whole mental world has gone hollow. The pre-Agricolan mind had preferred to think of books as saying something, of sentences as expressing something, and of words and ideas as "containing" nothing at all but rather as signifying or making signs for something. After Agricola the notion of content can serve for and level out all these diversified modes of conceptualization.[29]

In such a hollow mental world where things slip inside other things like prefabricated shipping units, it is no wonder that structuralists and deconstructionists revolt and avow the *non*-content of signs. Though one may argue that in so doing one kind of hollow world has been substituted for another, it remains true that the idea of a knowing subject (and that truth exists as a relation of intellect and object) is lost.

The hollow world bequeathed to posterity by Agricola and Ramus was entirely in step with other cultural features of the late Middle Ages and early Renaissance. Ong notes that the habits of mind encouraged through the writings of Agricola and Ramus were encouraged by other things as well. There was increased interest in texts apart from persons or living entities. There were also the diagrammatic products facilitated by printing which helped to "spatialize" the imagination. Ong notes the "humanist determination to make the measure of all speech a fixed *written* tradition. . . . This is the age which will become marked by the idea that the Bible--become itself a kind of commonplace--is the sole rule and depository for faith and morals."[30] Knowledge (and thus faith or moral doctrine) is content, stuff, as it were, to be inserted into receptive minds and fixed in determinate, written (even printed) form. Again, we see today this idea fully developed in the sense of publication as a permanent--and inherently valuable--thing. A published author has made a permanent contribution to the intellectual life of the era; on the other hand, an unpublished intellectual is often regarded as an abortive thinker, one whose thoughts (or energies) must be too undeveloped to merit permanence, regardless of that intellectual's interaction with persons. Knowledge is content of mind, and discourse is the laying out, the *dispositio*, of that content in an advantageous way. The very word "examination" acquired in the Middle Ages and renaissance its modern meaning: picking out the contents of an individual's mind relative to a subject matter. The classical *examen* means a swarm of bees, or "at best such consideration or weighing of matters as might enter into judicial decisions."[31]

Today the difficulties inherent in the objectification of knowledge, its de-personalization and mechanistic conceptualization, are a persistent thorn in the side of university pedagogy. It has resulted in a kind of see-saw. The inadequacy of such conceptions of knowledge persistently breeds insurrection and revolt. The revolt takes the form of advocating subjectivism and relativism in an attempt to find a place for the personal in the educational milieu. The reigning mechanistic and "knowledge-as-content" schools of thought despise such educational "personalism" as a soft, unreal, and sentimental approach to knowledge and pedagogy. The extremes co-exist in a somewhat stable equilibrium, each reacting to the other.

Historically, the same bifurcation of the intellectual world since the Renaissance is seen in endless repetition. In Newman's day the Benthamites and the romantics represented the divergent views, later to be taken up by the utilitarians and the liberal classicists. Mill's attempt at wedding mechanism to subjectivism (a description Mill would hardly approve) testifies to the unsatisfactory disunity of the intellectual milieu. Earlier, the German metaphysical romantics and the French methodical philosophers represented the extremes. In realist terms, the two camps or alternatives are reductionistic. In large part this accounts for Newman's being so frequently misunderstood; he was accused of being a mindless dogmatist at the same time as he was condemned for being a radical, relativist liberal. The intel-lectual milieu could only place a person in one of two limited camps. Newman did not seem to fit either one because he had a highly personalist approach to cognition while being utterly convinced of the objectivity of truth. This division is still felt today as critics label Newman a modernist and a romantic, or a reactionary and a dogmatist. Others attempt to settle the matter by invoking a label at once pacifying yet unsatisfactory: "moderate." All of this is the unhappy result of the de-integration of man, of knowledge, and of truth. It led ultimately to the utter schism of mind and heart, of fact and feeling. It has had the bizarre consequence of orthodox religion being attacked for contradictory vices: it is at once too abstract and intellectual, and too sentimental and unthinking.

PETER RAMUS

Agricola's work prepared the way for Ramus. Ramus built upon and spread Agricola's basic logical and dialectical principles. The large-scale intellectual acceptance of these principles dovetailed with other cultural features, such that the conceptions of knowledge and discourse subtly but profoundly shifted toward the de-personal. Pedagogical practices, increased fascination with texts, and the onset of printing all encouraged objectified, impersonal concepts of knowledge and thought. Ramus' particular contribution was to magnify and heighten the significance of *topical* logic by developing the Agricolan rhetoricized dialectic.

Ramus, a student and later a professor at the University of Paris, was a dedicated humanist reformer who approached academic disciplines under the aspect of their pedagogical effectiveness. Primarily a logician and dialectician, he published numerous works including classroom textbooks that epitomize his work in many ways. In 1543, Ramus published *Structure of Dialectic* and a feisty *Remarks on Aristotle* in which he vigorously attacks the philosopher. This initiated a combative career that would become his trademark. He taught and wrote upon other subjects as well (mathematics, rhetoric, poetry), but his dialectical work is most significant.

Revised and republished countless times in his life, it was the *Dialectic* that introduced Ramus' all-important "method" to the Renaissance intellectual world. Ramus' method is the "orderly pedagogical presentation of any subject by reputedly scientific descent from 'general principles' to 'specials' by means of definition and bipartite division. . . ."[32] This method is more than mere technique; it is a universal tool applicable to anything and guaranteed to lay out a subject according to the subject's intrinsic nature. Indeed, therein lies the rub, for Ramus conceived that this method--a transparently pedagogical one--was in fact attuned to the intrinsic nature of each curriculum subject and, by extension, to knowledge itself. One begins to think of the old "science of sciences" phrase, and indeed method becomes synonymous with logic and dialectic. This is historically significant, for

> Here begins the practice of featuring a *tractatus de methodo* in logic textbooks, where Descartes was to find such treatises solidly entrenched. Here, also, begins the impression that, since such a treatise on method is featured as a part of logic, and is called logical method, what is purveyed in the treatise is a bona fide outgrowth of a strictly formal, scientific logic.[33]

The method increasingly dominated Ramus' work as his life progressed, and the highly diagrammatic twofold divisions it spawned were readily fashioned and distributed by the new printing industry. The "diagrammatic tidiness" of mechanical printing and Ramus' method were meant for each other, as it were.[34] "They were part of a large-scale operation freeing the book from the world of discourse and making it over into an object, a box with surface and 'content' . . . which could be charted in a 'table' or ranged, now for the first time, in a 'place indicator' (*index locorum*)."[35] Even the titles of books reflect this change; titles had commonly been "De" or "On" something, which suggests not only speech or dialogue but the fact that the subjects discussed "resided" in the minds of those discussing them. It was not long after printing became common that "On" was dropped and books were titled as *being* the subject: from "On Rhetoric" to "Rhetoric." The book became the subject.[36]

Ramist rhetoric (rather than his rhetoricized dialectic) was outlined, curiously enough, by Ramus' friend and associate, Omer Talon, whose avowedly Ramist text, *Training in Oratory*, was published in 1545. Ramus then goes on to explore, in commentaries on Cicero and Quintilian, the rather limited realm left to a despoiled rhetoric. Devoid of topics and invention itself, all that remains to rhetoric is ornament, elevation, and the study of tropes and figures. Oddly enough, even delivery gets short shrift, perhaps because it is not susceptible to diagrammatic description. Ramus' methodical thrust is nowhere better seen than in his study of oratory. His analysis of Cicero's *Plea for Rabirius* includes such methodical gems as:

> In tropes, the elocution is good and rich. Metonymy occurs sixty times, synecdoche about the same number of times, irony not once, metaphor eighty times. . . . Of the figures of sentence . . . *optatio* is not used, *prolepsis* occurs three times; prosopopoeia twice, but concealed as digression and *dialogismus*; *praeteritio* is used once, other figures of sentence not at all.[37]

As Ong wryly observes, "The 'scientific' approach to literature has arrived."[38]

In fact, Ramus' (and Talon's) opinion of rhetoric and literature is quite low. This is inevitable since the probabilistic reasoning proper to rhetoric had been assumed into demonstrative reasoning by Agricola and Ramus. Thus rhetoric--and also poetic, the reasoning of which is even more difficult to formulate--is regarded as a kind of broken or faulty dialectic. It is regarded with some suspicion, in fact, despite the high Renaissance value placed on oratory; one merely has to note the efforts of a Sir Philip Sidney in defending poesy to glimpse the extent to which non-scientific "reasonings" were considered suspect. In a simplistic and mechanical conception of reasoning, any kind of reasoning that does not fit "the mold" must be defective. Whatever reasoning poetry employs must be a stealthy, surreptitious kind of reasoning. Ramus describes the work of the poet:

> This is what the poet does as a major part of his tactics, when he sets out to sway the people, the many-headed monster. He deceives (*decipit*) in all sorts of ways. He starts in the middle, often proceeding thence to the beginning, and getting on to the end by some equivocal and unexpected dodge. . . .[39]

Sir Philip Sidney, who admired Ramus, would have done well to defend poetry from statements like this. Aside from the spatial description of plot and treating the story like a syllogism, the low opinion of poetry in this passage is clear; the poet tricks the audience, he dupes and deceives them into drawing some conclusion. The conclusion of a plot is rather simplistically assumed to be like the conclusion of a demonstration. The poet's greatest fault seems to be the *mis*-ordering of premises. As Ong observes, the poets (and rhetoricians) delight and move rather than *teach*, thus: "This qualifies them as deceivers--a thought which Ramus' Puritan followers would relish . . . because they [teach] in such a roundabout and underhand way. They 'ambush' their audience into drawing conclusions which the audience has no inclination to draw."[40]

By eschewing probabilistic logics, indeed by denying any such logic exists, Ramus is unequipped to deal with modes of discourse obviously dependent upon probability and the metaphorical "as if." Such things do not become subject to his method, therefore they don't exist. Even what might be considered methodical, diagrammatic aspects of rhetoric (such as the four parts of an oration) are confused in Ramus by being assumed into his dialectical definition-and-division procedure. The *exordium, narratio, confirmatio,* and *peroratio* are simply the "linking of arguments in an unbroken chain," the whole of which is labeled dialectical and left out of rhetoric.[41] This too has a debilitating effect on the oral and personalist characteristics of rhetoric. Ramus' interest in these four parts of an oration is strongly chronological, flow-chart like, and thus the "diverse psychological functions of the four parts are lost sight of. . . ."[42] These parts of an oration are more than just locations and times of arguments; they share an inherent significance relative to the movement of audiences' minds and the diverse ways in which people become convinced of things. They have a unique bearing on argument *relative to the audience*--a consideration, as will be seen, that Ramus is loath to entertain.

Another victim of Ramist rhetoric is the age-old *copia verborum* whereby "facility of expression" is aided through the ready availability (in the memory and imagination) of examples, means of expression, and devices of utterance. *Copia* was traditionally developed by retaining phrases, tricks of expression, aphorisms, and even stories that rhetoricians could use for "amplification."[43] Because *copia* was rooted in the topics, it also had to pack up and move to dialectic for Ramus. "This was the deathblow to profusion of expression as something consciously cultivated," says Ong, for the "riot of impressions" encouraged by *copia* is tamed "by the practice of analysis."[44] The word "riot" is well chosen, for it suggests the linguistic rabble that is *copia* and the personalist thrust of its sources and uses.

> The pre-Ramist commonplace tradition could be richly
> sonorous rather than merely 'clear,' for it was the echo of a
> cognitive world experienced as if filled with sound and
> voices and speaking persons. . . . With Ramus, the voice
> goes out of this world. The *loci communes* [the seat of
> copia] . . . provide not richness or vocal abundance, but
> arguments which can be hooked or 'glued' onto questions.[45]

REASON OUT OF ALL REASON

The final consequence (relative to Newman) of Ramist dialectic and rhetoric concerns audience. What had been the rhetorical necessity of tailoring one's rhetoric to the kind of audience at hand, the practice of "decorum," Ramus also takes into dialectic and dismisses as unnecessary. According to Ramus, discourse governed by method takes care of decorum automatically. This again shows a reductionistic conception of reasoning. It is supposed that different men do not think at all differently; if one has methodically analyzed a question, then the analysis has automatically "tailored" the discourse. Ramist decorum is the rhetorical equivalent of a stocking-cap: one size fits all. "Decorum had always involved a complex notion of adaptation, with a certain personalist valence, since the choice of style depended not merely upon some mechanically conceived adjustment but upon *ethos* or character."[46] Moreover, the audience's ethos or character is as important as the orator's. When all character is levelled on the uniform terrain of correct arrangement, rhetorical "personality" vanishes:

> This order in dialectic is, as has been seen, radically visualist and diagrammatic in conceptualization, so that the transfer of decorum from rhetoric to dialectic . . . is, in effect, an elimination of the vocal and personalist in favor of the diagrammatic within the concept of accommodation or adaptation itself.[47]

What is the historical effect of this?

> Out of this operation, emerges the Ramist plain style. . . . [which is] the verbal counterpart of the coming visualist universe of "objects," voiceless and by that very fact depersonalized, which would soon recommend to the Royal Society, as Thomas Sprat records in his history, "a close, naked, natural way of speaking," as near the "mathematical" as possible.[48]

The spread and influence of Ramus' and Talon's work was vast. Ong's *Ramus and Talon Inventory* charts the course of around 800 separate editions of these two authors during and after Ramus' life, as well as the works of almost 400 other authors distinctly Ramist in principle.[49] The Ramist passion for method swept into the Renaissance and was even instrumental in preparing the way for Descartes, a figure of pivotal intellectual importance for Western conceptions about knowledge.

> Ramus left on the scholastic and humanistic traditions a permanent and important mark. By hybridizing rhetorical organization with "logic," Ramist method widened the field in which the passion for at least superficial 'methodical' orderliness could play. It released enthusiasms such as that of Jean Bodin, who seeks to "methodize" man's understanding even of history, and prepared the way for the more gargantuan enthusiasms of the German systematic encyclopedists and thus indirectly for the still later French *Encyclopedistes*.[50]

The impersonal, schematicized world of knowledge established by Ramus and post-Ramist methodological philosophies was one where dialogue was lost and the "voice" had gone out of teaching and learning. Things known were little objects to be arranged and re-arranged, "corpuscular" in nature, and learned through the device of method.[51] For Ramus, method meant successive waves of definition and division until the subject was fully divided and (not coincidentally) readily memorized. The knowledge gained thereby was to be inserted into minds and inserted into books. Based largely on spatial/visual analogies, all knowledge was diagrammatic and precise. Thus ambiguity is the greatest evil, and for pedagogical effectiveness, Ramus mandates utter clarity--the kind easily derived from diagrams.

> Contrary to the common persuasion, the medieval
> scholastics, while they practice a certain amount of accuracy
> and certainly encourage it in their long-term effects, do not
> make an explicit shibboleth of it. Clear and distinct ideas
> would become a shibboleth chiefly in the age of topical logic
> and printing.[52]

The misappropriation of rhetorical topics into the realm of the categories
encouraged a visualist, impersonal perspective on thought. Instead of Aristotle's
demonstrative deduction where things were *said* of other things, a formal deduction
evolved where one hopped from place to place, from one intellectual corpuscle or
spot to another. One learns by initiating a mechanical process of thought that
terminates when the knowledge has been adequately "situated" alongside the rest of
the mind's contents. Here the intellectual process Aquinas calls "ratio"--discursive
reasoning--is everything, and the understanding or *intellectus* is gone. Discursive
reasoning is a necessary component of human thought "due to the material
component in man's cognitional make-up and in the make-up of the reality he is
immediately faced with."[53] But it is not everything. The *intellectus* is higher, and it
is that toward which the discursive reasoning "terminates and annihilates itself."[54]
Not so for the post-Ramus world which, according to Ong, insists that "it is
reasoning or ratiocination, not understanding, which differentiates men from
animals. . . ." In time, this legacy "leads into the eighteenth-century world of
'reason,' which proves to be a highly materialistic world."[55] Needless to say, the
eighteenth-century world established the intellectual milieu in which Newman was
raised. He imbibed to the full the post-Ramist conceptions of knowledge: the almost
unconsciously visualistic, impersonalistic, materialistic, and mechanistic conceptions. Though he may not have been aware of their history or development, he
imbibed them and knew them well. It is all the more remarkable, then, that he
rejected them.

VII. INTELLECTUAL ANTECEDENTS: PHILOSOPHICAL ROOTS, MECHANISTIC BRANCHES

> *There are more things in heaven and earth, Horatio,*
> *Than are dreamt of in your philosophy.*
> Hamlet I, v.

PHILOSOPHICAL MILIEU

The ideas about knowledge and discourse encouraged by various cultural and academic developments were given a more formal character in philosophical developments after the Renaissance. The visualist, mechanistic habits of mind saw their philosophical counterpart unfold in epistemological speculation. For the nineteenth century, the result was that "habits of mind" (what Ong might call archeology of thought) were joined by actual, formal philosophies which corresponded in principle to those habits. By Newman's time, mechanistic paradigms of thought and knowledge were so pervasive they constituted the intellectual background for almost any thinker. This background was not only an intellectual milieu, it was specifically articulated in concrete philosophies. Thus, Newman's intellectual world was "hemmed in" on all sides; general predispositions toward science and method were complemented by idealist and empiricist philosophies that advanced mechanistic models of knowledge. Newman's task as a proponent of a rhetorical, non-mechanistic access to truth or knowledge was, therefore, difficult, doubly difficult in being articulated largely *through* rhetorical, not philosophical, modes of argument. His arguments are most openly advanced in two works, the *Philosophical Notebook* and the *Grammar of Assent*. As we shall see, even when Newman goes "head to head" with the prevailing philosophies of the day, he ends up doing so rhetorically rather than through a consistent and systematic philosophy of his own.

In order to understand what Newman was up against, we must briefly explore the profound contribution Descartes and Locke made to that intellectual milieu. Newman did not write in a vacuum. The ideas of knowledge that Newman had to defy in attempting to create "room" for certainty and the illative sense were largely the products of these two philosophers and their successors. They set the stage for Newman's intellectual combat, and they did so largely by turning away from (or rather, ignoring) the metaphysical epistemology of Aquinas. It is this epistemology which allows man genuine access to the created universe and a genuine claim to knowledge and certainty about it. Newman's defense of rhetorical knowledge is in part an attempt to reclaim--not the specific epistemology--but the certainty that it allows.

AQUINAS' DISTINCTION

The philosophical traditions Newman imbibed were mixtures distilled through centuries of speculative thought. Widely different philosophies were held and discussed in the eighteenth and nineteenth centuries, but one philosophical school was almost entirely lacking: the Thomistic school. In fact, this lacuna was openly admitted. Philosophers and historians of thought unabashedly moved from Cicero to Descartes, often disregarding a millennium. Much of the Renaissance anti-schoolman prejudice persisted in the nineteenth century, and only began to dissipate after the neo-Thomist revival inaugurated largely by Pope Leo XIII (the same Pope who elevated Newman to the cardinalate). But there is a curious historical feature in the long absence of scholastic thought; ignored as the centuries between Cicero and Descartes may have been, the cornerstone of Aristotle's thought was also passed over. That cornerstone, of course, was his metaphysics, and this metaphysics was essentially adopted by Aquinas. Perhaps therein lies the explanation for this partial neglect of Aristotle; perhaps the disregard for Aquinas' scholastic manner was such that Aristotle's metaphysics was tainted by association. Whatever the case, the passing over of scholastic thought and the history of its reintroduction are very instructive. They underscore an essential difference between Thomistic philosophy itself and the philosophical principles that Newman's world (and our own) acknowledged. Those historians of philosophy who neglected the Middle Ages may have been poor historians, but they were astute philosophers. When they descended from their trans-millennial leap, they landed precisely upon a most significant philosopher: Descartes.

With the advent of Descartes, a great and sundering chasm in philosophical principles opened such that even today it is difficult to look at scholastic thought from a non-Cartesian perspective. Significant as was Descartes' mathematics program for the sciences (a program entirely harmonious with its mechanical, diagrammatic predecessors in Agricola and Ramus), the most important feature of his thought was his theory of knowledge, his epistemology. This is where the great chasm opened. Aided and abetted by the "mechanicism" introduced earlier, Descartes' epistemology constituted a framework for inquiry still largely used today and which radically altered the very starting point of philosophy. Indeed, he fairly invented epistemology.

Aquinas' philosophy of knowledge is so radically different from Descartes' (and that of various subsequent philosophers) that one hesitates to call it an epistemology. "Thomas voiced a very different theory of knowledge. It was in fact not at all a theory, that is, an epistemology (a discipline always tainted with the primacy of the Cartesian-Kantian cogito), but a metaphysics."[1] It was a metaphysics, as Jaki observes, because its principle was not a collection of neo-Platonic "clear and distinct" ideas, but the primacy and immediacy of being itself: "It is a metaphysics because, contrary to the fundamental tenets of empiricism, in the knowledge of reality not what is merely sensory is revealed but the intelligible nature of physical entities. Such a knowledge is the grasp of the being of things which underlies the grasp of any specificity evidenced by them."[2]

The criteria for a working metaphysics are severe. If metaphysics--the study of being--is to be properly philosophical, it must reason from first principles and treat universals. The reasonings must be formally correct and internally consistent. If not, the result is contradiction and ensuing philosophical absurdity. Owens warns of detours some metaphysicians take that either draw them away from metaphysics properly so-called or into fatal contradiction. "A metaphysics that aims to be an intuitive process beyond the reasoning of the intellect, or a historical cataloguing of pre-suppositions, or a type of literary creation in which prose borders on poetry," is doomed either to philosophical irrelevance or to trip itself up.[3] Though the author has Henri Bergson and R.G. Collingwood in mind here, the warning serves as a kind of summary of idealisms, historicisms, and even the contemporary literary rhetoricisms that are practiced upon metaphysical subjects. The warning even applies to Newman. As will be seen, his own metaphysical conceptions, born out of a rhetorical viewpoint, bear a literary and mental-historical (or psychological) mark essentially unmetaphysical in character.

The systematic nature of Thomistic metaphysics must not be confused with the Ramist habit of mechanized, schematicized thought. The two are philosophical night and day. Not only is Thomistic philosophy extremely unsusceptible to highly visual conceptualization (and strong in aural abstraction), but "systematic" is not properly synonymous with "mechanistic." The difference lies in the way intellect is regarded; systematic thought such as Thomistic metaphysics is *thought*, while mechanistic thought tends toward the employment of a device or "method." That is, the emphasis in the first is fully compatible with the idea of a personal intellect integrated with all the features of soul, mind, and body; the emphasis in the second is upon non-personal, abstract and "disembodied" technique (such as mathematical method). The scientific or systematic nature of metaphysics is derived from its subject--being--but its development is no tick-tock process wound up then set loose. It takes place in individual persons habituated to the kind of thought needed to treat universals yet remain cognizant of the reality of *things*:

> [S]uch a metaphysics [says Owens] has to be a living and
> when fully developed a creative habit, and so can live and
> function only in particular individuals. A habit, however, is
> specified by its object, and that object, in the case of a
> science, is something fixed in the nature of things and
> universally accessible to all.[4]

The integration in Aquinas' metaphysics appears clearly in the very opening of his "Treatise on Man" in the first part of the *Summa Theologica*. There, Aquinas addresses the nature of man and he at once defends the proposition that man is a composite, an integration of body and soul. Saying that man is composed of a spiritual and corporeal substance, he determines that the spiritual substance, the soul, is the principle of intellectual operation in man. The soul is both immaterial, a "not-body," and a substance--that is, a thing self-inhering. "It must necessarily be allowed that the principle of intellectual operation which we call the soul, is a principle both incorporeal and subsistent."[5] How the incorporeal nature of the soul is shown does not concern us here; suffice it to say that it involves the capacity for knowledge and the insusceptibility of material things to being known purely as or through their material natures. At the very beginning of his treatise, Aquinas has established principles that will be missed in Cartesian epistemology. He has affirmed the essential union of the corporeal and incorporeal, and the four-hundred year, post-Cartesian perplexity surrounding "mind-body, mind-world" divisions does not exist. The ties of integration between the spiritual soul and the material body will be drawn tighter yet, but first the fundamental Aristotelian distinction of form and matter must be explored, for both Aristotle and Aquinas treat soul and body as equivalent to form and matter.

MATTER, FORM, AND ABSTRACTION

Aristotelian "matter" does not at all mean what "matter" has come to mean today. In typically English terms, A.D. Nuttall observes that matter today is thought of as "bits of stuff"--perhaps, if one insists, very small bits.[6] But regardless of size, no bit of material can be called pure and unformed "first matter" because by the very fact of the material's determinate "piece-ness" it has its distinguishing form. "[T]o Aristotle matter is not hard but soft; as such it is mere potentiality which cannot grow into being [or act] without the imposition of form."[7] That is, Aristotelian first or prime matter is not what we would call mass or physical "stuff." For Aquinas it is that through which a form becomes actual and has undivided being. In this sense it can be said of prime matter that it is the individuating element of things.[8]

Matter is best understood, however, in relation to form. Form is the "thingness" or essence of an object. It is the internal principle of a thing and gives it its particular nature; form is likewise the ground for all the properties and accidents inhering in a thing. Maritain explains that matter is simply "that *of which* things are made, which in itself is nothing actual, a principle wholly indeterminate, incapable of separate existence, but capable of existing in composition with something else," that is, the form.[9] In turn, form is

> an active principle, which is, so to speak, the living idea or soul of the thing, and which determines the purely passive first matter . . . constituting with it one single thing actually existent, one single corporeal substance, which owes to it [the form] both that it is this or that kind of thing, that is to say, its specific nature, and its existence. . . .[10]

All material things having form and matter, they necessarily have an immaterial principle (form) that confers actuality upon first matter and renders the composite a *specific* entity. However, form is not necessarily spiritual merely because it is immaterial. In natural objects form is not self subsisting, thus it does not or cannot exist divided from matter.[11] Thus matter and form in most natural things cannot actually be separated in fact but only in concept.[12] One cannot have a handful of un-differentiated matter in the left-hand, and a handful of un-individuated form in the right-hand.

The importance of form in the economy of knowledge is two-fold. In the first place, the integration of body and soul we have been speaking of is evident again in the soul as the *form* of the body. The disadvantage of regarding form spatially becomes obvious here. Aquinas refers to Aristotle's tenet that the soul is the *act*, the abiding principle or essence, of a "physical organic body having life potentially."[13] This applies to all living bodies, human, animal, and vegetable. The human soul or principle of actuality is a rational one that self-subsists; that is, it can exist apart from the body even though it is appropriate for it to be joined to the body. Animal and vegetable "souls" or forms cannot "exist apart from matter."[14] The fact that man's soul is rational does not interfere with the non-intellectual activity of the soul, "For the soul is the primary principle of our nourishment, sensation, and local movement; and likewise of our understanding."[15] The form or soul of man, then, both brings the body into act and is the intellectual part of the corporeal/incorporeal composite.

The second role of form in the economy of knowledge also involves the body. In answer to the question: Is the intellectual soul properly united to such a body? Aquinas responds in part:

> Since the form is not for the matter, but rather the matter for the form, we must gather from the form the reason why the matter is such as it is; and not conversely. Now the intellectual soul, as we have seen above in the order of nature, holds the lowest place among intellectual substances; inasmuch as it is not naturally gifted with the knowledge of truth, as the angels are; but has to gather knowledge from individual things by way of the senses, as Dionysius says. But nature never fails in necessary things: therefore the intellectual soul had to be endowed not only with the power of understanding, but also with the power of feeling. Now the action of the senses is not performed without a corporeal instrument. Therefore it behoved the intellectual soul to be united to a body fitted to be a convenient organ of sense.[16]

This "convenient organ of sense" will become inconvenient indeed for Descartes, irrational for Locke, and summarily done away with by Berkeley. Though man might be "a little lower than the angels," he is lower enough to have to *acquire* knowledge.

It is one of the paradoxes of intellectual history that Aquinas, a philosopher who is often thought of as standing in the basket right next to Aristophanes' Socrates, should in fact describe a very down-to-earth, sensory starting place for human knowledge. Ultimately this has to do with Aquinas' view of the primacy of being--truly existent things deriving being from the divine source of all being. As with Aristotle, the first principle of knowledge is the senses. The operation of the senses initiates the process whereby man comes to know things and whereby the "tabula rasa" is written upon. We may be born "trailing clouds of glory," but Aquinas would have the glory consist of potentiality rather than an inborn presence of super-sensible forms. Knowledge itself, of course, is formal; it is the intellectual grasp of the immaterial form. Plato held this position as well, but in response to the difficulty of how material things can cause knowledge that is immaterial, he fell upon the idea of the direct participation in ideal forms. This is well and good, but as Aristotle was quick to point out, it left the body and all material things in a state of absurd superfluity. Aristotle, and Aquinas after him, rejected this expedient and sought to confront the "problem" of knowledge without ignoring the role of the composite being--body *and* soul--in the process. The first constituent in solving the difficulty is simply the definition of form itself--it is immaterial by nature. The form is the non-material essence, "soul" or "quiddity" of the object. It is, as it were, its definition. "Now a thing is known in as far as its form is in the knower," says Aquinas, and in this Aristotle and even Plato agree.[17] What the intellect grasps is forms (or species), not particularities, for particulars are the material component of objects and unintelligible by definition.

The form does not "float" or emanate from the object and enter the intellect; such a Democritean conception threatens to materialize forms and spatialize the act of knowing. However, forms do not exist apart from their matter either. An essence cannot exist without a particular being--in the case of natural things, a material being. How then does the intellect "obtain" those forms? The senses provide the knower with the materiality of an object. They bespeak the particular and individual matter before them. The object thus presented to the knower is in itself unknowable precisely because it is in its "material condition." Of itself then, the object is not in any way intelligible to us. "We must therefore," Aquinas concludes,"assign on the part of the intellect some power to make things actually intelligible. . . ."[18]

There must be some power within the intellect capable of lifting out of the materiality and particularity of the thing that which is intelligible--its form or essence. This power is known as the *intellectus agens*, the agent intellect, a name intended to convey the idea of the *active* power of this intellectual faculty. Rather than merely receiving impressions from without through a radically passive function (if anything so radically passive can be said to have a function), the intellect possesses of a power to penetrate the sensory data and lift out that immaterial form which can then be received into the intellect as intelligible. Thus there is an active *and* a passive function to the intellect. The necessity of the *intellectus agens* is absolute.

> [S]ince Aristotle did not allow that forms of natural things exist apart from matter, and as forms existing in matter are not actually intelligible; it follows that the natures or forms of sensible things which we understand are not actually intelligible. Now nothing is reduced from potentiality to act except by something in act; as the senses are made actual by what is actually sensible. We must therefore assign on the part of the intellect some power to make things actually intelligible, by abstraction of the species [form] from material conditions. And such is the necessity for an active intellect.[19]

Later, Aquinas re-affirms the part of the senses in this process, referring to their data as "phantasms":

> According to this opinion, then, on the part of the phantasms, intellectual knowledge is caused by the senses. But since the phantasms cannot of themselves affect the passive intellect and require to be made actually intelligible by the active intellect, it cannot be said that sensible knowledge is the total and perfect cause of intellectual knowledge, but rather that it is in a way the material cause.[20]

The agent intellect, then, abstracts the form or species from its material particularity to supply the intellect with knowledge of the object.[21] Abstraction is the key, and in this specifically philosophical sense, abstraction is the very source of the intellect's ability to know. The somewhat pejorative sense the word has acquired (a sense Newman often employed) does not refer to this fundamental act of the intellect. Newman refers to a much "later" post-abstraction process whereby qualities of things are deliberately "shorn off" in order to isolate a particular aspect of a thing. This process is a psychological one, *not* epistemological or meta-physical, and should not be confused with "abstraction" as the activity of the agent intellect. As Gilson blandly remarks, "To abstract is not primarily to leave something out, but to take something in, and this is the reason why abstractions are knowledge."[22]

Indeed, when the agent intellect has abstracted the form and made it its own, the form is "its own" in every sense. The form as the essence or "this-ness" of a thing cannot be assumed into the intellect without the essence of the thing actually existing in the intellect. This is no mere redundancy but the key to the genuine and objective character of knowledge. The intellect actually becomes the thing it knows. The intellect, taking in the essence of a thing, possesses in itself the nature of the thing. Harold Weatherby underscores the same point, emphasizing that "knowledge means that the knower enters into a real union with the form of the thing known.

Thus, in Gilson's words, 'to know a thing is to become it.'"[23] The importance of this cannot be overstated. Weatherby's warning against spatial/imaginative efforts to construe this process is well founded; though we must use such words as "in" and "form," there is no spatial transfer involved.[24] Forms do not drift about and fall into the ready net of the soul; the soul becomes the essence of the thing known. "[I]n the soul," says Aquinas (quoting Aristotle), "is there something by which it becomes all things. . . ."[25]

It is noteworthy that the means of acquiring knowledge described in Aristotle and Aquinas is a true "golden mean." On the one hand is the idealist, Platonic extreme that postulates independent forms and direct participation, and on the other hand is the materialistic, Democritean system that postulates "emanations" from objects and banishes all intellect by quantifying the immaterial. In each case, either mind or matter is destroyed or rendered irrelevant. For this reason Aristotle has sometimes been called the philosopher of common sense. He does not, certainly, speak of a non-rational intellectual intuition called common sense (as does Thomas Reid), but his analysis of knowledge gives mind *and* body, sense and intellect, their due. What is therefore known as "metaphysical realism" not only integrates the physical and intellectual properties of man into a consistent, harmonious operation, but it philosophically validates the ordinary man's assumptions about his knowledge of reality. The Platonic idealist buying a gallon of milk is embarrassed by its necessity; the materialist is embarrassed by his concept of "milk"; the realist alone is content to both conceptualize milk and drink it.

Another important aspect of "form" and knowledge relates to what was said earlier about universals. There are several senses of the term "universal," and the form as universal is one of them. Philosophy deals with the universal in another sense, in that it treats of things that are what they are necessarily--that is, apart from any contingency. It is the necessity of philosophical matters, as well as their "generality," which makes them determinate, definite, and knowable. But even things contingent and particular are determinate and knowable insofar as they are universal too, though in the former sense. The particular, in having form, has a universal. In being cognizant of that universal, one truly has a definite, determinate knowledge of particular things. Maritain cautions that this must not be considered direct knowledge of the individual alone, or knowledge of the individual in the aspect of its individuality.[26] We devise such knowledge by abstracting the universal; then, as Aquinas says, we know the singular in the aspect of its individuality "by a kind of reflexion" from turning toward the phantasm.[27] Thus there are two kinds of proper knowledge of individual things: 1) that of the universal in the particular, knowledge properly so-called, and 2) that of the individual in its individuality, by reflexive use of the sense-phantasm. This is especially important in view of Aristotle's many statements about all knowledge being of universals, and the indeterminacy of particulars. A later discussion of Walter Jost's rhetorical approach to Newman will develop this point; for now it is sufficient to grasp the very real and determinate intelligibility inherent even in particular things.

DESCARTES AND THE LOSS OF ABSTRACTION

A little-known article in Aquinas' *Summa Theologica* serves as a good transition from the world of the schoolman to the world of Descartes and post-Cartesian philosophy. In Part 1, Question 85, Article 2, Aquinas addresses a question seemingly tailor-made for those who delight in hurling charges of logic-chopping: "Whether the intelligible species abstracted from the phantasm is related to our intellect as that which is understood?" In fact, this question addresses the epistemological concerns that would consume Europe for four hundred years, especially those of John Locke and the British empiricists. The question is a subtle one, but it essentially poses the empiricist dilemma: if what we know originates in the senses, do we not know merely our perceptions? How can we be said to acquire knowledge of exterior reality? To put the question in scholastic terms, if the intelligible species of an object resides in the intellect, is not what we know the intelligible species and *not* the exterior object? Aquinas answers thus: "The intelligible species is to the intellect what the sensible image is to the sense. But the sensible image is not what is perceived but rather that by which sense perceives. Therefore the intelligible species is not what is actually understood, but that by which the intellect understands."[28] The distinction is critical; though we say that one knows the intelligible form or species, what that means is one knows the object by means of its intelligible species. If the species were itself the object of knowledge, all knowledge would be of one's own cognition. One would be confined to the prison-house of the isolated intellect. That this is not the case Aquinas shows by two arguments: first, if one's knowledge were so confined, the fields of knowledge or the sciences would not apply to exterior reality as it is universally taken they do; second, the law of non-contradiction would be violated, for contradictory impressions would be equally "true," thus resulting in logical irrationality. One knows *by means* of intelligible species, not the species itself. Knowledge terminates in the object; predicate knowledge of the intelligible species itself and the result is a cognitive infinite regress: knowing the species, which knowledge is knowing a species, which knowledge is knowing a species, on back through successive layers of knowing and species.

The bottomless pit of infinite regress will appear in full force with John Locke and empiricism, and will do so in spite of the rugged "common sense" Locke believed to be bringing to philosophy. Aquinas' little known article could have headed-off such a foray into empiricism, but his entire metaphysics was largely lost (despite thriving schools in Spain) in the refuse-heap of scholasticism. It is fair to ask whether his metaphysics was "found" even in the Middle Ages, for the history of this period is littered with nascent idealisms. But the confused morass of warring philosophies was permanently altered with the work of Rene Descartes. We pointed out the curious justice of historians of philosophy who skipped from ancient Rome to Renaissance France. In descending upon Descartes, the historians landed upon the one thinker universally acknowledged as the starting point of modern thought.[29] This philosopher forever changed the course of thought by means of a subtle yet radical shift from realism to idealism. True, idealisms of various sorts flourished from Plato onwards, and the full-grown idealism of Descartes was not without "infant" medieval predecessors. Numerous neo- or even pseudo-Platonisms surfaced in the works of such philosophers as Duns Scotus, Abelard, Bonaventure, William of Ockham, the Franciscan Roger Marston, and others. Indeed, it seems that all the different shades and types of philosophies can be "boiled down" roughly to two basic varieties: idealism and realism--the ancient debate between Plato and Aristotle continues.

It was, nevertheless, Descartes who cast the world of thought into a "new" mold, and he did it by beginning not with things, as did Aquinas and Aristotle, but with thought. The world of Aquinas was a world of independently existing things the being and essences of which were apprehended by man's intellect. Thought was second; things, as it were, were first. Material and exterior reality provided the starting ground for all thought, all knowledge, all philosophy. Knowledge begins in the senses. With Descartes, knowledge begins with innate, "clear and distinct" ideas, the most famous of which is the "cogito." In fact, the most important "clear and distinct" ideas are one's own existence (*cogito ergo sum*) and the existence of God. Most knowledge is derived from these two unimpeachable starting points. The consequences of this are both simple and immediate, and occupied many subsequent philosophers' thoughts. By "making the cogito the starting point of philosophy," says Jaki, external reality has been lost to the intellect.[30] Things, objects, and entities are not inherently intelligible for the simple reason that the mind has no access to them.

Descartes' famous rejection of all assumptions based upon sensory data and experience, and his parallel rejection of any reasoning based on such assumptions (a kind of predecessor to Kant's critique), is intended to leave the mind stripped of "peripheral" and unreliable thought. The resulting clear ideas are the only reliable elements of cognition and are to govern all thought by means of strict mathematical demonstration. Nowhere does the reality exterior to the mind enter into this foundation of all knowledge. The world of things is lost (and, indeed, rendered irrelevant) as concerns knowledge. Descartes did not, thereby, question the existence of exterior reality; rather, his second distinct and innate idea, God, would suffice to guarantee it. Based on God's non-deceptive nature, exterior reality must be as its appearances lead us to believe. Thus the world is offered to us on God's credit, as it were, and that should be good enough for any man--or so Descartes thought. Descartes' confidence in this cannot be overemphasized. He rested convinced he had settled the matter of knowledge once and for all. Despite the obvious "theologism" (as Gilson would call it) of his account of knowledge, Descartes was sure it was truly disciplined philosophy purged of scholastic cobwebbery.[31] The fact is that this account effectively rendered the world largely superfluous--after all, all true cognition began from innate ideas that had no connection to the exterior world. Indeed, the mind was cluttered and distracted by false knowledge mistakenly thought to originate from experience. *True* knowledge must have no such base ancestry; it can only be the result of strictest reasonings upon "clear and distinct" ideas. As to how we even know the world exists, the answer is a simple: "We wouldn't, if God had not told us."

When he turned man into a creature of essentially spiritual knowledge, he never tried to reintegrate the corporeal and incorporeal elements of things he had divided. He steadfastly ignored the problem of how the incorporeal can know the corporeal, despite the fact that the question was put to him directly.[32] He did not ignore the problem out of intellectual dishonesty; rather, he could not conceive of it as being a problem. The corporeal, too, was thought of in terms strictly "philosophical." It was merely a matter of three-dimensional extension, and as such was perfectly governed by the rules of geometry. Therein lies a key to the Cartesian revolution, for the confident philosopher's assurance derived from a very simple conviction: truth was essentially and mathematically demonstrable. Gilson points out that "the whole philosophy of Descartes was virtually contained in that initial decision [truth being equal to mathematical demonstration], for the *I think, hence I am* is the first principle of Descartes' philosophy, but it is his pledge to mathematical evidence that led Descartes to the *I think*."[33] The philosopher said as much himself, elevating mathematical knowledge above any other "not, indeed, that arithmetic and geometry are the sole sciences to be studied, but only that in our search for the direct road towards truth, we should busy ourselves with no object about which we cannot attain a certitude equal to that of geometry."[34] In a pithy summary, Gilson syllogizes: "true knowledge is necessary; mathematical knowledge alone is necessary; hence all knowledge has to be mathematical." He adds, significantly, "Whatever such a reasoning may be worth, the fact remains that Descartes was thereby eliminating all that was mere probability."[35]

Gilson is too modest. Far from "merely" eliminating probability--grave as such a fiat is--Descartes has eliminated man's capacity to know the independent natures of things. Even exterior reality has been lost, and the motivating force behind this philosophical development is noteworthy. The mechanical, mathematical or geometric paradigm driving Descartes to imprison the intellect in the solitary confinement of its own ideas was well prepared for. Descartes' mathematicism is Ramus' reasoning machine grown into a colossus. The full force of a mechanistic conception of thought, knowledge, and the intellect itself is revealed in Descartes' words "the direct road towards the truth." There is here the sense that the important thing is not the truth so much as the "direct road" towards it. A caustic wit might assail such an approach as "short-cut science," yet Descartes' emphasis is unmistakable. The mathematician's impatience with intangibles and discursive thought has crystalized the elements brought into solution by Ramus; knowledge is now a simple, if elaborate, mechanical sequence of equations. Even the seemingly mechanical syllogism is bereft of its personal aspect. While knowledge lost its voice as a personal enunciation in Ramus, Descartes takes a further step and reduces knowledge to a narrowly mathematical field. Though the matter never arose, of course, this transformation of knowledge results in there being no possible distinction between "artificial" intelligence and natural. Would Descartes have loved the computer? Fully wrought, too, is the disintegration of Aquinas' knowing subject; man is divided up into operative, relevant parts on one hand, and superfluous, irrelevant parts on the other.

CONSEQUENCES AND DESCENDENTS

The mind, divorced from the body and self-sufficient in the acquisition of knowledge, becomes a curious entity in itself. Aside from rendering the body, the passions, and other human attributes superfluous, the disembodiment of the mind makes the entire idea of process in thought something of a problem. As Ong points out, "the presence of discursive reason in the human intellectual apparatus is due to the material component in man's cognitional make-up and in the make-up of the reality he is immediately faced with."[36] Embodied intelligences proceed through reason and rest in understanding. A pure intelligence grasps essences and understands immediately, without having to go through a process. Thus, it is curious that Descartes' procedure of the *cogito* not only cuts man off from exterior reality, it also makes impossible the very process--the mathematical movement of reasoning--of which Descartes was so enamored. It is still more curious that his ideas of the intellect and knowledge are in fact described by Aquinas in his treatise on the angels. Descartes had given man an angelic intellect.[37]

The crack Ramus opened in thought has grown to a great crevasse: knowledge has become data, what is knowable has shrunk to the strictly demonstrative, and certainty is confined to sciences on a par with mathematics. The kind of thinking Descartes consciously cultivated would in time become unconscious habits of thought for an entire culture. Many of the presumptions about knowledge against which Newman would fight originate here. By the nineteenth century, these presumptions (or even attitudes) had penetrated the culture so deeply, that in large part Newman's appeal for knowledge not devised "scientifically" would sound like an attempted defense of irrationality.

Like the profusion of Ramus' texts and "method" throughout Europe, Descartes was the match igniting the philosophically parched world. Descartes' conception of man as an angel, or a disembodied thinking substance, swept Europe and was soon received as immediately self-evident by the greatest thinkers of his time. Stripping themselves of their bodies, they become magnificent minds, which, theoretically at least, did not feel indebted to their bodies for their ideas. Leibniz in Germany, Malebranche in France; Spinoza in Holland, were all descendants of Descartes and began with innate ideas. For them, too, Cartesian mathematicism cast its spell.[38] Once it was placed on the table, the *cogito* as a principle seemed obvious, and unavoidable. It made any conception of the knowing subject or the integration of mind with body fairly unimaginable.

Nevertheless, Descartes' inability to see the consequences of his principles was not shared by his successors. Much of the activity of those who operated from essentially Cartesian standpoints was aimed at trying to secure the reality Descartes lost. Cartesian idealists clearly saw that the difficulty of accounting for incorporeal knowledge of the corporeal had not been solved simply by coming down on one side (the incorporeal). Leibniz proposed a "principle of pre-established harmony" whereby God ordered the "coordination between things and thought."[39] This differs little from Descartes' saying that God secures the objective existence of material reality for He would not lie. Not only does it repeat the irony of post-medieval philosophies being far more dependent upon God than medieval ones, but it again employs God to shore up an impossibility. Coordination or not, the human intellect still does not, *in itself,* have any contact with material reality. Malebranche also attempted to solve the problem, though he did so by inserting God into the process of thought. This remedy suggested that physical, sensible phenomena do not impinge upon the mind, but do provide "an occasion for God to produce a corresponding change" *in* the mind.[40] Here the mind is still imprisoned, but Malebranche's "occasionalism," as it is called, provides a divine go-between. Jaki comments that this is "a mere atomization of the pre-established harmony advocated by Leibniz," and indeed it seems little different even from Descartes' position.[41] Yet another, more daring attempt was made by Spinoza, who eradicated all difference between mind and body, the incorporeal and the corporeal, by assuming all reality into a pantheistic, divine nature. Perhaps this is "theologism" in epistemology gone mad, but it is still a conscious effort at accounting for the existence of knowledge. Moreover, Spinoza knew exactly what this postulate meant in relation to the history of thought. He observed correctly that "The Scholastics start from things, Descartes from thought, I start from God."[42]

The idealism inaugurated by Descartes bounced from person and place, and transformed itself in protean fashion. Kant, for instance, developed an elaborate theory of reason and sensibility in response to Humes's skeptical empiricism. His response, however, also re-asserted the intellect's self-contained or self-sufficient operation--with a little help from Newtonian physics. Postulating *a priori* forms of time and space in sensibility, and *a priori* forms (the categories) such as substance in the understanding, Kant erected an elaborate idealist platform the rigors of which do not eliminate its *cogito*-centered principles. The *a priori* components of sensibility and understanding do not make experience intelligible, they *constitute* experience.[43] The mind itself is still isolated from the world. By the twentieth century, several shifts in the history of thought had occurred, not the least of which was the widespread devaluation of philosophy in general and metaphysics in particular. (This devaluation had a long head-start. Hegel's idealism--the pattern for many nineteenth-century idealisms--was motivated by his desire to rescue metaphysics from irrelevance.[44]) In part a consequence of progressive material science, philosophical subjects and issues were increasingly marginalized. However, Cartesian idealism continued to have grandchildren in such systems as Husserl's phenomenology. Like most philosophers of the twentieth century, Husserl tried to put aside metaphysical and epistemological questions in order to pursue a "method." The resulting quasi-philosophical (and mathematical) phenomenology "bracketed" all questions of objective reality and sought a merely descriptive "science" of consciousness. But the accessibility of reality returned to haunt him:

> Having performed his *epoche* [bracketing] Husserl was, predictably, assailed by an anxiety to secure the objectivity of the public universe and was forced by his chosen method to look within consciousness itself for a guarantee of the independent existence of its objects. Predictably, he failed.[45]

EMPIRICISM'S REPLY

Idealisms invariably strive to overcome the solipsism inherent in their philosophical principle: thought. Whether they draft God to secure correspondence between mind and reality or postulate innate forms to do the same, all dis-integrate and de-personalize man by making him a being of incompatibles. The harmony and unity found in Aquinas is gone, as is the very accessibility to the "public universe" and the possibility of genuine knowledge. Newman was not aware that European idealisms had their answer in Aquinas, but neither did an obscure English tutor and medical practitioner who set out to refute Descartes. This physician established a school of thought famous for being the great opponent of Cartesian idealism, all the while operating on principles no less solipsistic. His refutation captured the imagination of Europe, especially Britain, and almost single-handedly established the philosophical milieu of Newman's world. This was, of course, none other than John Locke.

The 1690 *Essay Concerning Human Understanding* is justly considered one of England's premier contributions to the history of philosophy. It certainly established a "brave new world" in European thought and dominated philosophical speculation well into the late nineteenth century. The "huge, rambling work"[46] was known well to Newman, whose respect for Locke was great. Much of that respect was probably due to the highly "pragmatic" and English character of Locke's philosophy. Though the works of Locke were jubilantly greeted by such continentals as Voltaire, the English character of Locke's philosophy is such that the term "British Empiricism" is virtually redundant. It was the hard, sternly practical, no-nonsense quality of the empiricist that appealed to Newman, and one finds in Locke's motivation--a critical reaction to Descartes--enough to endear him to anyone wary of "unreal" or highly abstract systems.

Newman apparently read Locke during the summer vacation of 1818, and this was one of his first experiences with philosophy. More influential, however, was the simple fact that Locke was almost as important a figure in the early nineteenth-century intellectual environment as Aristotle. Newman praises Locke's "manly simplicity of mind and his outspoken candor" and laments having to treat him as an opponent.[47] But Newman's other comments regarding Locke are not so enthusiastic; he considered the empiricist a cornerstone of contemporary liberalism in philosophy and religion.[48] Though Sillem thoroughly outlines Locke's influence on Newman, his critique is weakened by a strained attempt to divide Locke and Newman where the two are not so readily distinguished. Suffice it to say, for our purposes, that Newman was not aware of the metaphysical consequences of Locke's thought. He thought Locke solid in his grasp of the real, tangible world through experience. As has become clear, this is hardly the case.

Locke, it should be remembered, was a physician, and both the work of Newton and budding optics research informed Locke's approach to epistemological questions:

> He undoubtedly believed himself to be cutting through the baseless metaphysics of the Schoolmen in order to clarify the simple facts. In him, as in virtually every major thinker of the seventeenth century, contempt for the scholastic tradition is automatic. Equally automatic is his reverence for the contemporary scientist.[49]

The result was a philosophical text replete with physio-biological principles and adorned with calm, seventeenth/eighteenth-century scientific self-assurance.

Whether Descartes' historical proximity to the scholastics made Locke consider him one is an open question, but it is certain that Locke's empiricist epistemology begins in rejection of Descartes' principles of innate ideas. For the

Englishman, ordinary experience simply did not confirm the existence of "clear and distinct" ideas innately present in the minds of men. Man begins with the famous "tabula rasa," and through experience acquires the ideas that are known. This "return" to common sense seemed to signal something acceptable to all and appeared immediately self-evident.

But the epistemology was not so simple. In fact, the Lockean empiricism, for all its sturdy pragmatism, was not so unlike Descartes and his idealist predecessor (Plato) after all, for in both Locke and Descartes knowledge was equated with ideas. Locke and Descartes merely disputed the origin of those ideas. While the essential ideas were innate according to Descartes, Locke insisted that ideas are derived from experience. And what constitutes experience? Locke's answer was: sense-perceptions. The significance of this cannot be overstated. What one experiences is *not* the "public universe," but one's own perceptions, and from these perceptions one derives the ideas that constitute "knowledge." Thus was a self-made trap closed, for there was no means of making determinate or validating that sense-experience. In the empiricist system, one experiences one's senses, not things; one sees the image on the retina, not the object. The connection between object and retinal image was purely a matter of postulation or assumption--not certainty. As Nuttall points out, "Locke's philosophy is an empiricism founded in the *subjective* experience of the perceiver [emphasis mine]," while Descartes' ideas at least had God to secure them.[50]

> The external world brings to the Cartesian mind a letter of introduction, so to speak, from the Supreme Being, and by this means both parties are protected, bound in an authorized epistemological contract. With Locke it is otherwise. His empiricism, as it is purer, so is it more naked, more defenseless. . . Locke could not tell whether his senses were telling him the truth or not. Thus the effect of his philosophy was to separate man from the real world.[51]

More on the consequences of this empiricism in a moment; first it is necessary to determine whether Locke's empiricism truly is so Platonic, even solipsistic. Leslie Stephen asserts that the "content" of knowledge for Locke--the "ideas"--are "unreal representatives of unknowable objects."[52] Locke himself is definite upon this point, as Nuttall indicates:

> In spite of the difficulties [Locke's empiricism] has generated, the doctrine can be stated very simply: we have no direct knowledge of anything in the external world, all that we know directly are ideas, that is, tiny representative

pictures of the world, relayed to the mind by eye, ear, etc. These and these only are the immediate objects of knowledge. In Locke's own words: 'Since the mind, in all its thoughts and reasonings, hath no other immediate object but its own ideas, which it alone does or can contemplate, it is evident that our knowledge is only conversant about them.'[53]

Furthermore, not only is knowledge confined to ideas, but the origin of these ideas is not the senses. As noted, experience is truncated in meaning for Locke; it does not mean experience of reality, an objective universe in which we participate. It is simply the tingling of nerve-endings, the sense-data irrespective of stimulae. This is entirely different from the Thomistic principle of knowledge beginning in the senses. The Thomistic principle bears

only a superficial resemblance to the one which was tried by Locke who declared the mind a *tabula rasa* and postulated the radical priority of sensations. Anyone aware of the difference between sensations felt by the subject and things, or objects, that give rise to sensations, will easily realize that Locke's starting point was merely a dialectical rewording of the Cartesian stance. The reasoning of Locke could provide no more assurance about the existence of things supposedly activating the senses acting on the mind than could the system of Descartes make appear plausible the mind's grasp of sensations, let alone of things.[54]

Thus, as Gilson observes, the old contraposition of idealism and empirical "materialism" is less of a real difference in principle than development of a single principle--that what we know are ideas.[55] True enough, Locke's interest in optics gave an oddly material, even physiological twist to the traditionally idealist formula, but this twist resulted in one of the more curious consequences of empirical thought--the perceptive infinite regress. The empiricist focus on perception as occurring in the senses--one sees what is on the retina, not what is outside the eye-- leads to the problem of what "eye" is beholding the retina? And how do nerve-stimulae become ideas? Is the image on the retina an idea?[56] "The infinite regress of any such description is evident. . . .[The depth of the confusion] is shown by the prolonged ponderings throughout the seventeenth and eighteenth centuries on the fact (in the circumstances delicious) that the image on the retina is upside down."[57] However perplexed empiricists might be about phenomena, one thing is certain: they, like Descartes, have no verifiable access to the public universe, nor even to any truth or knowledge properly so called. In Nuttall's analysis, empirical philosophy is even less capable of grasping reality than is Plato, for at least Plato's ideal forms--through which the intellect knows--were objective and "real." The world is lost, inaccessible to the empiricist, devoid even of its guarantee of a non-deceptive Divine Mind. "Once again," Nuttall observes

> we find reality slipping though our fingers, escaping our
> direct observation. One begins to feel that Lockean analysis
> is little more than a technique for losing the world. Who but
> a philosopher could lose so large a thing? Who so good at it,
> as an empiricist?[58]

Descartes had his descendants, and so did Locke. Though there is no need to detail the history of empiricism, it is noteworthy that the two most famous empirical descendents, Berkeley and Hume, were both British. Bishop Berkeley stoutly defended the commonsense perception that exterior reality is known to man, and in so doing thought himself redressing the difficulty inherent in Locke. But the *manner* in which reality was "restored" tells all, for Berkeley's answer to the difficulty was essentially "Why bother?" Exterior reality is not necessary, is not needed, for all things can be seen in God. What we perceive need not actually exist at all--it is enough to say that God causes us to perceive it, and so its "validity" is thereby assured. This metaphysical coup illustrates the layers of paradox attendant upon forsaking abstraction and agent intellect. Essentially, Berkeley waived the attempt to connect ideas to the real by saying ideas *were* the real--one need look no farther. This empirical version of a Divine "letter of introduction" is clearly as solipsistic as the idealist version. Hume, on the other hand did not make ideas the reality; he merely forsook reality altogether in what is generally considered the ultimate expression of skepticism. The irony here is that Hume was also motivated by an attachment to "factual," empirical observation, the result of which was the ultimate denial of the referential character of experience. In a sense, Hume's empiricism was atomistic. By denying causality and making all mental activity a matter of simply greater and lesser vivacity of impression, Hume rendered experience a genuine, unconnected stream of consciousness. He "fragmented the world into a series of discreet experiences, having no logical connection but woven by the imagination into a web of fictitious causality."[59] Reality is gone, knowledge is impossible, thought is void of any but a formal, interim validity. It is no wonder, then, that Hume himself admitted his speculations were so terminal, so solipsistic, that he perforce must play backgammon to restore his sense of equilibrium.

PHILOSOPHY AND NEWMAN'S WORLD

Nuttall, in his analysis of English thought and its literary consequences, is at some pains to show that the philosophers and writers he speaks of never set out to "lose the world." No one seeks to banish concrete, public reality, unless it is a Berkeley who will replace it with ideas. In fact, as Gilson, Maritain, Jaki and others have shown, the furious activities of so many philosophers (and even literary artists) have been concerted--if strained--attempts at regaining access to the public universe. But how is it that it had to be regained in the first place? From Descartes on, philosophical exploration of thought and experience has constituted what amounts to a kind of philosophical cautionary tale. It is a tale illustrating the consequences of erroneous principles, of replacing metaphysics with epistemology, of rejecting the *esse* for the *cogito* or (even worse) the *sentio*. It is a tale whereby being is left aside as the beginning of inquiry, and thought or feeling introduced as a principle. With being is the concomitant essence, and the entire formal means of knowing outlined above. With thought one ends where one begins: thought. No amount of thought or circular "experience" will hurtle the thinker outside his own head and into the world. Philosophers who banish being find themselves in a curious world of existence-less-ness:

> Instead of attaching a central meaning to that little but most weighty verb *is*, they avoid other verbs as well, in order to be free for a clever game with nouns. Nouns disassociated from verbs are not images of things, that is, of reality. These are *mere concepts* [emphasis mine] that act in no substantive way whatever either among themselves or on the perceiving mind."[60]

With "verbs" lost, only the "nouns" were left to be endlessly re-arranged, whether by Descartes' mathematicism, Locke's empiricism, Kant's categories, or the great system-generators of the nineteenth century (Comte). The very idea of knowledge was increasingly problematic due to epistemological forays into "reality" and repeated failures to establish a beachhead there. Material science was a kind of refuge, despite the fact that it really possessed no philosophical underpinnings from the epistemologies available to it. Science, at least, "worked," never mind whether its "laws" were actual or merely probabilistic sequences of phenomena. The deep frustration with empirical thought was aggravated by empiricism's seemingly straight-forward, common-sensical appeal. It appeared so valid, so wisely based on "experience" and the senses; it appealed to English "manly simplicity." So why, then, did it breed repeated and persistent efforts at "firming-up" its hold on material reality? Just when things became so solidly empirical, why did the intellectual world become so persistently troubled about the possibility of knowledge, the existence of the public universe, and the place of man amidst all this? These frustrations frame the intellectual world Newman entered, and their metaphysical answer was not forthcoming during his lifetime.

As philosophy--however paradoxically--became even more solipsistic and skeptical, as "verbs" were lost and only "nouns" remained in a kind of existential vacuum, as material science developed and progressed, man's intellectual environment was such that system became everything. "Nouns" might be arranged in dazzling array, for there were no bothersome "verbs" to control their action; science might be the sovereign "truth," for consistently interacting phenomena satisfied the burgeoning mechanistic habits of thought. The deep, underlying skepticism about the possibility of knowledge and access to the public universe actually increased the importance placed upon material science. Like an intellectual stock-market, epistemological failure caused a high premium to be placed on knowledge strictly and materially demonstrated, scientifically certain, experimentally observed, regardless of the lack of an epistemology to justify such certainty. It was a kind of compensation for philosophical uncertainty. People whose hearing is failing place a high premium on precision of diction, and gladly dispense with the individual oddities of accent, idiosyncrasy, and tone. A culture of deepening skepticism places a high premium on precision of demonstration and material science, and places little value on personal modes of knowledge and its communication. When people are weak they must have strong machines; when personal access to truth is in doubt, mechanistic access will be exalted.

So Newman's world was one of increasing intellectual de-personalization, skepticism, and mechanism. He could not avail himself of the former integrated, personal conceptions of knowledge, where knowledge was participated in. There was no metaphysics of knowledge available that satisfactorily explained formal abstraction and the agent intellect. The patristic and medieval eras had enjoyed personalist discourse in the communication of knowledge, the integration of faculties inherent in verbal/aural discourse, and the different modes of apprehension and truth-telling discourse. The person, in such an intellectual environment, is potentially a mighty knowing being indeed. He is free to roam from dialectic to poetry, rhetoric to philosophy, and is capable of grasping and communicating truths through a rich variety of means. In such an environment, the truth in the pathos of

Dido's tears is no less a truth in its own sphere, than is the truth arrived at in a Euclidean theorem or philosophical demonstration. In fact, the highly experiential, connatural grasp of truth proper to poetic discourse (and often found in rhetorical discourse) is present even in philosophical argumentation. As universal experience has shown, philosophical argumentation is neither produced nor understood immediately; it must be participated in over time, experienced, as it were, before being fully comprehended.

But unaware as Newman was of the metaphysical and cultural principles behind the cognitional de-personalization of his time, he was aware of the process underway and its harmful consequences. Action breeds reaction, and much of nineteenth-century history is a record of attempted re-assertion or reclaiming of the personal--as witnessed in the Romantic movement. Newman's intellectual mission was largely an attempted restoration of the highly personal modes of rhetorical knowledge and discourse.

Nuttall has observed that when epistemology falters from false principles, psychologism enters in. "We . . . have seen that temperamental solipsism tries to resolve pre-empirical questions by specifying psychological contents."[61] Whether Newman was a "temperamental solipsist" is an open question. From Nuttall's point of view, it would seem likely. It is quite true that when Newman attempted to philosophize, he largely began where Descartes and Locke had begun--with thought or the content of the mind (it is difficult to imagine how anyone in the nineteenth century could do otherwise). His statement that the two "luminously self-evident beings" in his mind were God and himself, may be read as just short of true solipsism. Here again, however, the comment is experiential to the point of being a poetic, rather than a philosophical, remark. But does the remark bespeak a solipsistic temperament, in Nuttall's terms? Newman may have been influenced by seemingly straightforward empirical principles, but temperament is revealed in a man who delights in natural beauty, in one who wonders at his mistaking good coffee for bad tea, in one who ponders personal perspective in regarding the letter "B" as looking "forward" or "backward." That temperament is not one of incommunicable solitude divorced from the public universe. There is too much of this world's "stuff" present in easy and natural fashion in Newman's thought (and even speculations) for his temperament to be one of lurking distrust as to the world's actuality. As will be seen later, Newman does openly speculate on the unreality of the world, but there is simply no sense of the speculations running deep, or of a mind uneasy and in need of solace in a distraction like backgammon.

There is no sense of a mind cultivating intensity of experience in a kind of psychological compensation for distrust of reality.

Newman was never satisfied that epistemological questions had been answered--by himself or anyone else. It is highly probable that he considered the questions ultimately unanswerable, this side of the grave. Nuttall observes, "To say 'We *do* know and there's an end on't' is not to resolve the philosophical problem. Rather, it is a refusal to do any more philosophy."[62] This could well serve as a summary of Newman's position; much as we might prefer to have Newman a philosopher who "did" philosophy and "solved" the problem through a restoration of pre-empirical metaphysics, the fact remains that the clergyman left the philosophy undone. He fairly gave up epistemology in the manner Nuttall speaks of, asserting that we *do* know, but at a loss to say exactly how. The loss was not a terribly disturbing one, however, for "how" did not concern Newman so much as "what happens when." In parallel to "temperamental solipsists," Newman focused on "psychological contents"--matters entirely proper to rhetoric. The flash of insight Newman speaks of as coming to him in Switzerland when he suddenly realized that his approach to the question of truth should focus on "certitude," occurred at the moment Newman framed the question in the rhetorical mode.

The psychological, reflexive resonance of "certitude" and "assent" belong intimately to rhetorical modes of knowing. They are what the rhetorician strives for. They are not so often brought about by demonstration as by the convergence of a hundred probabilities, a thousand suggestions, a varied assembly of poetic associations. This is not philosophy (nor even strictly psychology), but it is rhetorical, personal, general yet individual, interior yet predicated on the public world. When Newman leaves philosophy for rhetoric, one can detect a sigh of relief in his works. Some may regret that Newman approached intellectual matters rhetorically, but in so doing they regret that Newman was Newman. So rhetorical was his habit of mind, that even when trying to untangle philosophical difficulties, Newman produced speculations that were wonderfully persuasive, telling in motive and purpose, well aimed at the times, but which were utterly wretched philosophy. In other words, he did not produce philosophy at all; he produced rhetoric.

VIII. Newman's *Philosophical Notebook*

> *They say miracles are past, and we have our philosophical persons, to make modern and familiar things supernatural and causeless. Hence it is that we make trifles of terrors, ensconcing ourselves into seeming knowledge when we should submit ourselves to an unknown fear.*
>
> All's Well that Ends Well II, iii.

Weatherby's Newman

[T]he great Newton's authority was squarely behind that view of the cosmos which saw in man a puny, irrelevant spectator . . . of the vast mathematical system whose regular motions according to mechanical principles constituted the world of nature. . . . The world that people had thought themselves living in--a world rich with colour and sound, redolent with fragrance, filled with gladness, love and beauty, speaking everywhere of purposive harmony and creative ideals--was crowded now into minute corners in the brains of scattered organic beings. The really important world outside was a world hard, cold, colourless, silent and dead; a world of quantity, a world of mathematically compatible notions in mechanical regularity.[1]

We have seen that this cold, mechanical world was not simply a creation of Newton's, but was largely readied by philosophical conceptions of knowledge that depersonalized the intellect (and its objects) and transformed into a "method" the processes of learning and knowing. It is against this world and these narrow intellectual confines that Newman rebelled, persistently striving to restore intellectual legitimacy to the "whole man" and the personal, rhetorical grasp of truth. Before we take a critical look at Newman's concerted attempts at philosophical speculation, a few preliminary points are in order concerning the Thomistic point of departure employed here.

To date, the most thorough Thomistic study of Newman has been that of Harold Weatherby in *Cardinal Newman in His Age* and *The Keen Delight.* Weatherby embraces the metaphysical/epistemological principles of Aristotle and Aquinas, and critiques Newman from that standpoint. His analysis is thorough and

detailed, yet its thesis can be simply stated: Newman was a philosophical modernist
who attempted to harmonize skeptical philosophy with doctrinal orthodoxy. As the
two are incompatible, the result was disastrous. One senses a great deal of
frustration in Weatherby, for he quite justly observes that many who regard
Newman as a failure do so for the wrong reasons, while many who regard him as a
success are faulty in their reasoning as well. Weatherby notes that some have seen
philosophically modernist elements in Newman and concluded he must be
religiously heterodox; the Modernists (Loisy et al.) regard Newman as a useful
predecessor. Those who are convinced of Newman's orthodoxy (they are more
recent) and

> sympathetic toward it, have given him a fairer reading. . . .
> In doing so, however, these commentators have overlooked
> the fact that Newman's philosophy *does* present problems.
> That is not to say that they have ignored his philosophy or
> failed to recognize its modernity; on the contrary, the
> strongest emphasis in recent Newman studies is
> philosophical and epistemological, and the modernity of that
> philosophy and epistemology has been generally
> acknowledged.[2]

The difficulty, says Weatherby, is that these critics also try to harmonize skeptical
philosophy with doctrinal orthodoxy. In this Weatherby is quite correct, and
Sillem, for instance, falls into this category.

Weatherby is attempting to clear out a true rat's nest of conflicting criticism,
but as noted earlier, his own reading of Newman as a philosopher forces him--
despite disclaimers--to place Newman more toward the heterodox side, albeit a
"philosophical" heterodoxy. Openly declaring Newman "the most important
English theologian of the last two centuries," (not "religious figure" but
"theologian") Weatherby perforce reads Newman for systematic thought. He
concludes, not surprisingly:

> Newman's particular achievement may prove to be in the
> long run to be an index of his peculiar failure; namely, that
> he did not set his face resolutely against the whole course of
> modern thought. He was in a uniquely good position to have
> done just that, for he was unquestionably the most
> prominent, the most influential, the most nearly saintly
> theologian of the past two centuries. It seems to me to have
> been his great failure that . . . he omitted to bring to modern
> thought and modern literature what he alone could have
> brought, what no one else in his century or ours has been in
> a position or had the strength to bring--a thoroughly
> traditional Christian philosophy of nature and society.[3]

It goes without saying that Newman would be most surprised to hear that he did not "set his face resolutely against the whole course of modern thought" and that he "chose to make terms" with "the new world view."[4] What then, we can imagine Newman asking, has all this battling been about? It is also certain that Newman would wonder at the emphatic assignation of "theologian"--a title and claim he repeatedly and sincerely denied. In fact, it becomes clear that for all the acuity of Thomistic argument and observation concerning the *Oxford University Sermons* and the *Grammar of Assent*, the philosophical critique is seriously flawed. In what way was Newman "able" or "strong" enough to provide a Thomistic philosophy of anything? We have already seen his relative lack of contact with and training in Aquinas' works, and neither is there any suggestion of his comprehension of Aristotelian metaphysics. And as for no one else being capable of bringing a Christian philosophy to the world "in his century or ours," do the well-known works of Thomists such as Gilson, Maritain, Pieper, Owens, to name a few, count for so little?

Happy as the sight of a serious Thomist on the critical horizon is, one detects here a peculiar rigorism inimical in fact to Thomistic principles. There is in Weatherby's critique of Newman the sense that metaphysics is more akin to a post-Ramist *method* than a pre-Ramist philosophical system. System and method are not at all the same; in a Thomistic context, they are as different in action as is the orderly sweep of a scythe from the movement of a self-propelled lawn mower. Weatherby's conception of metaphysics and epistemology does not distinguish what is philosophical in attribute and what is philosophy itself.[5] As will be seen, Newman's "philosophy" is not philosophy at all, but at most a philosophical *rhetoric*. The distinction is an important one that should be kept in mind while exploring the *Notebook*.

THOMISTIC PARALLELS

It turns out, however, that Newman and Aquinas occupy much common ground. Newman's purposive rhetorical concerns often led him to highlight the limitations of man's intellect. The prevailing over-confidence in scientific reasoning and highly mechanistic conceptions of knowledge moved Newman to emphasize the partial character of what men know.[6] His focus on this is largely responsible for frustrating Weatherby, who indicts Newman's "philosophy" for its incipient skepticism. However, the principles of Thomistic metaphysics themselves carry much the same caution as did Newman's protests about reality's mysteriousness. Seeming to anticipate just such a mechanistic reading of Aquinas, Maritain cautions:

> [One] must always bear in mind that, if philosophy enables the human intellect to apprehend with absolute certainty the highest and most profound realities of the natural order, it cannot therefore claim to exhaust those realities by making them known to the utmost extent of their intelligibility.[7]

The contemporary Thomist who discusses this point most thoroughly is Joseph Pieper, in a book titled *The Silence of St. Thomas: Three Essays*. This small book directly addresses the venerable stereotype of scholastic thought that sees Thomism as a dry, mechanical series of formulae whereby everything is "figured out." Going directly to Aquinas' observations about existence and the creation, Pieper stresses that even material creation is deeply mysterious by virtue of its having been created by God. Like Aristotle's exposition of the virtues, there is a prized middle ground to be held in discussing man's ability to know things. Things are both intelligible and mysterious--which is to say, not irrational, but beyond our powers to comprehend. Because things are created, they have "on the one hand their ontological clarity and self-revelation and, on the other hand, their inexhaustibleness; their knowability as well as their 'un-knowability'."[8] This "unknowability" is derived directly from the participation of each thing in the mind of the Creator; the essences of things are only partially intelligible to us because their sheer created intelligibility exceeds our power of intellectual vision. Pieper summarizes Aquinas: "Our minds are too crude and obtuse (*imbecillitas intellectus nostri*) to read in things even that information concerning God which they really contain."[9] Nor is the "*imbecillitas nostri*" confined to the "information concerning God"; even the information in things concerning themselves is brilliant beyond our capacity to see them entirely.

Though mystery is that aspect of reality which is beyond our power of understanding, it is not irrational:

> [F]or St. Thomas, the unknowable can never denote something in itself dark and impenetrable, but only something that has so much light that a particular finite faculty of knowledge cannot absorb it all. It is too rich to be assimilated completely; it eludes the effort to comprehend it.[10]

Thus man's intellectual powers are limited and only partially comprehend what is intelligible. Nevertheless, the opposite extreme is also dangerous. What man does know, is legitimately known:

> The essence of things, insists St. Thomas, cannot be completely grasped but it is not unknowable. Man's intellectual power enables him to penetrate to the essence of things; there can be, therefore, insights and assertions concerning the nature of things which, though not exhaustive, are nevertheless true.[11]

We have, therefore, a kind of "middle height" where knowledge is possible but mystery abides. Man knows, and is incapable of knowing exhaustively, as Pieper, Maritain and Gilson maintain.[12] The fundamental mysteriousness of reality is a theme Newman frequently employed precisely for its being so forgotten in his day.[13] The theme doesn't seem to be remembered in our own day either, for Pieper felt compelled to describe modern consciousness in words equally applicable to Newman's time:

> The world in which man today leads his ordinary life is becoming more and more a purely technological one. The things with which he is concerned are artificial; they are artifacts, not creations. The danger inherent in this situation is that man might, erroneously, come to regard the world as a whole and the created things with it--above all, man himself--in the same manner in which he regards, correctly, his own artifacts belonging to the technological sphere; in other words, man is beginning to consider the whole of creation as completely fathomable, fully accessible to rational comprehension, and, above all, as something which it is permissible to change, transform, or even destroy.[14]

While Newman was not in the least bothered by science--he was a somewhat bemused spectator of the squabble over evolution--he was deeply anxious about the habit of mind encouraged in a world dominated by science. Empiricism and science "removed nature from the human," says James P. McGowan, and they too easily fell into place with the deepening public perception that knowledge was a mechanical product, arrived at and transmitted through schematic method.[15] Despite, or rather because of, philosophical skepticism, materialistic approaches to everything blossomed, forcing the range of legitimate intellectual operations to narrow. The idea of a rhetorical, personal grasp of truth was absurd. Even poetic truth became dangerously "sentimental," and in many instances, poets sought respectability in poetic obscurity. So Newman, like Aquinas, was often at pains to emphasize the limits of man's intellectual powers, even concerning material things, while defending man's intellectual capabilities regarding immaterial things. To be sure, Aquinas' emphasis upon man's capacity--

its limits and powers--was philosophical, while Newman's was rhetorically (and even pastorally) motivated, but the similarity in emphasis is unmistakable.

Another area of common ground is in the idea of teaching, the teacher, and the relation of teaching to knowledge. Joseph Owens describes metaphysics as a *habitus*, a "living habit of thinking," which is "not a collection or systematic [read methodological] organization of data either in print or in the memory."[16] This might well summarize Newman's idea of a liberal education in general. As seen, the "gentleman" Newman held up as the proper product of education is not a man stuffed with knowledge. His intellect is not just a memory filled with Ramistic diagrams, charts, and lists. In fact, education involves much more than memory, for as a *habit* it is something active and not simply a storage-house. This is why even the Thomistic mode of exposition, for all its systematic and philosophical qualities, retains much of the personalistic idea of knowledge described in an earlier chapter. Pieper asserts that the

> scholastic *articulus* has retained, and not merely in external form, the character of a genuine conversation or dialogue, that is, the character of reflective meditation, which makes no claim to possessing a definitively formulated answer.[17]

While saying there is no claim to a definitive answer, Pieper does not, of course, suggest that no answer is given or that an answer is not "correct." He means that the answer given may be true and correct, yet not be exhaustive. What is too often forgotten is the dialogue or conversational form of Aquinas' works. The works hardly appear conversational to us (nor did they to Newman) for they were composed in "hand-book style" and were meant to be used by those in daily contact with the scholastic debates.[18] But the works reverberate with the "sounds" of arguments proposed, objections raised, and errors exposed. They echo--even if faintly for us--voices raised in lecture halls and in academic controversy; the "*respondeo quod*" is that of a teacher speaking to students. For all the formality of the discourse, even the "external form" of Aquinas' works exhibit the personalistic and verbal thrust of the scholastic educational mode.

Although Newman complained of finding little *personality* in the texts of Aquinas, he recognized the personalistic mode of instruction implied in them and frequently referred to the medieval schools as being the ideal educational environment. For St. Thomas, says Pieper,

> Teaching is a process that goes on between living men. The teacher looks not only at the truth of things; at the same time

> he looks at the faces of living men who desire to know this
> truth. Love of truth and love of men--only the two together
> constitute a teacher.[19]

This statement could just as easily describe Newman's pastoral/educational idea of a teacher. Because a liberally educated person possesses the intellectual habit of learning, and habits are best acquired "live," the best learning occurs within the living interaction of a teacher and a student. Texts do not have the flexibility a teacher has to assess--in rhetorical fashion--the current state of students' minds and to adjust the matter under instruction accordingly.

SILLEM'S INTRODUCTION

Sillem's two volume edition of *The Philosophical Notebook* is one of the most useful studies of Newman's "philosophy" because the longer first volume consists entirely of the editor's introduction. The introduction, titled "General Introduction to the Study of Newman's Philosophy," goes far in bringing together the various influences, threads, and themes in Newman's writing, while providing numerous examples from his texts and letters. Though his claim that Newman was strongly influenced by Abraham Tucker seems overstated, Sillem provides a wealth of general intellectual background on his author. He draws attention to Newman's personalism, noting that the kind of thought most interesting to the clergyman was concrete and particular, especially as witnessed in the dialogue between minds.[20] The editor also underscores the practical, "missionary" motivation behind much of Newman's work. "Newman was a man of action rather than a pure thinker," Sillem warns, and to forget that his works were products of a rhetorical occasion or purpose, is to misunderstand the fundamental motives behind those works.[21]

One such motive, of course, was to temper the extravagances of rationalism by showing forth the intellect's limits or weaknesses while creating "room" for mystery. Sillem gives this purpose some attention, quoting a passage from the *Grammar* that might well be mistaken for Pieper: "No mind, however large, however penetrating, can directly and fully by one act understand any one truth, however simple."[22] The truths and even objects that the scientist proudly points to as the material of his knowledge are not, Newman says, so readily appropriated after all. While the popular conception of knowledge placed materialistic science "at the top" so to speak, full as it is of hard, real things, it relegated religious knowledge to a level more or less equivalent to opinion. Newman, emphasizing the

whole man in acquisition of truth, turns this hierarchy topsy-turvy. Sillem illustrates this with a passage from the Tamworth Reading Room letters:

> This is why Science has so little of a religious tendency;
> deductions have no power of persuasion. The heart is
> commonly reached not through reason, but through the
> imagination, by means of direct impressions, by the
> testimony of facts and events, by history, by description.
> Persons influence us, voices melt us, looks subdue us,
> deeds influence us. Many a man will live and die upon a
> dogma; no man will be a martyr for a conclusion. . . . No
> one, I say, will die for his own calculations; he dies for
> realities. . . .[23]

Charts and tables are not "realities"; they are deductions and conclusions.
What Newman considers realities are those things brought to us through rhetorical
(or poetic) modes of reasoning rather than strictly scientific ones. Notice the
integration of human faculties implied in the excerpt; a reality is brought home to us
through the simultaneous action of head and heart, through the testimony of our
senses, of witnesses, of history. While Newman's purpose often led him to take
aim at the suppositions behind materialistic rationalism, his own exposition of the
"way people think" is sharply "historical," personal, and psychological. Sillem
quotes from the well-known *University Sermons*:

> The mind ranges to and fro, and spreads out, and advances
> forward with a quickness which has become a proverb, and
> a subtlety and versatility which baffle investigation. It passes
> on from point to point, gaining one by some indication,
> another by a probability; then availing itself of an
> association; then falling back on some received law; next
> seizing on testimony; then committing itself to some popular
> impression, or some inward instinct, or some obscure
> memory; and thus it makes progress not unlike a clamberer
> on a steep cliff, who, by quick eye, prompt hand, and firm
> foot, ascends how he knows not himself, by personal
> endowments and by practice, rather than by rule. . . . And
> such mainly is the way in which all men, gifted or not gifted,
> commonly reason--not by rule, but by an inward faculty.[24]

This inward faculty Newman would later call the "illative sense," and it is worth
noting the high profile in this passage of things like "probability," "testimony,"
"popular impression," etc., things that either belong properly to rhetoric or are often
employed in rhetoric. This is how people "commonly reason." Moreover, the
processes described here are almost automatic, matters of personal endowment, or
habitual. "As truth is discovered not by reasoning, but by habituation, so it is
recommended not by books, but by oral instruction. Socrates wrote nothing."[25]

The features of mind Sillem describes, and in the texts he employs for introductory material, display much that confirms the centrality of personalistic rhetoric in Newman. But the word "rhetoric" hardly appears. In fact, Sillem rejects the concept of the literary (or rhetorical) nature of Newman's ideas. This is doubly unfortunate, for at times Sillem appears to be describing Newman's rhetorical approach without realizing it. Of Newman's "ideology" he says:

> Newman conceived the entirely original idea of studying his problems concerning the relations holding between faith and reason, not theoretically or speculatively, as the theologian considers the natures of faith and reason *in abstracto*, but concretely, that is to say, as mental activities going on in the minds of people believing and thinking and finding themselves unable to believe.[26]

The observation is just. Though Sillem says *in abstracto* (where I have used *per se*), the suggestion is the same. Even while describing Newman's approach to theoretical matters (not limited to theological ones, I should add) as not speculative but "concrete" in the minds of persons, Sillem describes the "*per modum*" quality of Newman's interests. That is, Newman's inquiries into properly speculative matters do not consider those matters in and of themselves, but the inquiries focus on the mode or manner of apprehension in persons. This focus allows Newman to say a particular person's embrace of something (the doctrine of the Trinity, perhaps) may be true but unreal. The person has a formula down pat, without "filling out" the formula with an imaginative, personal grasp of its meaning or even its mystery.

The "*per modum*" focus of Newman's "speculative" inquiries give them a peculiarly psychological turn. It is not difficult to see the particular pastoral effectiveness of such a turn, for the casting of one's self into the mind of another is supremely useful in determining the "what" and "why" of another's religious thinking. Likewise, the necessary rhetorical antecedent to effective persuasion is the proper "sizing-up" of the audience. But is this *per modum* business a legitimate field of intellectual inquiry? Can it really be studied at all or is it simply the device of an incipient relativist? In answer, it should be noted that Aristotle says some things are known better in and of themselves, while other things are known better *to us*. The knowledge of the metaphysician--rare as that knowledge is--is better known considered *per se* because it concerns the highest knowledge naturally possible to man. Nevertheless, things known better to us are those intermixed with particulars of person and circumstance. Newman's interest in how things are apprehended and known in concrete cases (that is, in actual persons) clearly demonstrates that his focus is on the "to us" part of the equation. Aquinas' principle that knowledge is in the knower according to the mode of the knower is similar in distinction. Not only does knowledge exist, it exists in persons in a fashion particular to themselves. From the foregoing analysis it should be clear that this distinction does not imply a lurking relativity. The "particular fashion" in no way militates against the true universality of the thing known or the actual possession of essences by the intellect. It merely points out what should be almost self-evident. Persons are particular and arrive at their knowledge through their own sequence of intellectual events. What they know is universal; how they come to know is a process involving different particulars. Philosophy, by nature, deals with the "what." Newman, by inclination, deals with the "what happens when" or the "how" considered not epistemologically but regarding particular persons. This "how" in its particularity is neither philosophical nor dialectical, although it may frequently touch upon these sciences; immersed as it is in the personal (albeit general), the psychological, and the motivational, this "how" is properly rhetorical.

Despite his usual acuity of perception, Sillem misses this important distinction. This results in the transference of "*per modum*" to philosophy: "His [Newman's] philosophy is thus the quest for a consciously 'realized' personal metaphysics based on as clear a vision of existent realities as the mind can reach from its own lived experience."[27] What can this mean? As seen, the word "experience" is philosophically problematic, and the phrase "as clear a vision of existent realities as the mind can reach from its own lived experience" does little to resolve the difficulty. It has the peculiar inward-turning reflexivity seen in Locke; it begins and ends in the mind. The universe expressed in that passage is not one of objects but of thought. The feeling that Nuttall describes of being closed-in and isolated is all too prevalent here. Sillem is trying to make a metaphysics out of Newman's rhetorical personalism, and in so doing paints a picture of a poor "philosopher" indeed. What begins in the mind can only end there, and we are left with the odd term "personal metaphysics."

Sillem explains the personal/rhetorical thrust of Newman's emphasis on conversation in the same way. "He sought objective truth by the method of dialogue, in and through the experience of inter-subjectivity (to use the modern jargon), that is to say in the intercourse of man with man, and the action of mind on mind."[28] Jost will make the same point later, looking to "inter-subjectivity" to secure knowledge of reality. The difficulty here is precisely that no amount of "inter-subjectivity" suddenly or magically yields "objectivity." If one begins in the world of the mind rather than the world of things, of objects, one cannot embrace "objectivity" regardless of intellectual effort. One is reminded of the comical phrase "pooling our ignorance." If people are ignorant of objective truth to begin with, pooling their ignorance of it in inter-subjective dialogue will not produce it. These are the kinds of problems generated in an epistemology haunted by skepticism. But the difficulty in Sillem's analysis lies ultimately in his conception of "truth."

Truth is not "decided upon" by subjective intelligences; it is objective in the sense of being a grasp of the real. While truth is the adequation of mind to things, it does not follow that truths are "automatically" grasped. The mind has to be "adequated" or made fit to receive many truths. Again, we are not dealing with a baldly mechanical process at all. The particular dignity of rhetoric is that its supreme utility is in adequating or preparing the mind for truth. Thus the connection between rhetoric and teaching is a most intimate one, and Newman's interest in both is hardly coincidental.[29] In the pattern of Peter of Spain, Agricola, and Ramus, Sillem has taken a legitimate (rhetorical) field of intellectual endeavor and given it the crown of philosophy. In doing so, both rhetoric and philosophy suffer.[30]

GENESIS OF THE *NOTEBOOK*

Newman's *Philosophical Notebook* is unquestionably the most deliberately philosophical text of his opus. There are a great many philosophical themes in a great many of his works (notably in the *Grammar* and the *Oxford University Sermons*), but no other text enjoys the distinction of being avowedly philosophical in entirety. It is quite a hodgepodge of manuscripts, notes, drafts of essays, and stray thoughts on philosophical subjects. Much of the *Notebook* consists of notes drafted between 1859 and 1860 when Newman was considering writing a book on metaphysics. These notes, entitled "Descriptive Enquiries on Metaphysical Subjects," represent thoughts *not* designed primarily as history, apologetic, or psychology. They are meant to treat "philosophy" and are valuable in providing a glimpse of Newman's mind when so engaged.

Though the glimpse of Newman's mind is a good one, the tentative nature of the text should be remembered. Newman affirms little, choosing to interpret "speculative" quite literally as applied to the conjectural, exploratory aspect of his work. He left the unpublished *Notebook* with a written caution that the text was not meant or readied for publication. Just the same, as an incurable organizer and arranger, Newman had many opportunities to dispose of the *Notebook* along with many other papers he thought would be of no use or interest after his death. He knew scholars would pour over his papers, and the fact that the *Notebook* was carefully preserved implies that Newman felt the text would be of interest and use. In the end, however, he did not write his book on metaphysics. The idea came to write a different kind of book, one on "the popular, practical, and personal evidence of Christianity," which, interestingly enough, turned out to be the *Grammar*.[31] The "Discursive Enquiries" were dropped, although he continued to add stray thoughts periodically.[32] Nevertheless, the text more than amply displays Newman's habit of mind, and as we shall see, it is a deeply rhetorical habit, even when applied to philosophy. His approach to philosophical questions possesses the same evidential, probabilistic (even testimonial) thrust seen in his thoughts upon education, pastoral activity, and the Oratory.

MATTER AND SPIRIT

The manuscript *Notebook*, published in entirety for the first time in 1970, does not itself contain the "Letter on Matter and Spirit" with which Sillem concludes the volume. The inclusion of the letter is justified, however, for it is in many ways an apt summary of Newman's thoughts as expressed in the rest of the text. Written in 1861, to an unidentified recipient, the letter attempts to lay before its reader Newman's thoughts concerning the intelligibility of material reality. The central purpose of the letter is to explain his thesis that "the objects of the senses [are nothing] more than phenomena, not things in any true sense" and that there is "no such one thing as Matter, any more than there [is] any one thing called Soul or Spirit. . . ."[33] Such statements are indeed startling, sounding very much like a paraphrase of Berkeley. But Newman clarifies the issue, saying that the word "matter" does "not express a real essence, but stands for all material substances viewed as one. . . ."[34]

Although it is interesting that Newman immediately focuses on what words mean rather than what things are, his observation appears to be that matter is not some "stuff" that material objects have "scooped-up" and possess. Likewise, spiritual beings do not grab a bit of (doubtless ethereal) stuff and thereby become spiritual beings. Matter and spirit do not have their own essences; that is, in accordance with the Thomistic doctrine, matter does not exist in itself apart from form. Every material thing has an essence, and its material is its individuating substance. Take away the form or essences and one is not left with matter; one is left with nothing. This seems to be Newman's meaning here, for he affirms that material things do in fact exist ("material substances indeed there [are] innumerable"[35]). Just a few pages later, however, Newman changes the sense of the term "matter" and employs it to mean material substance, for he speaks of the relation of matter to perception. Here we see Newman struggling with the barrier placed between the senses and reality by the empiricists: "And now first I shall take for granted that matter is not an object of direct perception by means of the senses, is not identical with the impressions of sense, is not demonstrated to exist by the mere fact of these impressions."[36]

Material substances *do* exist, says Newman, but we cannot know that they do by reason. Reason cannot possibly ascertain any connection between our sense impressions and the objective existence of things outside of us. We are back to Berkeley and Hume! But on what grounds does Newman affirm the existence of material things? Reality is confirmed to us by revelation--that is, scripture and tradition. "I am not bound to believe the existence of material substances a natural truth, because it is a supernatural truth."[37] So Newman's position here seems to be that matter doesn't exist by itself, but exists in conjunction with essences, that our senses are incapable of ascertaining the objective existence of the things they perceive, and that this lack is made up for by revelation which affirms that what we perceive is actual.

Are we then left with a Malebranchian philosophical skepticism rescued by religious faith? Fortunately or unfortunately (depending on how one looks at it), it is not so simple. Newman flips again (in the same letter) and comes down on the side of our perception of reality being naturally trustworthy. However, it is trustworthy not on account of *reason* (which cannot ascertain the existence of external reality) but of *instinct*. "I certainly grant the instinct in our minds by which we spontaneously believe and cherish, as a first idea, that matter exists[,] our impressions of things derived thro' the senses are not merely subjective."[38] While he maintains the accuracy and propriety of this instinct, Newman cautions that such an instinct cannot "be called properly a proof. Considered as an instinctive conviction, or what is often called an intuition, it is not a conclusion but a first principle or premise; and the existence of matter is not proved but assumed."[39] The objective reality of material substances is thus guaranteed for Newman by this two-fold assurance; the testimony of revelation and our natural "instinct" that such substances exist.

Though Newman clearly believes he has affirmed the common-sense view of reality, as philosophy his statements straddle several fences. First of all, the terms "instinct" and "intuition" are highly problematic. Strictly speaking, instinctive material is neither subject to nor available for reason. One cannot philosophize from the starting point of instinct or intuition. However, if, as Newman suggests, we are to understand instinct as "first principle," then it may be employed as a basis for reasoning. But we seem to have it both ways; there is at once the sense of the non-rational nature of the instinct and its being a first principle.

Secondly, the philosophical nature of a first principle seems confused here with the logical nature of a premise. In philosophy, a first principle is beyond proof, indeed, but it is also a self-evident truth. One cannot prove "the whole is greater than the part" but neither does one *need* to. For the Thomist, objective reality is a first principle; all attempts at "proving" the existence of reality are futile from the start, for it is that which is *prior* to proof of any sort. This is why a first principle is absolutely distinct from an assumption or postulate.[40] First principles and assumptions are similar only in their actions in syllogisms; as intellectual entities they are utterly different. To put it simply, an assumption or postulate is a given only for the sake of the argument that follows; a first principle is purely a given in itself. This vital distinction is blurred here as, again, Newman employs first principle and assumption in a dual fashion. On the one hand, there is the sense of the rational legitimacy of the principle; on the other hand is the sense of a mere premise, a starting point simply assumed.

Thirdly, note the philosophical import of Newman's position. Reality exists, we can be assured, because revelation says so, and because we all instinctively know it does. This is exactly the kind of thing Nuttall speaks of when he says "to say 'we do know and there's an end on't' is not to resolve the philosophical problem. Rather it is a refusal to do any more philosophy."[41] At the core of Newman's most considered "epistemology," at least in reference to perception of reality, lurks instinct, a form of "we *do* know, and that's an end on't." Indeed, any Thomist would agree with the assertion itself. It is the philosophical status of the assertion that is questionable.

Despite Newman's philosophical intentions, what is in fact taking place here is rhetorical argument and not, as Weatherby would have it, philosophical skepticism. The appeal to or affirmation of instinct is the formal counterpart to the rhetorical appeal to a commonplace. The orator's assertion that "we all know . . . " is a forceful appeal combining a kind of mass authority and immediate testimony. It points to something rhetorically self-evident. Newman argues for the reality of material substances with the rhetorical argument: we all know. True, the argument is couched amidst many denigrations of reason. It is the irony of Newman's day that philosophers felt compelled to exercise mechanistic reasonings in an attempt to prove the unprovable--reality's accessibility. More ironic still is Newman's combat with this mechanistic reasoning, for he was correct about the unprovability of reality, but he was right for the wrong reasons. Rather, it is more accurate to say he was right for *rhetorical* reasons, not philosophical ones. As noted, even the Thomist would agree that everyone knows reality is "out there." It is just that such a formulation can hardly be considered philosophy.

MATTER AND SPIRIT: RHETORICAL PURPOSE

A more subtle rhetorical aspect of Newman's argument is its purpose. Clearly, having a purpose or motive for something does not automatically make it rhetorical, but purpose *per se* is so highly rhetorical that it can color a discourse very easily. In Newman's case, purpose is so strong in his reasoning that it palpably shapes the mode of argumentation. Newman's motive in limiting or fencing in the power of reason is not so much his attachment to principles of skepticism but his alarm at the "natural" gradually elbowing aside the supernatural. The rationalistic complacency encouraged by mechanistic conceptions of thought can be shaken up by limiting and weakening the claims of reason. It might be argued that reason requires very little weakening in an age of philosophical skepticism, and indeed Newman will use that skepticism as a kind of "cold shower" for his day, reminding his contemporaries how "uncertain" an intellect's grasp of reality is. As we have seen, though, complacency as to the powers of a mechanistically conceived reason is strengthened, not weakened, by prevailing skepticism.[42] Newman's particular thrust here is to combat the disproportionate sway of material things (and sciences) in the nineteenth-century imagination, by challenging the claim of reason to be so automatically adequate to material reality. Newman is saying, in effect, "Compile data all you will; in the end what have you got? Your reason cannot even prove the data actually relate to anything real." Again, Newman insists that the "instinct" for objective reality is legitimate; he simply will not allow reason any claim to it.

It may well be argued that Newman's rhetorical procedure in such arguments is counter-productive, that weakening the claims of reason in a scientific and mechanistic era can only backfire in the long run. While this may be true, it bears noting that Newman's frequent critiques of reason must be balanced not only against his purpose in saying so, but also against his frequent assertions of the dignity and power of reason. Once again, statements that might appear contradictory when placed side-by-side usually are consistent when Newman's purpose is kept in mind. The purpose continues to influence his rather empirical critique of a kind of complacent, cultural empiricism, as he delves into the relation of the senses to material objects. While affirming the objective existence of material reality (as justified by revelation and instinct), he says "our senses tell us that matter exists, but they tell us no more. They do not tell us what matter is, or what it is like."[43] The argument is that the essences of things are not brought to us by our perception of those things. Material substances act like causes, the effect of which is our perception. According to Newman, this is as far as one may safely go. Effects are not at all like their causes ("no image," as he says) and thus we have no purely natural guarantee that the things around us actually are what we normally take them to be.

There are numerous difficulties here, not the least of which is caused by the absence of the agent intellect. If essences are unavailable to us, then Newman's scenario of a mind filled with images wholly unlike their causes is conceivable. It is conceivable, but not likely, for the second assertion is also problematic. Though he offers several examples of effects being unlike their causes (such as the sound of a bell and the pulling of a bell-chord), Aquinas would disagree as to the principle exemplified. What Newman treats rhetorically, the bell-chord example, Aquinas would treat systematically, breaking the example down into kinds of causation. The efficient cause (pulling the rope) is indeed like the efficient effect (the movement of the bell) while the final cause (the intention to produce the sound) is also like the final effect (the sound).

Newman's comments about the senses and material substances lead up to an argument central to the purpose of this letter. In fact, it is not so much an argument as an observation, not so much a proof as a "speculation." The senses, we are told, give us different kinds of perceptions or impressions. Olfactory impressions give no indication, for example, of spatial extension. The smell of a rose gives no clue as to the appearance of the rose. Were we limited to one or two senses, our perception of material reality would be enormously different--and poorer--than it is with five. The power of vision revolutionizes our perception of the world. What might happen if we suddenly possessed a sixth sense? What untold revelation in our perception of reality might occur? How might our entire conception of material reality alter if we perceived aspects about it now inconceivable to us?

Newman is saying first that our senses do not tell us what things *are*, and second that we have no idea what our perceptions might be of this same material reality if we possessed additional senses. It is in this context that Newman says (to the horror of Weatherby) that our ignorance of essences is so profound, that for all we know, what appears to us as a rose might in fact "be an angel; it may be the soul of a child; it may be as I have hinted above, one of the innumerable immediate acts of the Everpresent Creator Himself. There is nothing absurd or impossible in the idea."[44] Indeed there is nothing absurd in the idea, if phenomena are just phenomena and do not reveal essence. Oddly enough, there is some justification for the suggestion concerning angels in the writing of Aquinas. His treatise on the angels expounds upon the proprietary, mediatory role of the angels with regard to material creation. Clearly, though, the idea that material things have no essence of their own, that they are phenomena *generated* by spiritual beings, is dangerously akin to Berkeleyism.[45]

Newman frequently hedges or moderates his assertions in order to preserve a rhetorically useful "middle ground." He is careful to assert that, yes, the senses *do* tell us something of material substances, and he even goes so far as to contradict his earlier pronouncement on the dissimilarity of cause and effect. Noting the consistency of sense impressions, he says "the effects of a cause have a certain likeness to that from which they proceed. . . . " Then openly admitting the difficulty here, he inserts in brackets: "I can't get at the bottom of this. . . ."[46] The patterns revealed in the discussion of matter, essences, and sense are typical of the letter as a whole. There is little actual assertion, and a great deal of "problem posing." The method is one that creates questions and exposes difficulties relative to a complacent reliance on material phenomena.

From a Thomistic standpoint the letter possesses layers of philosophical difficulties, if not outright contradictions. Even the speculations on the senses are problematic, as Aquinas argues for the propriety of the five senses and the impossibility of there being more.[47] There are unannounced shifts in the meaning of terms and subsequent confusions about "matter" and material things, there are confusions of distinctions such as principle/postulate where dual yet incompatible meaning is required to make the argument "go." Not least, there is an over-all ambivalence as to the objective character of material substances. Newman asserts and affirms the existence of exterior reality, even going so far as to pronounce it beyond reasonable question. Yet he tries to whittle away at the solidity of that existence, not so consistently or thoroughly as Berkeley, but by means of prodding and posing difficulties. In fact, it appears he wants to "have it" both ways. Though he pronounces reality beyond question to the empirical skeptic, he swoops down on the rationalistic materialist with nagging questions and belittling paradoxes. He does not demonstrate or prove, for both his approach and his objective is largely negative. Why? What is the ultimate purpose here? Some indication is given where Newman says the senses betoken the unknown, but they do not reveal it.[48] This resembles the Thomistic principles so well enunciated by Pieper: we do know, but not exhaustively. Newman reveals here his objective--to give the man's senses and intellect their due, but to prevent (or retard) presumption upon them.

This, of course, is fully in keeping with Newman's life-long mission of securing an intellectual middle-ground between man considered potentially omniscient or utterly "nihiliscient." Man's natural powers are powerful, but only to an extent. His purpose is to reduce the naive presumption upon material reality as being wholly adequate for human nature and by so doing create room in the imagination and reason for the immaterial and the supernatural. It is noteworthy that his technique is to pose questions structured in probability and analogy, not definition and demonstration (the letter on Matter and Spirit makes large use of analogies, and the final third is devoted to analogy and the senses). Newman proposes early in the letter than "I am not proving what I [am] advancing. . . . Let us put aside proof for the present."[49] The rhetorical nature of his intentions is clear not only in his reluctance to enter fully into philosophical combat, but in the "utilitarian" motive for his speculations. He speaks of his "arguments" as "conceivable" and declares his reasonings non-conclusive: "[T]o go as far as this without demonstrating has its uses, a clear vivid conception may be mistaken for proof, but it has its uses short of it."[50]

Newman is working on the nineteenth-century rationalistic *imagination*. His assertions and examples are imaginatively striking more than philosophically consistent, and this, as he says, is useful. It can be employed to prepare minds to receive truths or to be sensitive to matters otherwise alien to them. The contradictions, ambiguities and ambivalences of this letter, its confusions and twists, make it difficult to call "philosophy" at all. It is an excellent example of something being "philosophical" without being philosophy. The rhetorical nature of its purpose and approach to the issues is its most palpable aspect. The rest of the *Notebook* is much the same; the patterns of inconsistency, probability, analogy, the appeal to imagination through commonplaces, and a strong rhetorical motive pervade the text.

BLENDING PRINCIPLES

The *Notebook* is filled with unusual combinations of philosophical doctrines that are sometimes contradictory and often confused. Early in the manuscript, within a segment titled "Elements of Thought," a note is recorded in which we see Newman "blending" principles by asking a kind of rhetorical question:

> If our consciousness of our existence is to be taken as true and trusted, then our consciousness of something external to us, answering both to phenomena and to typical principles or ideas is true and to be trusted. We must take ourselves for what we are--we cannot divide between the mind and its gifts--we only know the mind through its gifts and powers.[51]

In a sense, Newman seems to be reaching for a Thomist or realist principle of being. By asking "if we trust we exist, what ground do we have for distrusting the existence of exterior reality?" Newman suggests that there is a ground common to ourselves and everything we perceive; that ground would be being. Newman reaches but does not attain this. He instinctively grasps the reasonableness of this "being" as something common between ourselves and the exterior world, but his grasp is rhetorical; it is expressed essentially as a rhetorical question "Why not?" He does not land upon "being" as the answer and principle; he simply asks a general, "common-sense" question that points up the improbability of finding a cause for "distrust." Of course, this is thoroughly rhetorical in approach, but the passage is still peculiar for its confusion of principle. Despite the reach for a realist principle, the starting-point remains the *de rigueur* ground of "our consciousness." We are still trapped inside ourselves, and there is a hint of Cartesian "clear and distinct ideas" in Newman's "typical principles or ideas." Thus one has a curious blend of metaphysical realism and Cartesian idealism in a single proposition.

The same mixing of philosophical principles occurs earlier still, when Newman's speculations treat the ancient and thorny question of individuals and classes. "Classes" writes Newman, "are not external facts, but ideas derived from the sight of resemblance, purely mental, and without corresponding objects. Individuals are the only facts."[52] One hears here echoes of Abelard and William of

Champeaux wrangling about the logical nemesis of scholastic thought, nominalism. In fact, Newman's formula is classically nominalistic: there are only individuals, not genera or species. The philosophical position seems clear enough. Note, however, the very next paragraph:

> When Mill, vol. 1, p 121 [*A System of Logic*] is severe upon essences of things, and essential predications, I would ask, whether we cannot contemplate an individual . . . and whether we have not the idea of a unit. Unit and essence are equivalents. The unit is open to changes--those changes are accidents, and do not interfere with its individuality, i.e. its essence. Much more when we compare units together, and find that they only differ from each other as they differ from themselves, which is, as I have said, in *accidents*. When then men are like each other except in accidents, I would say they are like in essences. This is quite consistent with holding that we cannot fully attain to the essence, as Mill says, though we may get at some differentia.[53]

Never mind that Abelard's old trap of dealing with philosophical problems with a logician's tools reappears in the first sentence, what is noteworthy here is the resuscitation of classes. Though we were just told classes are not external facts, Newman here reverses the nominalist stance and asserts that men are alike in essence. The assertion does not get at the bottom of individuation, but neither does it have to. What is important is that we have such a rapid and radical juxtaposition of contradictories, without correction, emendation or adjustment. No less noteworthy is the psychologism used to counter Mill. Newman again turns not to philosophy *per se* but to the experience of cognition--what happens when we contemplate an individual or when we compare units. The old sensitivity to the workings of other's minds is evident here, as is the appeal to common experiences. The last sentence is almost classic Newman; he wants to defend man's claim to know reality, yet limit that knowledge so as to prevent intellectual presumption and to allow for the reality of mystery.

RHETORICAL FIGURING

More rhetorical philosophizing occurs when Newman makes use of analogous reasoning to prove a point. In "The Unseen World" the reader sees Newman seeking out ways to jar or jolt the materialist, to make room for the immaterial, and to do so through means largely conditioned by the materialistic habits of mind so pervasive at the time. He uses analogy in a fashion typical of the

Notebook. Newman opens this "note" with a summary statement of an imaginary opponent's position (note the debate format): "I deny that there is any world but the sensible world. A Creator, Personal God, Angels, Souls, are mere traditions and fancies."[54] The reply is an amusing "Is this so?" followed by the assertion that the invisible world is as thoroughly "inferred" as the visible. Here is the same tactic seen earlier; weaken the case for visible reality (make its existence an inference) and show invisible reality meeting the same criteria. The philosophical weakness is typical of a post-empirical argument: exterior reality is inferred, not apprehended.

But Newman's main argument follows, and it is a superb example of effective rhetorical argument employing analogy. Newman asserts that "The . . . mind of each individual is at once a reality, yet to all others . . . a hidden reality."[55] People hope, fear, love, like and dislike all the time, yet we have no direct knowledge of those interior mental activities except in ourselves. We know others' minds exist and that they have these activities, but it is an unseen existence. Its reality is inferred from what we do see. Of this unseen world Newman exclaims "How infinitesimal is the knowledge I have of it in its details and fulness!" The unseen world of "God, then, Angels, devils, &c &c," is much the same. It is real, but not seen directly. It is not a strong idea or fancy at all "but a carrying out of a conception, which experience has brought home to us together with a knowledge of the visible world."[56] In other words, we have here a rhetorical counterpart to the old Thomistic proof of inferring the existence of God through "a knowledge of the visible world."[57]

Analogy has a place in philosophy, of course, but its rhetorical utility is clear. Newman's use of it is not demonstrative but figurative. He does not demonstrate the existence of the unseen, supernatural world by means of the Thomistic "analogy of being" or other proofs. Instead, he creates a figure or "shape" of argument that imposes upon the reader another kind of rhetorical question; "If here, why not over here?" That is, if we come to know something (anything) unseen, we have no ground therefore upon which to disclaim all knowledge of the unseen.

Newman's reply to the hypothetical materialist does more than simply point up the illogic in saying "I believe nothing I cannot see." Because it shows how *in fact* the unseen is believed by everyone, the reply conditions, as it were, the imagination to receive a possibility or probability. Much of Newman's thought upon faith and assent to the reality of the supernatural is just this sort of conditioning of the imagination. He tries not to prove so much as he tries to prepare minds to receive proofs.

This hearkens back to the personalist, integrated conception of knowledge. Newman's conception of human reason is not the typical nineteenth-century mechanistic conception. In the *Grammar* he will "buck the system" by showing that, rhetorically, a thing may be known without being "proved" and it may even be "proved" without being "known"--as when the grasp of an abstraction is purely conceptual. More than mere reason enters into most human cognition. The assent to a truth in most people is a complex affair involving, among other things, the ability to *imagine* a thing as true. The philosopher or theologian may well develop irrefutable arguments for the existence of an unseen world, etc., but the arguments can fall onto infertile ground. Enter the rhetorician whose concern is preparing the ground. Newman's reply to the materialist creates a possibility in the mind of the materialist. It elbows aside the doctrinal presumptions of the nineteenth-century mind in order to establish room for probabilities and movements of the intellect that appeal and "warm." Before the reason can properly assent to a truth, the person's (whole man) motive for rejecting it and imaginative capacity to accept it have to be seen to. This is why Newman's psychological sensitivity was so beneficial to his rhetorical purposes. Analogous argumentation is an excellent means of preparing the imagination because, like metaphor, analogy calls upon the imagination to present similarities for recognition. Newman's rhetorical intellect relies heavily upon analogy for this reason, and his interest in the pre-conditioning of the mind for assent is omnipresent in his texts.[58]

Again treating an imaginary opponent's proposition, Newman's habitual rhetoricism reveals itself in full regalia when he considers a source of misapprehension as well as some concomitants of religious faith:

> "Catholics do not honestly seek truth." This misapprehension arises from the fact that religion is not solely a *philosophy*, but also a *devotion* and a party adherence or a fellowship. Devotion brings in hope and fear--and fellowship beings in fear of scandal. In philosophy there is no fear or consideration of anything but "is this so or not"? but devotion brings in the fear of error and its consequences, and fellowship introduces the necessities of all moving together--the duty of deference to superiors, and consultancy for the interest of our neighbors.[59]

Note that the assertion here is beyond strictly philosophical or theological bounds. Religion is not being treated purely as a system of supernatural truths--it is a devotion and communion. One may have emotions regarding it (Newman inserted the word "passions" above "devotion"), and there are other people that one must look out for in it. Newman felt that the intellectual validity and rationality of the faith were perfectly capable of exposition and that, in a sense, the rationality of faith could take care of itself. His missionary, rhetorical purpose is seen in his inclusion of passions and corporate unity. Again, the whole man is involved in possession of faith, not merely the intellect. It is interesting that Newman immediately follows the above with an observation about the role these extra-intellectual faculties play in the initial assent to supernatural truths. We are back to pre-conditions;

> [I]n religious and moral matters we gain truth *not without* devotion and social interchange of thought--e.g. not without a good life and prayer for grace, and availing ourselves of the judgement of the wise and waiting for the consent of the many, i.e. the consent of doctors and the *sensus fidelium*; the voice of authority and the "*securus judicat orbis terrarum*".[60]

We recall Newman's advice that inquirers should pray for enlightenment as much as they should read books on the faith. We also recall the importance he placed on personal discourse in communication and education. It is clear that these concerns dovetail neatly with his rhetorical personalism in their emphasis on the manner in which things are learned and known.

CONSCIENCE AND THEISM

The longest section of the *Notebook* is titled "Proof of Theism." Here we see in condensed form the argument Newman will develop in the *Grammar* advancing the existence of God through the evidence of conscience. Newman's famous proof from conscience is fairly novel from an historical point of view, and he believed the argument was most effective in his day. Still little more than a collection of notes, the "Proof of Theism" exhibits the same odd combination of mixed principles, dual starting-points, and difficulties with the multiple meanings of terms seen elsewhere in the *Notebook*. As will be seen, the "Proof" also possesses a personal valence and psychological sensitivity so rhetorically useful to Newman.

Not surprisingly, this series of notes begins with an actual controversy in which the fence-straddling of principles is evident. Newman uses his argument with W. G. Ward's *On Nature and God* as the occasion for these notes. The debate with Ward is a rat's nest of argument concerning what it means to "have faith in one's existence"--i.e. the nature of consciousness and how one "trusts" one's consciousness. The details of the debate are unimportant for us here, except that one sees again the strong combination of a realist starting-point in sensible reality and an almost Berkeleyan disregard for the existence of non-spiritual natures. But the result of Newman's argument is a simple position upon which he based his argument for the existence of God.

Newman asserts that one's consciousness is comprised of "sensation, memory, thought, reason," all of which are "essentially bound up" in the very idea of our existence.[61] They are all self-evident things that require no "trust" at all in order for one to know one exists. They are "primary conditions of mind which are involved in the fact of existence."[62] Newman does not say memory, sensation, thought and reason exhaust the primary conditions of mind; they are just examples of things automatically bound up with the idea of our own existence. In a sense, Newman is arguing that the operation of the mind is self-evidently indicative of its existence. While he mentions "*cogito ergo sum*" and "*sentio ergo sum*," he seems to diminish the "*ergo*" in such a way that one does not conclude or believe in one's existence whatsoever. One apprehends it at once with the operation of mind. The truly important step in the argument is taken when Newman identifies "conscience" as one such primary condition.

Conscience Newman defines as "the discrimination of acts as worthy of praise or blame."[63] He asks in a footnote "What is praise or blame?" but his real interest is in taking this faculty for discrimination to the very heart of consciousness. "Now such praise or blame is a phenomenon of my existence, one of those phenomena thro' which as I have said, my existence is brought home to me."[64] The importance of this to Newman cannot be overstated. He argues that conscience is as inherent a faculty as is reason or memory; it is in everyone. This is not to say it is the same discrimination in everyone. Typically practical in inclination, Newman does not ignore the fact that in concrete persons, the dictates of conscience are not the same. For the purposes of Newman's argument, however, the dictates do not have to be the same; the relevant fact is not what conscience dictates but *that* it dictates:

> all men know what the feeling of a good or bad conscience is, though they may differ most widely from each other as to what conscience injoins. That is, this sense of a particular judgement or sensation on the quality of action is part of myself in the same way that existence, in the same way that sensation, consciousness, reasoning, memory are part of

myself . . . and it is . . . unmeaning to say I have faith in it. .
. . It is bound up in the very idea or fact of my existence.[65]

Newman maintains, then, that this discriminatory faculty is as inherent in man as existence itself. The status of this assertion relative to synderesis in the works of Aquinas is not material here, for another hinge of Newman's argument is yet to come. How do we get from conscience to God? Upon the answer to this does Newman's argument turn, and the shift into rhetorical argument is rapid and radical. Note that for his answer Newman turns to one of his *Occasional Sermons*, fifth edition, volume five, page 73: "Man has within his breast a certain commanding dictate, not a mere sentiment, not a mere opinion or impression or view of things, but a law, an authoritative voice, bidding him to do certain things and avoid others."[66]

The hinge is "voice." Newman proceeds from conscience as a faculty to the inference of God's existence by identifying conscience as a voice that commands. The highly personalist valence of "voice" is in its being the act of a person, an act direct and willed. It is also noteworthy that Newman chooses to say "voice," not vision or apprehension. His pre-Ramist aural inclination regarding knowledge and the discrimination of moral truths is evident here, and it fills out the personalist thrust of his description of the conscience. It suddenly transforms the argument from an anatomy of faculties into an identification of sources--or rather, source: a personal being.

Newman's quotation from the sermon continues, rounding out the conception of this voice. The passage is significant in the "Proof of Theism" for not only is it the hinge of his proof, but it takes us out of the perplexing trenches of arid epistemological wrangling and into the clear air of Newman's oratory:

> I do not say that its [conscience's] particular injunctions are always clear or that they are always consistent with each other; but what I am insisting on here is this, that it commands; that it praises, it blames, it promises, it threatens, it implies a future, and it witnesses of the unseen. . . . The man himself has not power over it, or only with extreme difficulty; he did not make it, he cannot destroy it. He may silence it in particular cases or directions; he may distort its enunciations. . . . He can disobey it; he may refuse to use it; but it remains. This is conscience, and from the nature of the case, its very existence carries on our minds to a Being exterior to ourselves; for else, whence did it come? . . . Its very existence throws us out of ourselves and beyond ourselves, to go and seek for Him in the height and depth whose Voice it is. As the sunshine implies that the sun is in the heavens, though we may see it not, as a knocking at our

> doors at night implies the presence of one outside in the dark
> who asks for admission, so this Word within us, not only
> instructs us up to a certain point, but necessarily raises our
> minds to the idea of a Teacher, an unseen Teacher, etc.[67]

The movement is very clear; conscience is a voice (so personal that by the end of the passage it merits a capital "V") that bespeaks a Person, a Being both teacher and judge. This Being is God, of course, and it is difficult to imagine an argument more patently rhetorical. Even ignoring the suggestive fact that Newman turns to oratory at the very hinge of his argument, the case presented has all the marks of rhetorical demonstration rather than philosophical demonstration. It is important to remember that rhetoric is not "weak philosophy." It possesses its own logic and generates its own proofs and demonstrations based on that logic. The province of rhetorical logic is probability, and in Newman's argument we see an extremely well-turned case based on probability and metaphor. This does not impugn the validity of the argument in the least. Again, to sneer at "mere probability" is to relegate an entire mode of legitimate knowledge to the dust bin of intellectual endeavor. Newman's argument is not properly a philosophical one for it turns upon the personalistic, metaphorical suggestion of "voice" and the probability of its divine origin. There is not demonstration of a universal, here, but the argument is no less valid. Indeed, the argument is an excellent one, and even the most narrow, crabbed philosopher must concede its force, especially as expressed in the *Grammar*. Newman's rhetorical proof of theism exemplifies his use of a philosophical rhetoric to reach his audience of rationalistically "locked-in" contemporaries. Since it is tailored to an educated, intellectual audience, its philosophical aspect is a well-aimed rhetorical use of subject matter

Again, Newman's motives and feelings toward his proof of theism reveal a great deal about its rhetorical character. Toward the latter part of the "Proof," Newman describes his attraction to the argument from conscience he has just elaborated:

> I am led to it, not only by its truth, but by its great
> convenience and appositeness in this day.
>   1. It is a proof common to all, to high and low, from
> earliest infancy. It is carried about in a compact form in
> every soul. It is ever available--it requires no learning--it is
> possessed by pagans as well as Christians.
>   2. And next, it is intimately combined with practice. It is
> not some abstract truth wrought out by the pure intellect, or
> wrought out theoretically, as that from design. It goes to the
> root of the matter, and is the source of practical religion as
> well as speculative.[68]

RHETORICAL "NOTES"

This key passage presents in miniature many points of importance maintained throughout this study. Newman's professed interest in his proof from conscience is its rhetorical utility. Of course, he is convinced of the truth of the argument, and as we have seen there is nothing about rhetorical argument that makes it unable to achieve or aim at truth. Yet the "convenience and appositeness in this day" of the argument is its principle recommendation. It is rhetorically suited to its times and audience. Indeed, due to the passage of time the argument might require modification to be effective in our own day. The twentieth century has a profound distrust of any interior faculty (not bio-chemically controlled) supposed to be as inherent in our being as existence itself. Rhetorical utility is paramount in Newman's criteria for good argument, and this proof possesses it. Note that philosophers and theologians like Ward and Perrone do not at all concern themselves with the effectiveness of their speculations. Their interest is in the speculative matter *per se*, while Newman's is eminently practical. The passage above highlights two other constituent elements of rhetorical discourse as well: practical subject matter and generality of application. Newman maintains that the utility of his proof comes from its source and appeal to people of all sorts. The generality of people is the source of the argument in that everyone discriminates action as praiseworthy or blameworthy; thus, the appeal of the argument is to the testimony of common experience. Because Newman is really speaking about what Nuttall calls "psychological contents"--the experience of conscience--the subject matter of the argument is general rather than universal. Likewise, since Newman appeals to action--albeit internal action--as the ground of his proof, it must be considered properly practical. That is, the proof is not only generated from Newman's practical intellect (note its design for utility), but it appeals to the practical intellect by investigating action of mind. As he says, it is not purely theoretical. It speaks to people's experience of their own internal promptings.

For all Newman's interest in the practicality and utility of his argument, his own temperament required no such supports. Proof of God's existence was unnecessary for Newman, and this should be kept in mind when reading his occasional disparagements of such proofs. His oft-quoted remark about the two "luminously self-evident" beings in his mind (himself and God) illustrates his preference for the apprehension of God rather than the deduction of God. Here again the distinction between philosophical and rhetorical knowledge is important.

To himself (and for most people, Newman maintained) the existence of God
required no proof. It was a self-evident, never-doubted truth. Did he then disagree
with Aquinas for maintaining that the existence of God is not self-evident but
requires--and receives--demonstration? Not at all. For one thing, not even
Weatherby denies that Newman was careful to affirm the reason's ability to
demonstrate God's existence. Newman was too practical to say God's existence
was, *per se*, self-evident; too many people doubted that existence. The answer is
that philosophically, God's existence is not self-evident although it is capable of
demonstration. Rhetorically, however, for those whose practical intellects have
been properly pre-conditioned to receive and maintain this truth, and for those
whose "passions" and "social interchange" are likewise caught-up in it, the
existence of God assumes a self-evident character. It is a self-evident character *per
modum*, not *per se*, better known to us as Aristotle would say, or self-evident
according to the mode of the knower, as Aquinas would say. This is rhetorical
"self-evidence." It is general, not universal. It is how God's existence can be "as
plain as day" to an unlettered Irishman as well as an Oxford don, yet be obscure
and doubtful to another man. The philosophical mode of knowledge is a legitimate
mode, but so too is the rhetorical. Though their means differ, their object--whether
attained or not--is the same; the adequation of mind to reality.

Newman is so rhetorical in mind that he even reverses the Ramist
absorption of rhetoric into dialectic. Newman virtually (though not completely)
takes philosophy and turns it into rhetoric. He openly announces his focus on
probability in the *Notebook*, and in so doing he comes dangerously close to
equating all philosophy with probability:

> All I aim at is to draw out a case, or a "probable doctrine"
> and I think this enough, because there is very little teaching
> in this subject matter, which is more than probable, though
> one system or theory may be more probable than another. I
> am not speaking of *particular* doctrines, but of a system of
> philosophy.[69]

Newman is so caught up in the probable mode of argumentation that he
comes close to considering philosophy itself a kind of probability. That he does not
do so ultimately must be gleaned from the context of the entirety of his writings.
There is simply too much affirmation of the demonstrative certainty of reason and
philosophy for Newman to relegate the whole to probability. There is likewise too
much affirmation of the weakness of philosophy or reason for anyone to assume
Newman was comfortable with those departments of knowledge. Jost will maintain

that Newman indeed does precede in thought contemporary theorists who declare "Probability is all." That assertion will be taken up later, but it remains that even in this passage Newman reserves some philosophical teachings as being beyond probability. He also is speaking pointedly of systems and schools. In short, Newman's saying "most philosophy is probability" is another instance of his rhetorical habit, for he is clearly referring to the practical fact that differences exist between systems and philosophies. Not everyone agrees in philosophy, so he will treat the subject in controversial fashion as a matter of probability (a very similar procedure will be seen in the *Grammar* regarding first principles).

Thus Newman underscores his own, rhetorical approach to the subject and identifies his assertions as probabilities. It is no coincidence that this modest disclaimer (he had just finished saying he would merely present his own notions of psychological facts) is itself effective rhetoric. It disarms philosophical opponents who are no longer facing one about to demonstrate them into a corner. His technique here, as elsewhere, is not confrontational but invitational. Newman confesses his motives and means are rhetorical. Indeed he may not say as much; he may be convinced that the efforts in the *Notebook* are as philosophical as anyone else's efforts. Nevertheless, it is clear that these discourses are ever profoundly probabilistic, practical, and designed to effect assent in a variety of people.

PHILOSOPHICAL RHETORIC?

Finally, this brings us to the question of whether "bad philosophy" can be "good rhetoric." We have seen contradictions, blendings of incompatible principles, and near rhetorical usurpations of philosophy. From a Thomistic standpoint, treating Newman's "philosophy" as a failure seems justified. But this is justified only if one insists on reading Newman for philosophy. Enough has already been said here about the irreducibly rhetorical nature of these "philosophical" discourses to make reading Newman for philosophy extremely precarious. The very question "can bad philosophy be good rhetoric" is wrongly stated. Though Newman considered these discourses philosophical, they cannot properly be required to do the work of philosophy. Theirs is a different task. Still, can something so philosophically influenced by dubious principles be good rhetoric? The answer must be "yes." The purpose here is to identify and characterize Newman's habit of mind, not to evaluate it; but one can say that good rhetoric may be derived from questionable philosophy. In fact it happens all the time. The notion of reality as "flux" may be discredited philosophically, but it can be most useful in sensitizing an audience to very real conditions of our experience. There is an old saying that any good sermon could be convicted of at least three heresies. Religious dogma is too full and multi-faceted to be completely laid out with theological precision in a single sermon. Rhetorical discourse (and thought) can often make good use of ideas incomplete or even incorrect considered in the light of more formal, especially philosophical, modes of reasoning.

It is difficult to believe that, had Weatherby's wish come true, had Newman been a sound Thomist in philosophy, he would have been able to reverse the course of nineteenth-century skepticism. Contrary to Weatherby's assertion that Newman could have turned the tide of modernism, a mid-nineteenth-century Thomist would have been lost in a tower of philosophical babble. As the shoulder-shrugging comments of the theologians in Rome suggest, there was precious little room for serious Thomism even in Catholic Rome. Much less was England prepared to be informed and moved by a Thomistic scholar, no matter how prestigious of name. The twentieth century has seen great labors by such notable Thomists as Maritain, Gilson, Pieper, Owens and others who, while having an impact, have hardly seen the reversal of philosophical or theological modernism.

If Newman were to act according to his strong, even missionary sense of purpose, he perforce must jolt a culture fed on empiricism (and growing into materialism) into considering the possibility of the supernatural. To do this, the language employed must be recognizable to the audience. Newman did not consciously adapt the philosophical language of his contemporaries; he too grew up in the prevailing intellectual milieu and was thus "in his age." But his own habit of mind was of another age, and as such he used the terms familiar to his audience while employing them for his own purposes. He not only used nineteenth-century philosophical principles to create rhetoric, he advocated rhetorical modes of thought as well. Using language familiar to his peers, Newman communicated to them things lost to the era--personalism in cognition, the non-scientific aspects of certain "logics" or modes of certainty, the necessity of moral and imaginative preparation for kinds of knowledge and faith, the limits of demonstrative or scientific reasoning, the dignity and certainty available to probability, the hollowness of naive empiricism and rationalism, the possibility of the supernatural and the unseen. Newman may have failed. If success means effecting a large-scale realization and recognition of principles hitherto unacknowledged, then Newman failed. The world did not turn around, did not, as a whole, accept rhetorical modes of thought, certainty, and knowledge. But at the very least he confronted the growing scientific materialism and mechanistic rationalism with arguments and questions it could not answer. Indeed, to this day, despite the change of time and particular circumstances, Newman's questions remain largely unanswered by a scientism at once more popular yet more vulnerable than its nineteenth-century antecedents.

IX. Newman's *Grammar Of Assent*

> *You do yet taste*
> *Some subtilties o' the isle, that will not let you*
> *Believe things certain.*
> Tempest V, i.

The *Grammar's* Purpose

There is a very real sense in which Newman's *Essay in Aid of a Grammar of Assent* is the principal work of his life. Although his *Apologia* is most often read, and the various collections of sermons are most copious, the *Grammar* is the work closest to the heart of Newman's work as a thinker and author. It rolls into a single text his theory and practice of rhetorical personalism, the purposive character of his life's work, and his vision of fallen man in quest of rectification of mind and soul. The other texts were largely occasional, written upon a "call" to answer a particular need. While the *Grammar*, too, has a "call" and answers a need, it was an internal call felt by Newman to address a skeptical, liberal habit of mind creeping more deeply into the cultural fabric. As we have seen, this habit of mind was a Gorgon of misconceptions: mechanistic rationalism, material scientism, and depersonalized conceptions of mind and knowledge. The *Grammar* was a work Newman felt quite literally to be upon his conscience to write and confront these Gorgon braids of error. It was written not because of a particular occasion but because of a general attitude and creeping rigidity of thought.

Though a number of Newman's works were painful to write, without question the *Grammar* was the most difficult in the conventional sense. Newman worked on the text, off and on, for well over twenty years. He explored the preliminary ground for the book as early as the *Oxford University Sermons*, and large parts of the *Philosophical Notebook* are early, abortive approaches to the subject. The text, actually published March 15, 1870, had been begun in earnest four years earlier while Newman was vacationing in Switzerland. The topic had occupied Newman's mind for many years, but at Gilon in Switzerland "a thought came into my head as the clue, the 'Open Sesame,' of the whole subject, and I at once wrote it down, and I pursued it about the Lake of Lucerne. Then when I came home, I began in earnest, and have slowly got through it."[1]

The awkward, unwieldy title gives fair warning as to the seemingly arid subject of the book. Newman himself described it as dull and technical, though he consistently corrected any who thought it a systematic treatise; the emphasis, he insisted, is on essay or inquiry.[2] Despite the aridity of the text, and to Newman's surprise, the book sold well and was popular among educated readers.[3] Perhaps he should not have been surprised; after all, it was an attempt at combating what the author felt was a fundamental evil of the day. The "rhetoricality" of the text, though largely unexplored, has not gone unnoticed by critics. Edward P.J. Corbett asserts that the *Grammar* is "distinctively rhetorical in its province and its method." As a rhetorician, he notes that this province is perhaps unusually limited in Newman "to the exploration of how people are influenced to grant their assent to propositions."[4] J.H. Walgrave's oft cited *Newman the Theologian*, while appropriating Newman to theological science, still observes that the *Grammar* is a "markedly polemical" work that inquires "into the workings of [the] mind."[5] And in an excellent article on "Aristotelian Roots of Newman's Illative Sense," Gerard Verdeke affirms that the *Grammar* is "still coping with the topic of persuasion."[6]

Nevertheless, most critics have read this important text in a primarily philosophical or theological light.[7] This is natural enough, for the technicality and complexity of the work acts as both a lure to philosophers and, also, a repellant to literary readers. The text is philosophical, logical, but it is so in manner; its proper *subject* is, rather, rhetoric. In explicating the *Grammar*, Newman will be allowed to speak for himself whenever possible (it is difficult to elucidate one so preeminently lucid). But before we approach the actual analysis of the *Grammar*, the purpose of the book can reveal much about its rhetorical nature.

The reason for writing the *Grammar* was very much an apologetic one, despite its lack of an occasioned "call" or controversy. Its writing had for its background a deeper, more abiding controversy than some verbal conflict over a public event. The deeper controversy was that between the religious mind and the secular, materialistic, or rationalistic one. Broadly speaking, the *Grammar* constituted a refutation or reply to the rationalistic conceptual norms which increasingly were becoming the only *loci* or seats of thought about any subject. Characterized as it was by either the abstract empiricism of Locke or an abstract systematic rationalism of Kant, the scientific materialism of the day was most vulnerable in being so wholly abstract and removed from daily experience.

Newman recognized that a non-theological apologetic might well effect what abstract, systematic apologetic could not do: it could call into question the prevailing skepticism by striking at its abstractness. A swordsman can often defeat an enemy by selecting a weapon different from that being used by his opponent. But the apologetic was not merely a matter of argumentative tactics. The habits of mind resulting in de-personalized, non-, or anti-rhetorical assumptions about knowledge required emendation if religious discourse was to have any meaning. The point, Newman thought, did need to be made that the prevailing skepticism employed unreasonable and unworkable criteria for knowledge and certainty. As Francis Bacchus observes, people of Newman's generation virtually equated "Mathematical proof" with "Scientific proof."[8] In particular, Newman's old friend William Froude acted as an embodiment of these habits of mind and conceptions, for despite long correspondence with Newman and the Catholic conversion of his wife and four children, Froude remained convinced that religious skepticism was the single reasonable position. Though a great friend of Newman's and a sincere inquirer into the grounds for faith, Froude "stuck by his argument that the complete assent implied in Catholic faith presupposed absolutely certain proofs that no theologians could provide. Such," says Stanley Jaki, "was as rationalistic a posture as there could be."[9]

It is not difficult to perceive the imaginative strength of such a rationalistic posture. After all, it is only fair to require proof if one is to be convinced of something. The key, obviously, is what "proof" means with regard to what kinds of subject matters. A veritable mathematics of religion was what was required by Froude and others, and this, it is no surprise, was not forthcoming. So Newman's strategy was to focus on the idea of proof, not as it is in it itself, but as it affects the mind. Two important actions for Newman result from this approach. The first was to establish that (and explain how) people quite often follow formal demonstrations without giving assent to the conclusion. Even "mathematical proof" is not as simple as it may appear. Newman

> knew that there is a vast difference between understanding the meaning of a demonstration and assenting to its conclusion.... [He] knew full well that an intellect can find itself confronted with a truth whose extreme probability is a practical certitude, without finding in itself the strength required to give this an unconditional assent.[10]

Thus the first step was to weaken the rationalists' blind faith in the surety of "demonstration"--a parallel tactic to that at work in the *Notebook* where Newman tries to shake the materialists' bland confidence in material phenomena.

The second and more important action Newman took was to show that everyone, including these same strict rationalists, did not actually live in accordance to the dictates of rationalist philosophy. That is, in actual fact people gave full assent, were entirely certain of countless things, for which either they had no demonstrative knowledge or for which no such knowledge was even possible. In the words of Jaki, "The counterargument was to show that absolute assent is given on countless occasions in daily life as well as in general intellectual and moral domains, though absolute proofs are not on hand." He adds, pointing to the rhetorical consequence of Newman's procedure, "Dispensing with 'absolute' proofs would but invite a shift toward tactful persuasion."[11] Not only are assents given *sans* strict demonstration, but they are often given without conscious awareness of their grounds or evidence; there are many assents "*resting on premises mainly or partly implicit*, convictions grounded on evidence *incapable of being placed distinctly before the mind*, but which a man deliberately judges to be irresistible. . . ."[12] How does this happen? Newman's object in the *Grammar* is to show that the mind often comes to the recognition of truth not through scientific or philosophical demonstration, but through an implicit (illative) intellectual operation of evaluating the cumulation of probability. More about the intellectual character of this "probability" later; for the present it is enough to recall that it is precisely upon probable matters that rhetoric operates.

In taking up this strategy in his apologetic, Newman has brought the matter onto ground familiar and comfortable. He is back in the realm of the personal, individual mind and the concrete, practical situation. As Thomas Vargish notes, "His impulse is always to employ psychological discoveries as evidence for the truth of Christian doctrine."[13] The impulse confirms the rhetorical nature of this text as well as Newman's general habit of mind, for such evidences are by nature "probable" as distinct from "necessary," and "general" as distinct from philosophically "universal."

We miss the epistemological significance of rhetorical matter if we persist in thinking it "merely" probable and general; Newman's whole point is that this domain does attain certitude, knowledge. But the preliminary, rhetorical aspect of the *Grammar* is attested to by Newman's own description of the work. While mulling the matter over, well before his "Eureka" around the Lake of Lucerne,

Newman wrote his philosopher friend, Dr. Meynell, speculating upon the character of his contemplated book:

> If I wrote a new work, it would be on "the popular, practical, and personal evidence of Christianity"--i.e. as contrasted with the scientific, and its object would be to show that a given individual, high or low, has as much right (has a real rational grounds) to be certain, as a learned theologian who knows the scientific evidence.[14]

Ten years did not alter Newman's conception of the work: "I treat of propositions only in their bearing upon concrete matter, and I am mainly concerned with Assent; with Inference, in its relation to Assent, and only such inference as is not demonstration. . . ."[15]

Concrete matter is beyond or outside of philosophical demonstration, and throughout the work Newman testifies to the practical nature of his subject. Later in the text, Newman asserts what today might be considered a paradox: "Science in all its departments has too much simplicity and exactness, from the nature of the case, to be the measure of fact. In its very perfection lies its incompetency to settle particulars and details."[16] Such particulars and details include ethical and moral matters, matters that (as Newman reminds us) Aristotle assigns to judgment, a practical faculty of intellect. "[T]he philosopher refers us to no code of laws, to no moral treatise, because no science of life, *applicable to the case of an individual*, has been or can be written [emphasis added]."[17] This is because, as Aristotle and Aquinas maintained, there is no "science" of the particular. Newman writes here a rare and important footnote. He cites Aristotle's *Ethics*, affirming that the contingent matter Aristotle deals with is called "concrete" in the *Grammar*. He also makes an even more important assertion, implying how he will make explicit what is only implicit in Aristotle: "he does not treat of it [judgment] in that work in its general relation to truth and the affirmation of truth . . . ."[18]

Thus the epistemological/rhetorical province Newman will treat is outlined and defined. What he speaks of belongs to the practical intellect, is philosophically general and contingent, and is strictly psychological, descriptive, experiential. This is the ground of rhetorical reasoning and the matter of rhetorical discourse. All that is missing is the word "rhetoric." Again, in outlining the purpose and scope of the *Grammar*, and before plunging into an explication of the text itself, it is important to recall a prior distinction: a thing may be philosophical without being philosophy. The *Grammar* is an excellent example of a text philosophical in attribute but rhetorical in essence.

APPREHENSION, NOTIONAL AND REAL

Despite the complexity of the text itself, it is not difficult to summarize many (though by no means all) of its salient theses and points, especially with regard to rhetorical cognition. After looking at the text, we shall explore its significance relative to the idea of truth, skepticism, rhetoric, and rhetorical personalism.

The first important distinction Newman makes in the *Grammar* is the famous one between "notional" and "real" apprehension. He speaks here of how the mind holds or apprehends things and propositions, not things as they are in themselves. "Now apprehension, as I have said, has two subject matters:-- according as language expresses things external to us, or our own thoughts, so is apprehension real or notional. It is notional in the grammarian, it is real in the experimentalist."[19] This is followed by a series of examples, but Newman returns to clarify first real apprehension, then notional. "Real apprehension is, as I have said, in the first instance an experience or information about the concrete."[20] This includes the memory, for it recalls to us the information or experience of concrete things. Such may include objects, but also includes impressions or judgments ("The prospect is charming"[21]). It is interesting that, even when discussing real apprehension, Newman veers toward the consideration of the imaginative impact of such apprehension. He observes that the medical arts are filled with "shocking realities of disease and physical suffering"--they are experiential, but of necessity these arts employ a "notional phraseology" full of abstract Greek and Latin terms "stripped of the association of the facts" as a "protection to the practitioner."[22] Perhaps in order to work effectively, the physician must veil the real apprehension of his art in notional terms which enable him to de-personalize the suffering and distress inherent in his work.

Notional apprehension ("our own thoughts"), on the other hand, is not of concrete things but of abstraction. By "abstraction" Newman does not mean the agent intellect's abstraction of form, but rather the mind's removal of particularities for the apprehension of a class. "Experience tells us only of individual things, and these things are innumerable."[23] We are constituted, he says, such that we compare and contrast everything:

> Instinctively, even though unconsciously, we are ever instituting comparisons between the manifold phenomena of the external world. . . . In processes of this kind we regard things, not as they are in themselves, but mainly as they stand in relation to each other. We look at nothing simply for

> its own sake; we cannot look at any one thing without
> keeping our eyes on a multitude of other things besides.
> "Man" is no longer what he really is, an individual presented
> to us by our senses, but as we read him in the light of those
> comparisons and contrasts which we have made him suggest
> to us. He is attenuated into an aspect, or relegated to his
> place in a classification. Thus his appellation is made to
> suggest, not the real being which he is in this or that
> specimen of himself, but a definition. If I might use a harsh
> metaphor, I should say he is made the logarithm of his true
> self, and in that shape is worked with the ease and
> satisfaction of logarithms.[24]

Thus a notion is an abstraction in the sense of being "an aspect"; it is an abstraction
in the modern sense of "leaving things out" rather than the Thomistic sense of
"bringing things in."

Newman goes on to describe the effect notional apprehension has on the
imagination when things that are in themselves real are apprehended notionally:

> And thus it comes to pass that individual propositions about
> the concrete almost cease to be, and are diluted or starved
> into abstract notions. The events of history and the
> characters who figure in it lose their individuality. States and
> governments, society and its component parts, cities,
> nations, even the physical face of the country, things past,
> and things contemporary, all that fulness of meaning which I
> have described is absent, necessarily becomes to the
> multitude of men nothing but a heap of notions, little more
> intelligible than the beauties of a prospect to the short-
> sighted, or the music of a great master to a listener who has
> no ear.[25]

What is too rarely remembered is that Newman's description of notional
apprehension entirely leaves alone the truth of the apprehension. That is, Newman
does not say that the notional is untrue. Quite the contrary. His obvious disparagement of it has led many to equate it with "untrue," but notional apprehension is
belittled by Newman not for its lack of truth-value, but for its weak impact on the
imagination, its "unpersuasiveness," if you will.

This sensitivity to persuasion and the impact of the imagination on
Newman's part is further evident when he compares notional and real apprehension. In fact, most of his discussion here is just this comparison (almost as if
performing what he asserted to be so automatic a function), rather than separate
definition and description. "Of these two modes of apprehending propositions,
notional and real, real is the stronger; I mean by stronger more vivid and forcible
[not "more true"]."[26] He adds that "intellectual ideas cannot compete in
effectiveness with the experience of concrete facts."[27] Effectiveness for what? Here

the rhetorical thrust (and application) of the *Grammar* is made evident. The end of rhetoric is action.

Not that real apprehension, as such, impels to action, any more than notional; but it excites and stimulates the affections and passions, by bringing facts home to them as motive causes. Thus it indirectly brings about what the apprehension of large principles, of general laws, or of moral obligations, rarely effect. Neither "apprehensions" result in automatic action, but a rhetorician who strives to create real apprehension in his audience (in, say, epideictic circumstances: bringing an historical figure to life so that a monument may be erected) will be far more likely to succeed than one who cites the abstract principle of moral duty. Newman is describing his "whole man" here and how the man moves. There are passions and affections involved in action, not merely abstract principles, and this remains true even of internal actions such as assents. Passions will not (and should not) create the assent if it is rightly made, but they will assist in providing the motive cause, the sense of antecedent probabilities the illative sense will employ in evaluating concrete matters and previous assents.

The comparison continues in a manner often forgotten. While disparaging the notional, Newman carefully gives it its due, even revealing the weakness inherent in the real:

> Each use of propositions has its own excellence and service-ableness, and each has its own imperfection. To apprehend notionally is to have breadth of mind, but to be shallow; to apprehend really is to be deep, but to be narrow-minded. The latter is the conservative principle of knowledge, and the former the principle of its advancement. Without the apprehension of notions, we should for ever pace round one small circle of knowledge; without a firm hold upon things, we shall waste ourselves in vague speculations. However, real apprehension has the precedence, as being the scope and end and the test of notional; and the fuller is the mind's hold upon things or what it considers such, the more fertile is it in its aspects of them, and the more practical in its definitions.[28]

Newman had just finished saying "however divergent and independent in their [notional and real] direction they cannot really be inconsistent with each other . . ." --an idea which calls to mind the unity of truth detailed in the *Idea of a University.* Truth, it seems, is not a stranger even to notional apprehension, but the most important feature of Newman's notional and real apprehension remains its rhetorical distinction of force: "what is concrete exerts a force and makes an impression on the mind which nothing abstract can rival."[29]

ASSENT AND UNCONDITIONALITY

The features noticed in notional and real apprehension carry over, not surprisingly, into notional and real assent. Assent differs from apprehension in the tenor of its intellectual act. Apprehension is just what the term suggests--a holding. Assent is an act of acceptance. It depends upon apprehension, but assent is its own, separate intellectual act. Assent "is in itself the absolute acceptance of a proposition without any condition . . . it presupposes the condition . . . of some concomitant apprehension of its terms."[30] It differs from apprehension in pronouncing a verdict, as it were. "A spoon is a useful catapult of bread-crumbs" may be an apprehension; the assent to it would be "It is true that a spoon is a useful catapult of bread-crumbs." Thus assent is in itself an "absolute acceptance" and unconditional.

These are important points, and Newman is at some pains to clarify them. Assent is quite different from mere assertion, since "acceptance" presupposes "some apprehension of the matter" and not, as is possible in assertion, mere empty declaration. But assent is also more than assertion plus some kind of apprehension. As an intellectual act it has its own character, usually called "unconditional." Gilson summarizes the doctrine thus: "[T]he intellectual act of assenting itself does not admit of degrees. It is either given, or not given; that is all."[31] To indulge in a bit of mechanistic analysis ourselves, assent is binary, 0-1. There are no fractions. It may be supported or initiated by inference and evidence, but as an act of its own it is not dependent upon such preliminary matter.

> As apprehension is a concomitant, so inference is ordinarily the antecedent of assent;--on this surely I need not enlarge;--but neither apprehension nor inference interferes with the unconditional character of assent, viewed in itself. The circumstances of an act, however necessary to it, do not enter into the act; assent is in its own nature absolute and unconditional. . . .[32]

This is important, for Locke had pronounced that assent was of variable strength, a matter of degree, dependent upon the strength of the inferences leading up to it. Newman strenuously denied this position, insisting that it confused "conclusion" with assent, and did away with assent itself. If assent is not its own act, why do we even refer to it? In fact assent has no degrees and as an act is independent of any inferences and conclusions leading up to it. What Locke mistook for degree or variable strength in assent is actually the strength or vividness of the apprehension concomitant with--but distinct from--assent:

> I observe that it is this variation in the mind's apprehension of an object to which it assents, and not any incompleteness in the assent itself, that leads us to speak of strong and weak assents, as if Assent itself admitted of degrees. In either mode of apprehension, be it real or be it notional, the assent preserves its essential characteristic of being unconditional.[33]

And later: "But again, when we carefully consider the matter, it will be found that this increase or decrease of strength does not lie in the assent itself, but in its circumstances and concomitants; for instance, in the emotions, in the ratiocinative faculty, or in the imagination."[34]

Not being, then, a kind of by-product of inferences but being distinct from such conditionality, the concrete reality of assent begins to make sense. We begin to see how to account for the day-to-day assents people make without having to construct dubious logic-chains of inferences. Since assent is unconditional, that is, distinct from inferences, it can be given, fully and without degree, to many things incapable of syllogistic proof:

> Treating the subject then, not according to a priori fitness, but according to the facts of human nature, as they are found in the concrete action of life, I find numberless cases in which we do not assent at all, none in which assent is evidently conditional;--and many, as I shall now proceed to show, in which it is unconditional, and these in subject-matters which admit of nothing higher than probable reasoning.[35]

By "probable" Newman does not mean "uncertain"; he merely means distinct from syllogistic demonstration. We see the opening of one of the apologetic purposes in the *Grammar*: to describe a kind of knowing everyone employs with unquestioning certitude but which "violates" the demands of prevailing mechanistic requirements for certainty. Finally, assent as such (degree-less, unconditional) is incompatible with doubt because it is a complete, non-partial act in itself. If by doubt one means simply the study of an assent to determine what reasons are producible for it, it is not doubt at all, merely investigation--the assent still stands. However, if by doubt one means reservation as to the truth of the proposition, then no assent exists. Thus, in matters of religion, to "doubt" an article of the Catholic faith is to cease to be Catholic. One cannot assent and not assent at once:

> Thus it is sometimes spoken of as a hardship that a Catholic is not allowed to inquire into the truth of his Creed;--of course he cannot, if he would retain the name of believer. He cannot be both inside and outside of the Church at once. It is merely common sense to tell him that, if he is seeking, he has not found. If seeking includes doubting, and doubting excludes believing, then the Catholic who sets about inquiring, thereby declares that he is not a Catholic. He has already lost faith. And this is his best defence to himself for inquiring, viz. that he is no longer a Catholic, and wished to become one. They who would forbid him to inquire, would in that case be shutting the stable-door after the steed is stolen. What can he do better than to inquire, if he is in doubt? how else can he become a Catholic again? Not to inquire is in his case to be satisfied with disbelief.[36]

ASSENTS NOTIONAL AND REAL

Newman's next important distinction is between notional assent and real assent. These are simply assents made upon things apprehended, either notionally or really. The assents partake of the character of apprehensions. Both are full, unconditional, valid, complete intellectual acts of assent. Both have strengths and weaknesses. Notional assents are easy to argue and describe because they refer to terms notional and easy to formulate and manipulate. By the same token, such manipulations are often "cold" and unmoving. Real assents are more forceful and vivid, yet more difficult to formulate and describe to others. Again, Gilson is succinct:

> Real assent is not a more valid form of notional assent; it is an assent to realities. Notional assent is not a less valid form of real assent: it is an assent to notions, and its validity entirely depends upon that of its major and minor premises and conclusions. True enough, because it directly or indirectly bears upon realities, real assent (that is, assent to *res*) is more vivid, more impressive, and more striking that the mere apprehension of notional inferences, but the truth of notional inference does not require, *qua* inference, any further confirmation in its own line. This shows how completely irrelevant are the objections directed against the doctrine of Newman by those who reproach him with a leaning to fideism or with an ingrained mistrust in the validity of theological demonstrations.[37]

Like apprehension, real assent bears upon action or practice in a way notional apprehension does not, since it appeals to the imagination. Again, it does not produce action; it is an intellectual act "of which the object is presented to it by the imagination; and though the pure intellect does not lead to action, nor the imagination either, yet the imagination has the means . . . of stimulating those powers of the mind from which action proceeds."[38] This is why Newman calls real assent the "one secret of persuasiveness and influence in the public stage of the world."[39]

This does not mean that real assent is some sort of meta-rhetorical panacea; as appealed to or employed in rhetoric, real assent has its difficulties. Newman is quite consistent here. Although the imaginative, practical quality of real assent is persuasive, it is also difficult to marshall or wield effectively. The beauty of a syllogism is its ease of employment. The curse of real assent is its difficulty of employment. By definition, real apprehension and assents are personal almost beyond the point of communal recovery. Real assents

> are of a personal character, each individual having his own, and being known by them. . . . They depend on personal experience; and the experience of one man is not the experience of another. Real assent, then, as the experience which it presupposes, is proper to the individual, and, as such, thwarts rather than promotes the intercourse of man with man. It shuts itself up, as it were, in its own home, or at least it is its own witness and its own standard; and, as in the instances above given, it cannot be reckoned on, anticipated, accounted for, inasmuch as it is the accident of this man or that.[40]

Is there no common ground? Has Nuttall's "common sky" vanished into the night of incommunicable isolation? Not in the least. Because a common reality is the font of all personal experience, the commonality necessary for communication is inherently present in experience. In other words, people may experience things in their own way, but the things experienced are common. Newman asserts the control reality has over our individual, personal experience:

> If "five hundred brethren at once" saw our risen Lord, that common experience would not be a law, but a personal accident which was the prerogative of each. . . . [However,] at the same time it would necessarily be a principle of sympathy and a bond of intercourse between those whose minds had been thus variously wrought into a common assent, far stronger than could follow upon any multitude of mere notions which they unanimously held.[41]

Real assents, then are personal, individual, can be persuasively used or created, and are conducive to action. Nevertheless, the peculiar qualities inherent in real apprehension and assents that make them so persuasive and forceful also result in there being peculiar dangers. Real assent is not synonymous with "assent to something real or true." The imaginative basis upon which such apprehensions are founded can lead the "apprehendor" of them to assents beyond the reasonable claim of the apprehension. The forcefulness of the assent makes it particularly difficult to overcome such an error when it occurs. Heaven help the man, says Newman, who erroneously assents to something, thinking that he assents to it on the most obvious of bases.

> An image, with the characters of perfect veracity and faithfulness, may be ever so distinct and eloquent an object presented before the mind (or, as it is sometimes called, an "objectum internum," or a "subject-object"); but, nevertheless, there may be no external reality in the case, corresponding to it, in spite of its impressiveness. One of the most remarkable instances of this fallacious impressiveness is the illusion which possesses the minds of able men, those especially who are exercised in physical investigations, in favour of the inviolability of the laws of nature. Philosophers of the school of Hume discard the very supposition of miracles, and scornfully refuse to hear evidence in their behalf in given instances, from their intimate experience of physical order and of the ever-recurring connexion of antecedent and consequent. Their imagination usurps the functions of reason; and they cannot bring themselves even to entertain as a hypothesis (and this is all that they are asked to do) a thought contrary to that vivid impression of which they are the victims, that the uniformity of nature, which they witness hour by hour, is equivalent to a necessary, inviolable law.[42]

One's knowledge that physical nature has certain properties (be they sub-atomic or astro-physical) is just that: knowledge of particular properties, knowledge that material things interact in a certain way. Such knowledge cannot validly warrant the proposition that physical nature *must be* this or that way. Such a proposition clearly exceeds the limits of physical science, yet due to the imaginative force of seeing the consistency of phenomena, the leap is made without consciousness of the violence done to reason. Though philosophers of science have long known the untenableness of the idea of "laws of nature," the popular conception of them stands now just as it did in Newman's own day.

RELIGIOUS ASSENTS

Newman's discussion of real assent brings into sharper focus the religious aspect of the *Grammar*. Employing the distinction between real and notional assents, Newman carefully delineates the domain of the two assents within religion:

> We are now able to determine what a dogma of faith is, and
> what it is to believe it. A dogma is a proposition; it stands for
> a notion or for a thing; and to believe it is to give the assent
> of the mind to it, as it stands for the one or for the other. To
> give a real assent to it is an act of religion; to give a notional,
> is a theological act. It is discerned, rested in, and
> appropriated as a reality, by the religious imagination; it is
> held as a truth, by the theological intellect.[43]

By "an act of religion" Newman means the personal, imaginative, and even devotional apprehension of a supernatural truth. By "a theological act" he means the apprehension of the same truth in its abstract, more impersonal, notional aspect. It is important to realize that Newman does not create a bifurcated religious mind here; the *Grammar* is deeply integrated and unitive. He immediately emphasizes the whole man and the harmonious, simultaneous operation of both kinds of assent:

> Not as if there were in fact, or could be, any line of
> demarcation or party-wall between these two modes of
> assent, the religious and the theological. As intellect is
> common to all men as well as imagination, every religious
> man is to a certain extent a theologian, and no theology can
> start or thrive without the initiative and abiding presence of
> religion.[44]

Here we begin to see why Newman counseled inquirers, especially intellectual ones, to pray for a good will and for devotion to the truth. Purely notional treatment of religion threatens to obscure its "religious" or immediate and personal aspect. Thought must be joined to devotion. For this same reason, the best theologian is one who is also a saint. Newman constantly swerves toward the integration of human faculties even as he delineates their distinctions. He especially deplores the absence of an integrated religious life when bringing these distinctions to bear on contemporary English Christianity. The notional and real explicate Newman's famous criticism of English religion:

> Theology, as such, always is notional, as being scientific:
> religion, as being personal, should be real; but, except
> within a small range of subjects, it commonly is not real in
> England. As to Catholic populations, such as those of
> medieval Europe, or the Spain of this day, or quasi-Catholic
> as those of Russia, among them assent to religious objects is
> real, not notional. To them the Supreme Being, our Lord,
> the Blessed Virgin, Angels and Saints, heaven and hell, are

as present as if they were objects of sight; but such a faith does not suit the genius of modern England. There is in the literary world just now an affectation of calling religion a "sentiment;" and it must be confessed that usually it is nothing more with our own people, educated or rude.[45]

Conversely, a time or place of real religious assent without a balancing notional assent has its own dangers. Recall the weaknesses in the real: intensity can stimulate adherence to false assents, and real apprehensions or assents are often difficult to formulate. A religiously "real" but rather non-notional people will tend toward enthusiasm and religious excess. This is what Newman meant when he said a popular religion (including Catholicism) is ever a corrupt one. As he explained, he did not mean that such a religion ceased to sanctify or was corrupt *per se*; rather, an uneducated populace had a tendency to neglect the notional, thus falling prey to potentially false real assents--in mild instances such as calling a local favorite a "saint" without due investigation, or in severe instances, the actual mixing of pagan, animistic religions and Christianity. In this light--the unity of notional and real assents--Newman's famous declaration that his favorite "devotional formulary" was the Athanasian Creed makes sense. "It is not a mere collection of notions, however momentous. It is a psalm or hymn of praise. . . . It appeals to the imagination quite as much as to the intellect."[46] This is why a dogma (There are three Persons in one God.) must never be taught as a merely abstract truth. Newman insists that dogmas themselves are every bit as real as they are notional, and they call for real, personal apprehension and assent (as well as abstract notional comprehension and assent).

Finally, as regards assent, Newman addresses the fully apologetic purpose of his *Grammar* in asking how can one have any real apprehension and assent of the existence of God. Theologians may prove that God exists, but such proofs leave most people behind. What warrant do we have for a real as well as a notional apprehension of God's existence? "Can I rise to what I have called an imaginative apprehension of it? Can I believe as if I saw?"[47] Such a "high assent" requires some kind of experience. Are only mystics able, then, to attain a real apprehension of God? Not at all. There are a number of ways one can obtain such experience, but Newman's rhetorical sense brought him to advance a particular means of such apprehension: conscience. Conscience is something everyone knows and experiences. It is no secret that it was Newman's favorite apologetic tool:

As from a multitude of instinctive perceptions, acting in particular instances, of something beyond the senses, we

> generalize the notion of an external world, and then picture
> that world in and according to those particular phenomena
> from which we started, so from the perceptive power which
> identifies the intimations of conscience with the
> reverberations or echoes (so to say) of an external
> admonition, we proceed on to the notion of a Supreme Ruler
> and Judge, and then again we image Him and His attributes
> in those recurring intimations, out of which, as mental
> phenomena, our recognition of His existence was originally
> gained.[48]

Though Aquinas' *Summa Contra Gentiles* was written to combat Islam, it was not meant to conduct the actual argument; it was to be read by those who would in turn construct the required apologetic. The *Grammar* is much the same: it is meant as an exploratory essay into the "means of persuasion." Newman confesses here that, though he did not intend to "prove the Being of a God, yet I have found it impossible to avoid saying where I look for the proof of it."[49] Rhetorical habit indeed. As the tenth chapter of the *Grammar* demonstrates, our author cannot refrain from apologetic. Though the text is meant as an exploration of rhetorical knowledge, he concludes it with an extended rhetorical argument in favor of Christianity. That argument, as well as the details of his proof from conscience, do not concern us here, for this study is primarily limited to his idea of rhetorical knowledge itself. But it is worth noting the depth of his rhetorical habit, not just in theory, but in practice as well.

CERTITUDE

Newman's text explores two main theses, the nature of certitude and the illative sense. After so clearly expounding upon assent, Newman readily analyzes certitude. Certitude is a complex and reflex assent, a complete act of the intellect:

> Certitude, as I have said, is the perception of a truth with the
> perception that it is a truth, or the consciousness of
> knowing, as expressed in the phrase, "I know that I know,"
> or "I know that I know that I know,"--or simply "I know;"
> for one reflex assertion of the mind about self sums up the
> series of self-consciousnesses without the need of any actual
> evolution of them.[50]

It is a complex assent because of its reflexivity; it assents to an assent. Because it is a kind of assent, it possesses a fully intellectual character. It is not a feeling. However, "feelings" do result from certitude. One such feeling is "intellectual security"--the intellectual counterpart to the repose one experiences upon performance of a virtuous act. That is, as the object of the intellect is truth, the knowledge of attainment of the object yields satisfaction.

Because certitude occurs upon the recognition of one's holding a truth, it does not brook any contradictory proposition. "No man is certain of a truth, who can endure the thought of the fact of its contradictory existing or occurring; and that not from any set purpose or effort to reject that thought, but, as I have said, by the spontaneous action of the intellect."[51] The interesting thing about certitude, and what further demonstrates Newman's recognition of the value of the notional, is that all certitude is by definition notional. The certitude may regard a real assent, but in itself, the "It-is-true-that . . . " of certitude is a notional proposition; this is an essential observation and should be remembered while Newman makes his most important point about certitude. Certitude, Newman insists, is indefectible. It cannot change. Once someone is certain of a thing, he cannot become uncertain.

This doctrine is perhaps the most difficult to understand in Newman because it seems to defy common experience. First, let us see how Newman explains the indefectibility, then how he accounts for the experience of "changing" certitudes:

> It is the characteristic of certitude that its object is a truth, a truth as such, a proposition as true. There are right and wrong convictions, and certitude is a right conviction; if it is not right with a consciousness of being right, it is not certitude. Now truth cannot change; what is once truth is always truth; and the human mind is made for truth, and so rests in truth, as it cannot rest in falsehood. When then it once becomes possessed of a truth, what is to dispossess it? but this is to be certain; therefore once certitude, always certitude. If certitude in any matter be the termination of all doubt or fear about its truth, and an unconditional conscious adherence to it, it carries with it an inward assurance, strong though implicit, that it shall never fail.[52]

This sounds iron-clad, but is it all "unreal?" Do we not in fact feel certain about many things only to discover we were in error? It could be shown that Newman's answer implies that the problem lies in *feeling* certain. We confuse a feeling for an intellectual act. However let us confine the answers to those he explicitly states. First, in the order of logic, the observation that certitude cannot be indefectible because we change certitudes conceals a subtle but debilitating contradiction: "Because I have been mistaken in my certitude, may I not at least be certain that I have been mistaken?"[53] In other words, can one be indefectibly certain that certitude is defectible? Secondly, the apparent mistakes of certitude do not require that we reject the possibility of certitude; it merely requires that we exercise care in making such assents:

> Certainly, the experience of mistakes in the assents which we have made are to the prejudice of subsequent ones. There is an antecedent difficulty in our allowing ourselves to be certain of something to-day, if yesterday we had to give up our belief of something else, of which we had up to that time professed ourselves to be certain. This is true; but antecedent objections to an act are not sufficient of themselves to prohibit its exercise; they may demand of us an increased circumspection before committing ourselves to it, but may be met with reasons more than sufficient to overcome them.[54]

Finally, such errors are wrong because they are wrong, not because they are "wrong certitudes." If nothing else, at least we must admit that "*Usus non tollit abusus*," that even if certitudes do err, we have no right to deny the certitude of all certainties. "[I]f what may be called functional disarrangements of the intellect are to be considered fatal to the recognition of the functions themselves, then the mind has no laws whatever and no normal constitution."[55] That way the maddest, blankest, most despairing skepticism lies.

In fact, as G.R. Evans concurs, certitude is ultimately indefectible because it is the recognition of a truth. The unchangeability of truth gives certitude its permanence, not some force of the certain mind itself.[56] This will be discussed in more detail when we look at the matter of truth and rhetorical knowledge. Here, however, Newman's "hard case" should be given its due. He acknowledges that people seem to change certitude all the time. He insists, however, that they cannot in fact have been certitudes if they are changed. He takes for his instance changes in religion, describing how people would insist that they are unquestionably certain of a religion which, in time, they might actually reject for a different one:

> Now a religion is not a proposition, but a system; it is a rite, a creed, a philosophy, a rule of duty, all at once; and to accept a religion is neither a simple assent to it nor a complex, neither a conviction nor a prejudice, neither a notional assent nor a real, not a mere act of profession, nor of credence, nor of opinion, nor of speculation, but it is a collection of all these various kinds of assents, at once and together, some of one description, some of another; but, out of all these different assents, how many are of that kind which I have called certitude? Certitudes indeed do not change, but who shall pretend that assents are indefectible?[57]

What happens (and Newman himself may well be the best example) is that at the heart of one's religious attachment there may be a particular certitude or set of certitudes, which are true and therefore indefectible. The mind has a correct and actual grasp on the reality of these things about which it is certain. Collected around these certitudes are other assents not actually certain, which can and do change. Newman describes a person whose certitude that Scripture is the Word of God remains, while his other assents come and go--that congregationalism is enjoined by Scripture, that actually Anglicanism is so enjoined, etc. It is possible that this basic certitude will lead the person on to the recognition of other truths and new certitudes--the truth of the Catholic faith.[58]

FORMAL AND INFORMAL INFERENCE

Up to this point Newman has been detailing the way the mind builds propositions and acts upon them, all from a rhetorical-effectiveness point of view. What follows, his study of kinds of reasoning, maintains this point of view. Though Newman's readers should be highly sensitized to this manner of looking at things by this point in his text, the fact remains that Newman's treatment of "Formal Inference" or syllogistic reasoning is often misunderstood. The rhetorical, apologetic purposes behind the *Grammar* become more important than ever now, and they inform the meaning and intent of Newman's discussion. One of the primary purposes of the *Grammar* is to dethrone the tyrannical sway of narrow, mechanistic reasoning. The broad, cultural presumption that syllogistically demonstrative matters constituted all that could be known (as well, of course, as scientifically consistent empirical phenomena) may have been facilely maintained in Newman's day, but it was persuasive. It was the ultimate root of religious liberalism and indifferentism, and it was Newman's target. Confined to this straight-jacket, "reason" could not include the personal, everyday means of knowing and being certain. Newman's object was to show the reasonableness of such informal kinds of reasoning, as well as to show the hidden weaknesses of formal, inferential reasoning.

Newman's "critique of pure reasoning" (formal inference) will focus, as his analysis has all along, on effectiveness. Again, though he often seems to be speaking of formal inference *per se*, he is actually speaking *per modum*, relative to us, the "known to us" side of the intellectual equation. I stress this point because the discussion of formal inference that follows "certitude" is what curdles the unwary Aristotelian's blood. The Aristotelianism that identifies "reason" only with the philosopher's extensive and detailed accounts of scientific knowledge cannot

read Newman here without concluding--as Weatherby and others have--that the
clergyman is an irrational skeptic and nominalist. Certainly, there are many statements in this section that by themselves lend credence to the charge. Newman's
reaction against mechanistic reasoning is powerful enough to lead him into unwise
assertions and even bald contradictions.

Newman identifies formal, syllogistic, demonstrative reasoning with many
aspects of notional apprehension and assent. They share the same force and import,
as should be no surprise, since formal reasoning thrives on notional matter:

> [I]n other words, the nearer the propositions concerned in
> the inference approach to being mental abstractions, and the
> less they have to do with the concrete reality, and the more
> closely they are made to express exact, intelligible,
> comprehensible, communicable notions, and the less they
> stand for objective things, that is, the more they are the
> subjects, not of real, but of notional apprehension,--so much
> the more suitable do they become for the purposes of
> Inference.[59]

This is why logicians eventually abstract their terms to the point of symbols.
Indeed, when words are used in formal reasoning, they perforce must be definitive,
unequivocal in their reference, in order for logical relations to be valid and
comprehensible. This is nothing new, but note how Newman's expression of the
same fact, dovetailed with the characteristics of "notional" and "real," displays his
intention and purpose:

> Words, which denote things, have innumerable implications;
> but in inferential exercises it is the very triumph of that
> clearness and hardness of head, which is the characteristic
> talent for the art, to have stripped them of all these connatural
> senses, to have drained them of that depth and breadth of
> associations which constitute their poetry, their rhetoric, and
> their historical life, to have starved each term down till it has
> become the ghost of itself, and everywhere one and the same
> ghost, "*omnibus umbra locis*," so that it may stand for just
> one unreal aspect of the concrete thing to which it properly
> belongs, for a relation, a generalization, or other abstraction,
> for a notion neatly turned out of the laboratory of the mind,
> and sufficiently tame and subdued, because existing only in
> a definition.[60]

These are fighting words, and they almost--but not quite--assert that the
"unreal aspect" so described is un-true. But they don't, for that is not Newman's
point, though many have taken it as such. We recall that "unreal" does not mean
"untrue" for Newman; it is a term descriptive of imaginative impact and force,

descriptive of the effect of something on the mind, not an assessment of its objective truth or reality.

A similar tack is taken regarding first principles themselves. The undemonstrated, self-evident nature of first principles is the very heart of formal reasoning, and Newman affirms their nature again and again. Here, however, he goes on the offensive and seems to deny their claim to proving the truth of something syllogistically. Reduce the chain of logic to its first principles, according to Newman, and the mechanistic reasoner boasts "See? This kind of thought produces true knowledge! There we are at my undeniable, self-evident first principles. The chain runs with unquestionable validity on to its conclusion from these principles." If this kind of thought alone is the standard of truth, says Newman, we have real difficulties because first principles, "the recondite sources of all knowledge . . . are accepted by some, rejected by others. . . ."[61]

Although first principles are supposed to be self-evident, they are not in fact agreed upon. Even the self-evident is not self-evident to some. What are we to say about the reasoning that so entirely depends upon this disputed ground?[62] Even as he makes this argument, Newman reminds the reader parenthetically that, yes, he does hold that certain things are actually self-evident. This indicates that what Newman is doing here remains firmly in the rhetorical vein; he does not philosophically question the truth or reality of first principles. Instead, he is "shaking up" the narrow rationalist by taking from him the claim that formal reasoning offers a kind of universal and independent avenue to truth. How universal and independent can such reasoning be in practice (not in essence), Newman asks, when the very first principles acknowledged as the source of such reasoning fail to secure universal agreement? The emphasis is clearly on practice and effect, not the epistemological essence of first principles.[63]

It is unusual to look at philosophical matter from the standpoint of rhetoric, but Newman's practical and concrete focus does not allow any other interpretation:

> [W]hile we talk logic, we are unanswerable; but then, on the other hand, this universal living scene of things is after all as little a logical world as it is a poetical; and, as it cannot without violence be exalted into poetical perfection, neither can it be attenuated into a logical formula. Abstract can only conduct to abstract; but we have need to attain by our reasonings to what is concrete; and the margin between the abstract conclusions of the science, and the concrete facts which we wish to ascertain, will be found to reduce the force

of the inferential method from demonstration to the mere
determination of the probable.[64]

In the latter clause the paradoxical tenet of Newman's rhetorical analysis becomes
clear: what is philosophically demonstrative may be rhetorically only probable. The
rest of the text takes up the implied second-half of the paradox: what is philosophically "merely" probable (i.e., not "demonstrable") may be rhetorically certain.

Before leaving formal reasoning, Newman does temper and qualify his
"attack" on syllogistic thought. Perhaps the energy of his assault has incapacitated
devotees of scientific reasoning from being assuaged, but the Aristotelian should
take note:

> Every exercise of nature or of art is good in its place; and the
> uses of this logical inference are manifold. It is the great
> principle of order in our thinking; it reduces a chaos into
> harmony; it catalogues the accumulations of knowledge; it
> maps out for us the relations of its separate departments; it
> puts us in the way to correct its own mistakes. It enables the
> independent intellects of many, acting and re-acting on each
> other, to bring their collective force to bear upon one and the
> same subject-matter, or the same question.[65]

Oddly enough, his defense of formal reasoning is also to an extent practical
and experiential; in the final analysis Newman's appreciation of such reasoning may
stem from his sensitivity to its own "concrete reality." How can we deny it a place
when it is so pervasive, and at times even persuasive? "But reasoning by rule and in
words is too natural to us, to admit of being regarded merely in the light of utility.
Our inquiries spontaneously fall into scientific sequence, and we think in logic, as
we talk in prose, without aiming at doing so."[66]

INFORMAL INFERENCE

As Newman takes up his idea of rhetorical certainty, he does so while
leaning heavily on the distinctions and descriptions of thought and reasoning which
precede. He has laid ground for this unacknowledged mode of thought. Newman
has indicated the rhetorically limited and narrow range of the utility of formal
reasoning. He has sensitized the reader to the variability of impact regarding things
and aspects "real" and "notional." He will open his discussion of a mode of thought
and reasoning that he feels is actually used in concrete situations to determine
concrete truths. It is a mode most often used, but rarely thought of at all by
theoreticians of intellect (with some exceptions). It is largely what I call a rhetorical

mode, but Newman distinguishes it by its contrast to formal inference; informal and natural inference is in fact the kind of reasoning most often employed, and its basis upon probability identifies it as largely a rhetorical means of thought.[67] In describing what informal inference does that formal does not, Newman defines his term:

> It is plain that formal logical sequence is not in fact the method by which we are enabled to become certain of what is concrete; and it is equally plain, from what has been already suggested, what the real and necessary method is. It is the cumulation of probabilities, independent of each other, arising out of the nature and circumstances of the particular case which is under review; probabilities too fine to avail separately, too subtle and circuitous to be convertible into syllogisms, too numerous and various for such conversion, even where they are convertible.[68]

Informal inference, "the real method of reasoning in concrete matters," possesses certain characteristics relevant to the rhetorical nature of its method. First, it is not properly instinctual, but still inferential. It is inference *sans* abstractions, *with* realities and probabilities, "its premises being instinct with the substance and the momentum of that mass of probabilities, which, acting upon each other in correction and confirmation, carry it home definitely to the individual case, which is its original scope."[69]

Second, though informal inference is still inference, it is "a process of reasoning . . . more or less implicit, and without the direct and full advertence of the mind exercising it."[70] This inference has a "body of proof," but the mind recognizes only the outcome or whole, not the "constituent parts" of the body.

Third, and perhaps most important for our purposes is the fact that probability (not to mention particulars) is involved in this reasoning, which means that various minds will conclude variously despite similarity of matter. This is because the evaluation of and sensitivity to probable matter varies as the intellect has been well or poorly formed by experience (and interest):

> It follows that what to one intellect is a proof is not so to another, and that the certainty of a proposition does properly consist in the certitude of the mind which contemplates it. And this of course may be said without prejudice to the objective truth or falsehood of propositions, since it does not follow that these propositions on the one hand are not true, and based on right reason, and those on the other not false, and based on false reason, because not all men discriminate them in the same way.[71]

More about the variable discrimination of probabilities in a moment. For now, we should note that the "relative-to-us" nature of Newman's subject should be obvious; the "objective truth or falsehood of propositions" is not variable, but one's discrimination of them is. Also, the opening for the rhetor should be evident: what better way than rhetoric to realign discrimination of probabilities in accordance with reality? But to return: the implicit quality of informal and natural inference means that, as suggested above, we see things whole, at once, without sense of the massing of parts: "Such too is the intellectual view we take of the *momenta* of proof for a concrete truth; we grasp the full tale of premisses and the conclusion, *per modum unius*--by a sort of instinctive perception of the legitimate conclusion in and through the premisses, not by a formal juxta-position of propositions. . . ."[72]

 Per modum unius Newman recognized as Aquinas' "*cogitare cum assensu.*"[73] The examples given for this kind of reasoning and knowledge are surprising--deliberately so--for they constitute things about which everyone is certain, but in support of which no one can offer demonstrative proof. That Great Britain is an island, that classical works (such as Terence, Vergil, etc.) are not the forgeries of medieval monks, and that "I shall die" are all propositions everyone is certain of, yet where is the syllogistic proof? What can be scientifically determined about any one of these? True, one could charter a boat and sail around Britain, but Newman's readers, sitting in their libraries, parlors, or gardens, have in fact never taken such a cruise, yet they are just as certain of the fact as if they had. What one could do to prove a proposition is not the question. Here and now, as we speak, how does one know such things? Newman's point, of course, is that one does know, but not by any means accounted for by the scientific and theoretical rationalists. We gain this kind of knowledge by our trust of testimony, primarily, which trust and testimony fall under the categories of evaluation described by Aristotle in the *Rhetoric* and *Ethics*. I refer specifically to what is called "character": "We judge for ourselves, by our own lights, and on our own principles; and our criterion of truth is not so much the manipulation of propositions, as the intellectual and moral character of the person maintaining them, and the ultimate silent effect of his arguments or conclusions upon our minds."[74]

 The net is tightening around the rationalist, as he sees that "knowledge" and "certainty" are being treated in their concrete forms--what one actually knows, here and now--and not as products of aloof speculative philosophies. We do know that Britain is an island, and we do so through non-demonstrative reasons. Those who argue the unintelligibility of religious propositions because of their being non-demonstratively reasoned have just had their favorite argument eliminated. Likewise, those who insist that only the theologically trained can be called rational in their faith (with the result that the vast majority of Christian believers by necessity believe "irrationally") have been deprived of their argument as well. Newman is explicit:

> This certitude and this evidence are often called moral; a word which I avoid, as having a very vague meaning; but using it here for once, I observe that moral evidence and moral certitude are all that we can attain, not only in the case of ethical and spiritual subjects, such as religion, but of terrestrial and cosmical questions also.[75]

Moral certitude is not weak; it is truth itself and abides in a living intellect. The fact that people differ in so many intellectual as well as practical matters does not mean that there is no truth:

> Shall we say that there is no such thing as truth and error, but that anything is truth to a man which he troweth? and not rather, as the solution of a great mystery, that truth there is, and attainable it is, but that its rays stream in upon us through the medium of our moral as well as our intellectual being; and that in consequence that perception of its first principles which is natural to us is enfeebled, obstructed, perverted, by allurements of sense and the supremacy of self, and, on the other hand, quickened by aspirations after the supernatural? . . . [76]

In this passage, Newman opens up an issue of lifelong interest to him; truth is not the product of a data-gobbling mind. It is the proper relation of a personal, intellectual being with created reality. Knowledge is not acquired by an appetitive intellect in a vacuum. Again, in practical, factual, daily experience, one finds that truth is acquired by persons in the full exercise of their personalities, not in intellects alone. Newman rejects mechanistic models for ratiocination and posits--or rather, merely describes--the "whole man" as the agent in obtaining truth. The mode of thought he describes "is the mode in which we ordinarily reason" and is a "personal power" dealing with "things directly . . . in the concrete. . . ."[77] He maintains that this mode abides in everyone, lettered and uneducated, and like the intellectual gift for abstract reasoning, this natural reasoning varies in acuity:

> When it is characterized by precision, subtlety, promptitude, and truth, it is of course a gift and a rarity: in ordinary minds it is biassed and degraded by prejudice, passion, and self-interest; but still, after all, this divination comes by nature, and belongs to all of us in a measure, to women more than to men, hitting or missing, as the case may be, but with a

> success on the whole sufficient to show that there is a
> method in it, though it be implicit.[78]

Leaving aside the interesting note that women generally are more adept at natural reasoning than men, we must recognize several seminal attributes of the mode mentioned here. The first is that we are still involved with reasoning, inference of a sort, though it be implicit. Here is no made-to-order "instinct." Second, and what requires drawing out, this mode of reasoning is not infallible. This is where the "moral as well as intellectual being" enters the picture. We do not know mechanically. Our experience, our already existing opinions and biases, our cultural, mental habits all participate in the execution of this informal inference and the estimation of the weight and strength of probabilities. The "whole man" means intellect, passions, will, memory, intellectual habit, previous assents, prejudice, senses, everything. Our ability to discern concrete realities is influenced by our "moral" (in the broad sense) and mental make-up as well as a strictly intellectual make-up. This is true even of sense-perception. The image of the absent-minded professor is, of course, a srereotype, but it does seem that an abstracted intellectual is more likely to overlook things in the immediate environment than is someone whose thinking is more directly concerned with material surroundings.

Of course, not noticing things does not span the breadth of influence the "whole man" has upon knowledge, for as Newman makes clear, the most important consequence of the "whole man" rests upon the assents and certitudes he facilitates or hinders. The moral being of the knower influences his ability to make discernments in concrete matters, and this affects his entire ability to know and reason in the practical or rhetorical realm. Things known not by demonstration are susceptible to being truly and fully known, but when the knowledge of them depends upon an accurate informal inference and the due gauging of probabilities, twisted (fallen) faculties often get in the way.

There are, consequently, large differences of judgment among people about many different kinds of matters. Especially with more important things, such as religious truths, one has to be prepared to know them. One does not assent to religious propositions because they have been concluded through a chain of formal inferences. One can see such a chain and still not assent. The assent and certainty comes when one sees *per modum unius* the "necessity" of the Incarnation, through the perception of a fallen world. It all comes at once, as it were, and includes the ability to estimate innumerable concrete probabilities and the outcome contained in them. In moral matters it is much the same. Someone who consistently violates the moral law actually de-conditions himself from being able to perceive the truth of that law. The religious rhetorician, we might add, has many such obstacles to overcome in attempt to restore practical perceptions and sensitivities through his art.

This idea was not Newman's alone. As R. W. Church observes in *The Oxford Movement*:

> The Oxford writers had all along laid stress on the paramount necessity of the single eye and disciplined heart in accepting or judging religion; moral subjects could be only appreciated by moral experience; purity, reverence, humility were as essential in such questions as zeal, industry, truthfulness, honesty; religious truth is a gift as well as a conquest; and they dwelt on the great maxims of the New Testament: "To him that hath shall be given"; "If any man will do the will of the Father, he shall know of the doctrine."[79]

In an interesting (if unflattering) example of the range of influence ascribed to habits of thought, Newman once told Hopkins that contemporary intellectuals were far more likely to be "invincibly ignorant" as regards the Catholic faith than were the unlearned.[80] The reason should be clear by now; habituated to a false mechanistic rationalism, academic intellectuals were often blinded, by the thought incumbent upon their academic pursuits, to truths more immediate, more concrete, more pressing on the conduct of life. The importance of experience and habituation for rhetorical and practical knowledge must not be thought a religious invention, for the idea goes back to Aristotle. In the *Ethics*, the philosopher is quite explicit about the practical intellect itself requiring both right thinking and right desire. "Intellect itself moves nothing." Upon the point, Gerard Verdeke says, "Apparently what fascinates [Newman] is the intimate relationship between thinking and the whole personality of the knowing subject dealing with issues in which experience and practice play an important part."[81]

ILLATIVE SENSE

Thus there are many things one's practical intellect must be prepared to know, and the religious assents incumbent upon a just estimation of cumulative probabilities are intellectual acts dependent upon the right ordering of the mind and the will--the whole man. Men like Froude do not assent to religious propositions because they are trapped by a mode of thought which, if they were consistent, would prevent them from giving assent to almost any matter known through testimony--Britain is an island, this is a photograph of great-Aunt Mable, Caesar crossed the Rubicon. Other men are prevented from assent by their habituation to acts in themselves immoral, and who thus are often incapable of recognition when faced with a moral truth. Accounting for such phenomena is one purpose of Newman's *Grammar*, and now that he has done so through the analysis of assents and inferences, he goes on to describe his famous "illative sense" and pursue actual apologetic in natural and revealed religion.

"Natural Religion" includes Newman's discussion of purely natural evidences for religion in general. This is where he moves out of his analysis of rhetorical reasoning and into his more well-known practice of apologetic for religion. "Revealed Religion" picks up where "Natural" left off and seeks to explore the evidence for Christianity by weighing probability and testimony. These concluding segments will not be discussed here since they are beyond the scope of the description of rhetorical knowledge. They explicitly attempt to create--or rather allow for--such knowledge as regards Christianity. The matter of the illative sense yet remains.

Simply stated, the illative sense is nothing short of right reason in rhetorical or probable matters. Aristotle uses "right reason" to describe the proper operation of the intellect and refers to such reason even regarding the practical intellect. Newman notes the fallibility of informal inference, the "environmental" and habitual elements in it that can skew it from a perception of and assent to a truth. When it works properly, he calls it the Illative Sense. "It determines what science cannot determine, the limit of converging probabilities and the reasons sufficient for a proof."[82] Remembering that the conclusion of an argument is not the same as an assent--assent is a separate intellectual act--Newman details his doctrine on the illative sense emphasizing the personal power of mind in grasping a truth:

> Certitude is not a passive impression made upon the mind from without, by argumentative compulsion, but in all concrete questions (nay, even in abstract, for though the reasoning is abstract, the mind which judges of it is concrete) it is an active recognition of propositions as true, such as it is the duty of each individual himself to exercise at the bidding of reason, and, when reason forbids, to withhold. And reason never bids us be certain except on an absolute proof; and such a proof can never be furnished to us by the logic of words, for as certitude is of the mind, so is the act of inference which leads to it. Every one who reasons, is his own centre; and no expedient for attaining a common measure of minds can reverse this truth.[83]

Logic, an "expedient for attaining a common measure of minds," is employed by persons. While it may appear that Newman collapses all modes of knowing into rhetorical modes, he does not. He does not attempt to deny philosophy and logical argumentation its own, unique truth-finding capacity. Rather, he insists that all intellectual activities occur in persons, and the faculty of reasoning most employed by people and applicable to the vast domain of contingent, concrete, probable matter is this other form of knowing. He is fully in accord with Aquinas in saying that even philosophy has its personal, "contingent" aspect as regards the suitability of a particular person to make philosophic inquiry. Going on to the question of accountability, Newman asks if there is any *test* for informal reasoning. That is, how can we tell when it is properly working?

> But then the question follows, is there any criterion of the accuracy of an inference, such as may be our warrant that certitude is rightly elicited in favour of the proposition inferred, since our warrant cannot, as I have said, be scientific? I have already said that the sole and final judgment on the validity of an inference in concrete matter is committed to the personal action of the ratiocinative faculty, the perfection or virtue of which I have called the Illative Sense, a use of the word "sense" parallel to our use of it in "good sense," "common sense," a "sense of beauty," &c.;-- and I own I do not see any way to go farther than this in answer to the question.[84]

In a way, the answer to the question "Is there any criterion?" is "No." If by criterion is meant a systematic common measure that can be applied to a judgment which will determine its accuracy and truth, the answer must be "No." If there were, that would be a philosophical criterion for rhetorical matter. Newman must be given credit here for not succumbing to a very pervasive temptation for those who seek to justify non-systematic knowledge. He says he cannot go any further, which means he is aware that to do so would undermine his whole thesis. He will not assume rhetoric into philosophy. But in another way, the answer is "Yes," there is a criterion, and that is the illative sense. Though no systematic common measure, though a "personal action," the illative sense is a personal action of the "ratiocinative faculty"--i.e., a truly reasoning power. Again, rhetoric has its own logic, and when it works according to its proper nature, it is reasoning and attains truth. In a sense, the illative sense is to informal reasoning what certainty is to assent. One is certain when one knows he assents to a truth; one correctly reasons informally when the illative sense confirms the judgment.

Clearly, a short discussion of the rhetorical mode of thought enunciated and defended by Newman in the *Grammar* cannot do justice to the clarity of detail and wealth of examples he employs. Yet it should not be thought (from excluding the light shed by his examples) that he propounds a "rhetorical determinism." If we all employ informal inference, yet such inference is subject to the whim of experience and habit, is there any free ability to infer correctly? The answer is in the distinction between "subject to" and "influenced by." Ultimately, much comes down to the inclinations of the thinker's will. The extreme opinions of people whose sense of probability is deeply warped dismay others by their often unanswerable assertions. Chesterton remarks that the paranoiac is impossible to liberate from delusion precisely because he knows that the best way to destroy him would be to pretend to be a friend. How then can one argue? Where does one begin? Even in less extreme matters, matters that would appear "accessible" and simple, the judgments of ordinary people diverge. Is a particular politician a scoundrel or a saint? Does "progress" mean improvement? Should universities be trade schools? Newman does not suggest there are no answers, but he accounts for the disagreement in coming to an answer. Not forgetting his ultimate purpose in the *Grammar*, he even employs this universal variety of judgment as *prima facie* evidence in favor of a revelation:

> These instances, because they are so casual, suggest how it comes to pass, that men differ so widely from each other in religious and moral perceptions. Here, I say again, it does not prove that there is no objective truth, because not all men are in possession of it; or that we are not responsible for the associations which we attach, and the relations which we assign, to the objects of the intellect. But this it does suggest to us, that there is something deeper in our differences than the accident of external circumstances; and that we need the interposition of a Power, greater than human teaching and human argument, to make our beliefs true and our minds one.[85]

X. THE *GRAMMAR* AND RHETORICAL KNOWLEDGE

> *A good moral, my lord. It is not enough to speak, but to speak true.*
> A Midsummer Night's Dream V, i.

SKEPTICAL NEWMAN?

Religion is the ultimate focus of the *Grammar*, but a faculty of mind and mode of knowledge are its immediate subjects. Before, then, summarizing the "rhetoricality" of the *Grammar*, we shall address the status of "truth" in the text. Was Newman a skeptic after all, as Weatherby and others insist? To be sure, no one suggests Newman was a relativist or disbelieved in truth; Weatherby's thesis that Newman's religion saved him from the consequences of his deep skepticism posits dogmatism as a rescue of knowledge. Was there no natural access to truth in Newman's thinking? In fact, the idea that Newman was a skeptic is dependent upon a philosophical reading of non-philosophical matter. Newman does hold to a natural capacity for truth or knowledge of reality, even of the abstract, philosophical variety. Scholars who see skepticism in Newman perceive as philosophical what is essentially rhetorical and often openly apologetical discourse. The anti-mechanistic purpose in his texts is so strong that it is easy to lose sight of some essential assertions by Newman that demonstrate a non-skeptical mind. The *Grammar* has many such statements, a few of which will suffice.[1]

> By means of sense we gain knowledge directly; by means of reasoning we gain it indirectly, that is, by virtue of previous knowledge. And if we may justly regard the universe, according to the meaning of the word, as one whole, we may also believe justly that to know one part of it is necessarily to know much more than that one part.[2]

Somewhat later, he repeats the point, contrasting the knowledge of science to that known through probability or rhetorical knowledge: "Science, working by itself, reaches truth in the abstract, and probability in the concrete. . . ."[3] Again, it should be clear that the abstract truth referred to here is no less true than concrete truth. Yet Newman goes further than this, is more explicit as regards truth and the mind's natural capacity for it: "Now truth cannot change; what is once truth is always truth; and the human mind is made for truth, and so rests in truth. . . . [T]he intellect, which is made for truth, can attain truth, and, being attained it can keep it, can recognize it, and preserve the recognition."[4]

As the discussion of real apprehension and assent suggests, Newman's pseudo-skeptical comments about the unintelligibility of physical phenomena have to be taken with a hefty grain of salt. So do his denigrations of abstraction, universals, and formal reasoning. The reader must needs always ask, when Newman is pursuing these lines, what his object is. Having so patently rhetorical a purpose does not necessarily convert philosophical errors or confusions into sound reasonings, but it should alert the reader to suspend reading a text as essentially philosophical. In light of Newman's work as a whole, it is clear that whatever his pointed statements of a skeptical turn, his mental habit was thoroughly realist. He begins with reality, and spurns such skeptical standards as "criticism" and "doubt." Indeed, he has harsh words for doubt as a principle of any inquiry. Newman accuses the philosophical adoption of doubt as being baldly contradictory: "[T]here are writers...[who propose] that we have no right in philosophy to make any assumption whatever, and that we ought to begin with a universal doubt. This however, is of all assumptions the greatest, and to forbid assumptions universally is to forbid this one in particular."[5]

Doubt as a principle demands a suspension of certitude regarding not just knowledge of exterior things, but, as Newman is quick to point out, a suspension of one's natural operations, one's very being. Here Newman bridles because the integrated personalism he holds dear is sundered by such principles of inquiry as "doubt." Clouded by such a principle, we begin to ask wrong-headed questions, such as "How can we trust our perceptions, our reasoning, our thinking?" "It seems to me unphilosophical to speak of trusting ourselves. We are what we are, and we use, not trust our faculties. . . . We are as little able to accept or reject our mental constitution as our being."[6] In a stinging rebuke of Descartes (not by name, but idea), Newman declares:

> It is enough for the proof of the value and authority of any
> function which I possess, to be able to pronounce that it is
> natural. . . . [M]y first disobedience is to be impatient at
> what I am, and to indulge an ambitious aspiration after what
> I cannot be [Maritain calls Descartes's view of the intellect

"Angelism"], to cherish a distrust of my powers, and to
desire to change laws which are identical with myself.[7]

These powers include our sense-perception as well as reasoning.

In light of the fundamental acceptance of human faculties, Newman's
personalism can be called realist despite his alleged skepticism. It is true that he has
no consistent, sound metaphysics, and he is brim-full of comments belittling
abstraction and pretensions of "knowledge." But as shown, these are to be expected
from one whose thought is habitually rhetorical, whose aim is the restoration of a
personal, rhetorical mode of thought and knowledge, and who is immersed in a
culture where de-personalized, mechanistic thought has been enthroned. Stanley
Jaki approaches the idea that Newman's seeming nominalism is rooted in an
essentially non-philosophical attempt to combat an evil of the day. In a sound
Thomistic analysis of this nominalism, he attests to the garbled quality of
Newman's "metaphysics" but insists that, ultimately, Newman chose the objective
"thing" over doubt.[8] When Newman denies universals, though using language
proper to philosophy, the practical motive behind the denial results in very
problematic nominalism indeed. It becomes clear in "Formal Inference" that his
attempt is more to preserve the possibility of mystery in objective reality than
simply posit a pure nominalistic philosophy.[9]

The final answer to the charge of skepticism must remain, however, the
simple one that ultimately Newman is no philosopher, is not "doing" philosophy,
even when using terms proper to philosophy. This is not to deny that using such
terms obligates one to use them properly, nor that Newman is highly susceptible to
the charge of a misappropriation of philosophical matter for rhetorical purposes.
Nevertheless, to the question "Is Newman a skeptic either formally or
temperamentally?" the answer is "No." He is a rhetorical realist, not a philosophical
skeptic, and the ultimate indication of this is his own repeated definition of scope in
the *Grammar*.

PRACTICAL PROVINCE

In an article titled (appropriately enough) "Newman on Truth," Ian Ker
addresses the idea put forward by N. D. O'Donoghue that the *Grammar* is "bad
philosophy" because it fails as a systematic treatise. O'Donoghue affirms that the
Grammar lacks the "hardness of texture demanded by a theory of certitude."[10]
Ker's response, in essence, is that the text makes no pretence of being such a

treatise. It is a general, practical work, truly intended as an *Essay in Aid of a Grammar of Assent*. In fact, Newman repeatedly defines the scope of this work in such a way to act as a warning against misreading. He asserts that, unlike philosophers, he will deal with "psychological facts" in exploration of his subject.[11] Philosophers deal with "how representative symbols work" while his interest is "how the intellect is affected towards the thing which those symbols represent."[12]

In a long passage opening his discussion of the illative sense, Newman provides the most complete statement of the province of his work. He declares that his object has not been "to form a theory" to account for inference and assent, but "to ascertain what is the matter of fact as regards them, that is, when it is that assent is given to propositions which are inferred, and under what circumstances."[13] Openly sidestepping epistemology proper, he avows: "Earnestly maintaining, as I would . . . the certainty of knowledge, I think it enough to appeal to the common voice of mankind in proof of it. . . . How it comes about that we can be certain is not my business to determine; for me it is sufficient that certitude is felt."[14] Then relating this point of departure to philosophy, he classifies thus:

> This is what the schoolmen, I believe, call treating the subject *in facto esse*, in contrast with *in fieri*. Had I attempted the latter, I should have been falling into metaphysics; but my aim is of a practical character . . . I would confine myself to [probability and] the truth of things, and to the mind's certitude of that truth.[15]

This passage is critical for the whole of the *Grammar*, for it delineates the subject. Newman's is a practical study of certain mental phenomena, not as they are in themselves or absolutely, but as they are relative to those holding them, in the "fact of their being" or the circumstances of their existence. The formal, epistemological nature of knowledge and certainty is left aside for the most part, and one gets the impression that Newman is relieved to avoid it. Yet truth is his subject, and the fact that he spurns philosophy yet takes up the mind's certitude of truth--*in facto esse*--of practical (probable) matter, properly defines his topic as rhetorical apprehension of truth.

The latter part of the *Grammar,* where Newman advances arguments for Christianity based on the terms of probable reasoning, confirms the practical, rhetorical nature of his subject. He begins by saying that demonstration of God's existence and the truth of Christianity can indeed be made, but he is not so very interested in them because they, though true and valid, fail to persuade:

Truth certainly, as such, rests upon grounds intrinsically and objectively and abstractly demonstrative, but it does not follow from there that the arguments producible in its favor are unanswerable and irresistible. . . . The fact of revelation is in itself demonstrably true, but it is not therefore irresistibly; else, how comes it to be resisted? [Sounding here like Aristotle:] There is a vast distance between what it is in itself, and what it is to us.[16]

NEWMAN AND TRUTH

The charge of skepticism, then, does not seem to hold up under close scrutiny. Through sense we gain knowledge directly, according to Newman, and if he does not break down the process into its "parts" and metaphysical bases, neither does he erect a screen or barrier between reality and the mind.[17] But what is the "character" of truth for Newman, especially this truth appropriated through a rhetorical activity of mind? To a large extent the analysis of the *Grammar* already illustrates this, but some summary observation will clarify the point further.

Newman identifies certitude as a reflex recognition of a truth. But truth is not the object merely of certitude. The fact that even the sensory apprehension adequates the mind to reality demonstrates that the mind is in the province of truth far "earlier" than when it possesses certainty. This accounts for Newman's qualifying his "disapprobation" of notional apprehension. Early in the discussion of notional and real apprehension, Newman remarks, "Here then we have two modes of thought, both using the same words, both having one origin [objective reality], yet with nothing in common in their results."[18] The common origin--reality--of real and notional apprehension serves to quiet those who fear that Newman targets abstraction by the agent intellect when he denigrates the notional. But it also shows that the mind's adequation to reality does not begin with certainty but with the senses and proceeds on through the apprehension of propositions. Subsequent assent, like the intellect itself, also has truth for its object (without, however, being infallible). This applies to both notional and real assents as Newman indicates when he argues for the unconditionality of assent, its being a separate act of the intellect, and its absence of "degree." Gilson is quick to make the connection; assent has no degree, because truth has no degree.[19] In Newman's terms, "if assent is the acceptance of truth, and truth is the proper object of the intellect, and no one can hold conditionally what by the same act he holds to be true, here too is a reason for saying that assent is an adhesion without reserve or doubt to the proposition to which it is given."[20] When one adds to this that assent differs from mere assertion because it includes an apprehension of a thing,[21] there emerges a "truth chain" that can be expressed either backwards or forwards: reality permeates the mind through the senses, then apprehension, then assents. Or, truth is the object of assent, apprehension, and sense-data. Though (or rather, because) he is speaking psychologically, describing acts of the mind rather than the nature of intellect, there is little in this process to criticize from a Thomistic standpoint.

Keeping to his psychological province, Newman characterizes the truth that is confirmed in certitude (that is, not just a simple assent, but an indefectible, reflex one) in this fashion:

> [L]et the proposition to which the assent is given be as absolutely true as the reflex act pronounces it to be, that is, objectively true as well as subjectively:--then the assent may be called a *perception*, the conviction a *certitude*, the proposition or truth a certainty, or thing known or matter of *knowledge*, and to assent to it is to *know*.[22]

It should be clear, then, that the view of the mind taken up by Newman is one positively anchored by the idea of truth and the genuine capacity for knowledge at every level. It is too steeped in the real to be that of a skeptic, too public to be that of a solipsist. "We are sure beyond all hazard of a mistake, that our own self is not the only being existing; that there is an external world; that it is a system with parts and a whole. . . ."[23] Nor is this the grudging or relieved admission of a temperamental skeptic who, because of his adherence to religious dogma, asserts the capacity for truth. In the following summary of the rhetorical apprehension of truth advanced by Newman, it will be clear that his entire discussion avoids the customary epistemological and metaphysical departures familiar to the Aristotelian or Thomist. Nevertheless, the kind of knowledge or mode of thought Newman advances *does* belong in a Thomistic or Aristotelian schema when it is understood as rhetorical.

RHETORICAL KNOWLEDGE

Probability is certainly the key to the fundamentally rhetorical character of the knowledge Newman treats. Through the "accumulation of various probabilities . . . we may construct proof, sufficient for certitude."[24] We know what is meant by "certitude"--an objective truth. So, contrary to the almost unconscious beliefs of

Newman's contemporaries, truth is obtainable by means of probability, not just demonstration. Is this claim of Newman's borne out by the facts? Can so strong an assertion meet the test of the same concrete reality or facts that its author appeals to so frequently? Newman resorts to that reality to defend his claim. "There are many truths in concrete matter, which no one can demonstrate, yet every one unconditionally accepts. . . ."[25] These include the propositions mentioned earlier; that Britain is an island, etc. Later, in development of the same idea, he creates a lengthy list of things known by all, then moves gradually to things known personally (i.e., about individual circumstances). He then includes things known in the same way and felt the same way, yet which concern Christianity:

> We accept and hold with an unqualified assent, that the earth, considered as a phenomenon, is a globe; that all its regions see the sun by turns; that there are vast tracts on it of land and water; that there are really existing cities on definite sites, which go by the names of London, Paris, Florence, and Madrid. We are sure that Paris or London, unless suddenly swallowed up by an earthquake or burned to the ground, is to-day just what it was yesterday, when we left it. We laugh to scorn the idea that we had no parents though we have no memory of our birth; that we shall never depart this life, though we can have no experience of the future; that we are able to live without food, though we have never tried. . . . We may have an overpowering sense of our moral weakness, of the precariousness of our life, health, wealth, position and good fortune. We may have a clear view of the weak points of our physical constitution, of what food or medicine is good for us, and what does us harm. We may be able to master, at least in part, the course of our past history; its turning-points, our hits, and our great mistakes. We may have a sense of the presence of a Supreme Being, which never has been dimmed by even a passing shadow, which has inhabited us ever since we can recollect any thing, and which we cannot imagine our losing. We may be able, for others have been able, so to realize the precepts and truths of Christianity, as deliberately to surrender our life, rather than transgress the one or to deny the other.[26]

After his long list of facts and appeals to common experience, we are reminded of the single point that they have been summoned to support:

> On all these truths we have an immediate and an unhesitating hold, nor do we think ourselves guilty of not loving truth for truth's sake, because we cannot reach them through a series of intuitive propositions. Assent on reasonings not demonstrative is too widely recognized an act to be irrational, unless man's nature is irrational, too familiar to the prudent and clear-minded to be an infirmity or an

> extravagance. None of us can think or act without the
> acceptance of truths, not intuitive, not demonstrated, yet
> sovereign. If our nature has any constitution, any laws, one
> of them is this absolute reception of propositions as true,
> which lie outside the narrow range of conclusions to which
> logic, formal or virtual, is tethered; nor has any
> philosophical theory the power to force on us a rule which
> will not work for a day.[27]

Any philosopher's discomfort with this sort of statement is partially justified; what we have here is a kind of declaration of independence from the tyranny of philosophical theory. Do not ask something as concrete and real as Christianity to strive to justify itself according to abstract criteria that *no* concrete thing is capable of meeting. Like it or not, one's absolute certainty--a certainty Newman says is justified--that the moon is not made of green cheese rests on "probability," not formal demonstration. Insistence that rational conviction of some truth is possible only if it is clearly demonstrated is sheerest fantasy. Newman explicitly refers to Aristotle's affirmation that a truly well-educated man expects exactitude only "in every class of subject, according as the nature of the thing admits. . . ."[28]

Probability, then, as a basis for certitude (recognition of or assent to a truth) cannot be dismissed as a weak or inferior foundation for truth. It is the very stuff of our daily lives. It should be remembered that for Newman, "probability" does not mean "likelihood," but rather the indemonstrable quality of a proposition. Thus, what is philosophically "probable" may well be an objective truth one can be perfectly certain of, rhetorically, through the "logic" proper to rhetorical knowledge (the experiential and estimative work of the illative sense). What can be confusing is that, true to his non-systematic habits, Newman will use "probability" in another sense too, without warning or explanation. Thomists like Weatherby become exasperated when Newman coldly observes that metaphysics and any theoretical science are merely "probable." In part a result of Newman's desire to "bring down the proud," he applies the term to formal sciences but gives it a new meaning. We have seen Newman "deny" first principles their claim to universality not in themselves, but in their concrete acceptance by persons. What philosophically "succeeds" may rhetorically "fail." The same kind of shift of emphasis occurs periodically with the term "probable." Though normally used to mean simply "non-demonstrative," the word is employed by Newman as an index of rhetorical *persuasiveness* when applied to theoretical sciences. This is what was meant in saying that what is philosophically only "probable" may be rhetorically certain, and what is philosophically demonstrative may be, rhetorically, only "probable." It may not convince, persuade, carry the "inquirer" along to assent to its conclusion, however valid.[29]

A final indication that the truth Newman speaks of is known by the rhetorical intellect is the interesting fact that certainty, the ultimate, indefectible assent to a truth, has no exterior, universal "test" of its validity. The previous chapter remarked that Newman did not fall into the skeptics' trap of attempting a "verification" of knowledge to make up for the skeptical philosopher's inability to account for knowledge of exterior reality. Newman leaves certitude alone. He first asserts that he can offer no infallible token for the indefectibility of certitude, adding that certitude does not even admit of a test sufficient to distinguish it from false certitude. We can only discern negatively; if someone changes an assent, he was not certain of it.[30] These assertions seem unsatisfying at first, but they are *essential* if the kind of knowledge he is speaking of is to be properly rhetorical. If the certitude he speaks of is in the rhetorical province, rather than the philosophical, then there can be no critical test of it. Critical tests or verificational formulae of a truth, when speaking strictly, belong to formal, demonstrative reasoning. A rhetorical certitude cannot submit to an objective, absolute test of truth value for the same reason that something properly probable cannot become demonstrative. It can be argued for, certainly, but not objectively "tested," for that would be to judge the apple according to its orangeness. For Newman, certitudes correspond to reality, and that is all. His is a non-critical rhetorical realism: non-critical precisely because it is rhetorical.

RHETORICAL DETERMINISM?

An interesting question remains, the answer to which introduces us to the final discussion of Newman's rhetorical personalism in the *Grammar*. We have seen the position and character of rhetorical knowledge or truth, but is Newman's idea of this "practical cognition" in fact rather deterministic? That is, if certain things are best known through experience, if one's faculty of personal cognition must be prepared to see certain realities (i.e., religious ones), are we not "trapped" by our experience such that some can see and others cannot? In a way, the answer is "yes." This is what "invincible ignorance" means. When Newman stipulates the state of mind "in those who would inquire into the truth of Christianity," he describes a set of assents to "Natural Religion" that might cause an agnostic to think he was describing assents already specifically Christian. Newman says an inquirer, among many other things, must have a sense of the "Divine Presence," must admire "His Person," must be convinced of the preeminent importance of "the unseen world," and even must recognize the present lack of union with this Person and must desire a reconciliation.[31] These perceptions are almost necessary, he says, for an inquirer to be equipped to evaluate the evidence for Christianity. The accuracy of such an evaluation rests largely upon the inquirer's own character: "We judge for ourselves, by our own lights, and on our own principles, and our criterion for truths is not so much the manipulation of propositions, as the intellectual and moral character of the person maintaining [as well as evaluating] them. . . ."[32]

Thus in one of the most entertaining parts of the *Grammar*, Newman critiques Gibbon's assignation of the causes for Christianity's rapid growth; he scolds Gibbon for dealing with theories and disregarding facts. After analyzing Gibbon's "causes" one by one, Newman asks why, amidst the vast labor of Gibbon's works, did not the historian even inquire as to what account those very Christians gave for the growth? It seems poor history to simply disregard the ample historical testimony of the persons involved, yet this is what Gibbon does. He ignores a class of facts simply because they posit things supernatural; Gibbon, says Newman, is an example of one who "cannot even enter into [the testimonial data], because he needs the due formation for such an exercise of mind."[33]

It seems, then, that lacking a due formation of mind, one is fairly "locked in" and incapacitated to perceive certain aspects of reality. The proper answer is that no, one is not locked in: one is hampered. Not only is this doctrine consistent with Aquinas' description of fallen man's weakened intellect, it is also true to Newman's own idea of man's state. To be sure, we can come to the knowledge of God through creation, according to Newman, but it is a difficult task in a fallen world.[34] The particular utility of rhetoric is in its being an aid in overcoming the restrictions placed on our ability to "see" realities, as an aid in reformation of one's experience and perceptions. The first of Holloway's three "points" concerning the "sage" is just this note of rhetorical utility: a sage modifies "the reader's perceptiveness, from stimulating him to notice something to which he was previously blind."[35] Later on, Holloway exemplifies this activity of Newman the sage by observing that the clergyman's figurative language and examples "provide the mind with vivid particulars instead of abstractions"--harmonizing with Newman's own idea of how real assent is created.[36]

Rhetoric in action can "be a vehicle of thought," says Newman (speaking of an argument of Pascal's), which opens "the mind to the apprehension of the facts of the case, and to trace them and the implications in outline, not to convince by the logic of its mere wording."[37] This is precisely where a study of Newman's "poetic rhetoric" should begin, because the rhetorical enhancement of experience is not conclusive argument so much as it is ground-work preparation. It is the experiential, connatural formation of a mind such that it becomes capable of seeing facts and probabilities in their proper relation and proportion--rather like Newman's idea of a liberal education itself. But how does rhetorical art *do* this? The answer is clear from what has been already said: rhetorical art can create real apprehension and assents in an "audience."

RHETORICAL PERSONALISM

As we have seen, real apprehensions and assents do not compel men to action, but they are highly conducive to action--including, of course, interior actions such as complex assents regarding religious propositions.[38] Newman credits real assents as being the primary formative influence on the mind in its moral and intellectual character.[39] Heroes, saints, pioneers in science, great leaders are what they are largely out of their real apprehensions and assents--whether right or wrong.[40] Therefore, if one is to develop a people's character in such a way that it becomes capable of perceiving that to which it was blind, the place to begin is with the real in apprehension and assent, for by means of the real are minds formed. An instinctive recognition of this lies behind every frustrated composition teacher's cry "If you're going to convince me, use examples!" Newman says real assents

> excite the mind from their moral and imaginative properties, [such assent] has for its objects, not only directly what is true, but inclusively what is beautiful, useful, admirable, heroic; objects which kindle devotion, raise the passions, and attach the affections; and thus it leads the way to actions of every kind, to the establishment of principles, and the formation of character, and is thus again intimately connected with what is individual and personal.[41]

Finally, this rhetorical persuasion (or "rhetorical realism") should be understood as integrated--the human faculties are not treated in isolation despite the formulaic tone of the *Grammar*. Though Newman classifies and separates, he separates only to unite. The clearest example of this is the analysis of real assent with its emotional, intellectual, will-related, and imaginative aspects. In fact, even notional assents may be turned to real ones and thus made "operative."[42] The integrative approach explains why Newman rejects "method" in the sense it had acquired since the days of Ramus: a calculus of instrumentality. A magic, rationalistic wand waved over and ordering a subject (and resulting in "knowledge") struck Newman as unreal and dismissive of concrete, "whole man" modes of thought.[43] "Method" simply left nine-tenths of a man behind.

While logical arts have their utility, man's actual progress in knowledge is not "mechanical, nor is it of necessity; it is committed to the personal efforts of each individual of the species. . . ."[44] If one is to appeal to the "multitude," the appeal had far better be by the very means most people are to know most things, not a rarified "method." The ordinary means of cognition include the various mental faculties working together in integration upon concrete matter. What, for example, convinced the first generations of Christians of their religion (doing now what Gibbon failed to do)? The answer, quite apart from the truth or falsity of the religion, is not far to seek: "They preached Christ. . . ." They were persuaded by a *person*, by the "description of the life, character, mission, and power of that Deliverer, a promise of His invincible Presence and Protection here, and of the Vision and Fruition of Him hereafter."[45] The example is fortuitous because it describes as personal not only the religious certitude, but the *object* of that certitude as well. Many passages display how Newman pulls together human faculties into a unified means of attaining certitude, including such famous passages as this:

> The heart is commonly reached, not through reason [i.e., logical inference], but through the imagination, by means of direct impressions, by the testimony of facts and events, by history, by description. Persons influence us, voices melt us, looks subdue us, deeds inflame us. Many a man will live and die upon a dogma: no man will be a martyr for a conclusion.[46]

Note that the passage presumes upon "the heart" as having a role in reaching certitude (at least regarding real assent). This is shortly followed by a passage no work treating Newman's idea of rhetoric can leave out: "Logic makes but a sorry rhetoric with the multitude; first shoot round corners, and you may not despair of converting by a syllogism. . . . After all, man is not a reasoning animal; he is a seeing, feeling, contemplating, acting animal."[47]

Despite belittling reason, Newman does not, of course, mean to exclude formal inference from the process of coming to an assent or a certitude. It works in conjunction with the illative sense, which has cognitive value since it too is a kind of reason. Newman insists that the notional and real have each their proper domain, and in many matters both are mutually operative. Thus, regarding religion, both "belief" ("religion" or dogmatic assent or real assent) and notional "theology" are necessary. Reason acts as a "stay" for belief, to keep it from the excesses of imagination or emotion.[48]

There is, then, in Newman's idea of a genuine religious certitude a necessary combination of apprehensions and assents. While he does not propose to argue for the truth of Christianity by means of a "smart syllogism," neither does he mean to dupe the gullible by means of emotional manipulation. Just as, in reality, a man is intellect, passions, and will, so must a conversion to a real faith include the cooperation of intellect, passions, and will. All three, in integration, belong to man's common mode of thought regarding concrete things, and Newman will have them operating in regard to a concrete religion as well. "I do not care to overcome their reason without touching their hearts."[49] The will must also be well disposed, as seen by Newman's impatience with those "inclined to sit at home" passively waiting for revelation to present its credentials and humbly plead its case. "[T]hey expect its evidence to come to them without their trouble; they act, not as supplicants, but as judges."[50] Such a one will never be persuaded of a supernatural truth, not because he is a cool, hard-headed reasoner, but simply because he is not in the way of any kind of perception of something "above nature." Nevertheless rhetoric is not incapable of enhancing the perceptions even of such a hard case as this; it must take for its tools a different subject matter than the truth of Christianity, however. Such a one can be moved rhetorically by bringing to him a real apprehension of the limits and inadequacies of the very idea of proof and conviction he possesses. Leaving the supernatural well alone, the first step with the kind of individual Newman describes is to shake his "blind faith" in his own paradigm of reason and his own ability, as he stands, of judging the matter in question. Obviously, this is precisely the aim and object of the first two-thirds of the *Grammar* itself. So, not only does the text delineate and defend a rhetorical mode of reason, it is itself a very "rhetorical" text designed to make possible a persuasive yet rational access to the walled-in domain of the scientific materialist, the rationalist, the complacent agnostic.

The writing of the *Grammar* gave its author no pleasure. He thought it a dry, dull work that, however, he was obliged in conscience to write. It is not difficult to discern why. Dry as much of the work may be, the *Grammar* is all of a

piece with the entirety of Newman's writings. It is a book by a man with a strong
sense of motive, and the text itself possesses an unmistakably "pastoral" purpose.
As do so many of Newman's texts, the *Grammar* operates through a personal, even
conversational style, despite its largely technical nature. But it goes farther than
style, for it gives an account and defense of the particular cognitive potential of that
personalistic approach he so loved. Newman's sense of man's great supernatural
destiny and the difficulties in attaining it would not allow him to "write-off" a world
of ever narrowing ideas of truth. Though reintegration with the Creator was no
simple matter in the best of circumstances, the fact that his era was increasingly
prejudiced against religious assents only heightened Newman's insistence that man
must develop his entire range of sensibilities. The sense that man is a being in
motion and that motion has a proper end is never far from Newman's efforts in the
Grammar. Even when speaking of the natural development of the faculties, the
shadow of the supernatural end is not difficult to see:

> Other beings are complete from their first existence, in that
> line of excellence which is allotted to them; but man begins
> with nothing realized (to use the word), and he has to make
> capital for himself by the exercise of those faculties which
> are his natural inheritance. Thus he gradually advances to the
> fullness of his original destiny.[51]

XI. NEWMAN AND RHETORICAL REALISM

Man is not a mind that thinks but a being who knows.
E. Gilson

By the heart's still rhetoric disclosèd with eyes . . .
Love's Labor Lost II, i.

JOST'S NEWMAN

One very simple test can be applied to the *Grammar* that helps identify its essential subject as rhetorical: who is it that might best "profit" from the work? For whom is it most useful? Of course, in trying to weaken the strangle-hold of mechanistic conceptions of reasoning, Newman created a work of general utility or use. But who in particular would best profit from reading the *Grammar*, imbibing its spirit, then putting its tenets into practice? Clearly, the answer is: the rhetorician. Anyone who attempts to create assents concerning facts in the concrete and the conduct of life--teachers, apologists, priests, even politicians--employ an instrumental art (rhetoric) susceptible to enhancement and refinement through the insights of the *Grammar*. No one, not the philosopher, not the theologian, can convert the *Grammar* into as practicable an aid as can the rhetorician. Newman's own sermons are proof enough of this. Louis Bouyer likens the sermons to what the scholastics would call "an experience of appropriation," the outcome of which was the creation of "real assents."[1]

Throughout this study, we have inquired into the essential "rhetoricality" of Newman's mind both in its habitual operation and its particular interests. Though well-known as a "polemicist" and orator, Newman is regarded as a rhetorician primarily because of his excellence of style. Though some, as noted earlier, have hinted at his epistemological/rhetorical underpinnings, until the publication of Walter Jost's *Rhetorical Thought in John Henry Newman* (1989), nothing comprehensive had been attempted regarding the essentially rhetorical character of Newman's habit of mind. Jost's work is important in its scope and seminal in its opening fresh ground in Newman studies. Its thoroughness and seriousness is such that one cannot help but realize that there is "more" to rhetoric than commonly supposed, and that Newman's "rhetoric" deserves serious attention.

Jost's thesis proposes a new understanding of a rhetorical Newman:

> The central insight of the view offered here is that Newman's intellectual stance is thoroughly and persistently rhetorical. . . . That whatever Newman touched . . . he systematically operated with rhetorical principles and methods of inquiry, argument, interpretation, and judgment. He aimed, in fact, at a rhetorical ideal of mind. . . .[2]

These rhetorical principles are understood as classical in origin and constitutive of Newman's very mode of "conception" and argumentative proof.[3] Drawing this thesis out consistently, Jost maintains that: (a) Newman was not what should be considered a systematic (philosophical) thinker[4] and (b) that Newman's idea of knowledge was a personal one:

> Most of what is called knowledge is grounded in personal and interpersonal choices or construals of what is the case, and justified by a wide range of appeals--feelings, values, shared facts and opinions, probabilities, presumptions, interpretations--what we may call "all available means of persuasion."[5]

In light of this rhetoricism, Jost also notes that Newman's attacks on the abstract and notional have been seriously misunderstood (by Weatherby and others) as anti-rational and skeptical.[6]

WHAT IS TRUTH?

Difficulties loom quickly, however, as it becomes apparent that what is understood in Jost's text as "knowledge," "truth," and even "rhetoric" itself is profoundly different from those understandings best warranted by Newman's work. As we have seen, Newman's rhetoricism was a "realist" rhetoric; however much he might have despaired of getting to the bottom of metaphysics, it is clear from his texts (especially the *Grammar*) that *being* is the ultimate rule of Newman's habits and theory of rhetorical knowledge. Though he uses "being" infrequently, the operative control in all his works is the reality of objective creation and the adequation of the mind to it. He worried the terms about in the *Notebook*, virtually teasing the scientific materialism of his day with questions approaching "What do you mean 'reality?'" and such, but we have seen both the purpose and the philosophical incapacities of those speculations.

In fact, Newman was eager to challenge people's comfortable presumptions that they had "the world" figured out--even in its material phenomena--not because he thought the mind incapable of reaching reality, but because he feared it could be too easily seduced to a merely partial adequation to that reality. Truth, for Newman, is still the *adequatio rei et intellectus*. The "*rei*" is every bit as essential as the "*intellectus*." Hence, like Aquinas, he says that knowledge begins in the senses, and the appropriation into the mind of exterior reality is the principle and control of all cognition. Unphilosophical as he is, he remains careful to give such things as first principles and formal reasoning their due even though his interests lie elsewhere. As demonstrated by the doctrine of indefectibility, his entire idea of certitude rests upon the mind's actual grasp of an objective reality--a truth. "Being" (for something non-existent cannot be objectively known or indefectibly certain) is at the very heart of Newman's thought whether exercised on pastoral duties, means of knowing through probability, personal influence and discourse, or religion and spiritual development.

Indications that Jost misses Newman's focus on truth as knowledge of reality crop up very early and are soon confirmed. As early as the preface we see Jost straddling a philosophical fence. He seeks to defend Newman from the charges of skepticism and relativism posed by Weatherby and others. But he likewise seeks to defend him from contemporary critics who "find Newman infected" with the "metaphysics of presence."[7] "Newman is neither skeptically subversive nor dogmatic," asserts Jost; "on the contrary, he embodies the best in the modern turn to indeterminacy without sacrificing the intellect and the traditional search for truth."[8] Jost consistently assures the reader that both Newman and himself are exploring a moderate, "stable," middle ground between extremes. Though rhetorically effective, the "extreme" avoided--as we will see--is reality itself. For Jost, Newman "emerges as nothing less than the first modern epistemic rhetorician" and is in the same theoretical company as Kenneth Burke, Chaim Perelman, Michael Polanyi and others.[9] This may seem surprising company for Newman; certainly he becomes less recognizably "Newman" the more we interpret his writings in the light of such theorists. The epistemic rhetorician Jost most intimately ties Newman to is, ironically, the "Aristotelian" and scholar of rhetorical-history, Richard McKeon. Just as Agricola elevates dialectic into philosophy, McKeon elevates rhetoric into "an architectonic philosophic principle capable of coordinating all our knowing, doing, and making."[10] By so doing, philosophy is effectively collapsed and rhetoric takes its place as the meta-mode of discourse and thought.

Telling as this procedure is, the difficulties soon compound when we find that what is meant by "knowledge" is quite at odds with what Newman meant. All knowledge is rhetorical, says Jost, because the mind knows by means of "the persuasive determination of the indeterminate in any problem."[11] The rhetorical intellect is constitutive of knowledge, since what is to be known is itself indeterminate. Though the term "indeterminate" may have an ominous ring for the realist, it has legitimate uses especially when employed in reference to something indeterminate relative to something else. Instead of defining the indeterminate relatively speaking, Jost (and McKeon) use the term to concretize their theory with the result that the very idea of "truth" is dealt a fatal blow.

Identifying Newman with McKeon, Jost affirms that indeed the mind does know, and that truth is its object. But what is this truth? What is meant by "knowledge?" "[F]or McKeon rhetoric aims at truth-through-communication. What is known or knowable must survive the crucible of argument and persuasion; intersubjective agreement over time by qualified inquirers who have accepted the evidence and arguments is the test of truth."[12] The precision of this statement must not be underestimated. Because "epistemological absolutism" has been "exploded" by Burke and Richard Rorty, and because the "will to power" they advocate is repugnant, a middle ground must be sought, according to Jost, where we can claim to know but not be subject to the "absolute" quality of any knowledge.[13] McKeon provides this middle ground, but like the pea under the shells, whenever we lift a shell to find truth or knowledge, it is gone. For Aristotle and Aquinas, what is known does or can survive the crucible of argument because of the real being of the thing known; here, what is known *must* survive the crucible, that is, it is not actually known until after the "proving" has occurred. This is confirmed by the following clause. The test of truth is--dress it up how you will with argument and evidence--*intersubjective agreement*. Truth is known as such not by the intellect's grasp of a truly existent thing, but by the intersubjective agreement of persons. As we have seen, however, no amount of subjectivity can result in objectivity. Once locked inside the mind, always locked inside the mind. It must be remembered that Jost and McKeon are speaking of truth itself, all truth, *per se*, and not, as with Newman, the "history" of holding a truth within persons. Jost has made the "history" the essence, and thus the reality of truth is lost. Truth has been deconstructed and all one is left with is agreement among persons equally incapable of adequation to beings other than themselves. Descartes is back.[14]

INDETERMINACY, INTERPRETATION, AND THE CONCRETE

It is interesting how the incipient skepticism of this "middle ground" is hinted at by the verificationism so prominent in the passage above. The skeptic will always try to verify knowledge despite his radical inability to do so. Occasionalists called on God to secure knowledge, while McKeon settles for agreement among men, albeit "qualified men." The unfolding of the skepticism in Jost's study continues, for while "truth" is emptied of meaning the troubling echo in the word "indeterminacy" becomes ever louder. Rhetoric deals with indeterminacies in the same sense that it deals with probabilities. We have seen that what is "probable" philosophically speaking may nonetheless be a fact, objectively real. The indeterminate is similar in that, as Jost notes in one place, "purely theoretical investigation and logical deduction cannot force one to view [it] in a certain way."[15] Something indeterminate then, is only indeterminate from the standpoint of theoretical science. As philosophy deals in universals, anything particular or contingent is "indeterminate" from the standpoint of philosophy. That does not mean, however, it is indeterminate in and of itself. Jost misses this point, as he understands "indeterminate" as applying to everything *per se*. As Aristotle notes, even the particular can be known, although not philosophically, because it has the universal *in it*. Likewise, an historical event, though not known scientifically, is nevertheless wholly determinate of itself.

Jost overlooks these distinctions, which leads to a profound miscasting of Newman's thought. Trying to find corroborative expressions in Newman, Jost calls our attention to two passages in the *Grammar* that support his view and use of indeterminacy as the cornerstone of thought and knowledge. Newman, he says, "suggests in chapter III of the *Grammar*, the apprehension of reality is in some measure indeterminate, since the real requires ongoing interpretation from the perceiving subject (*G.of A.*, 23, 30)."[16] In saying so, Jost employs two terms essential to his study, "indeterminate" and "interpretive." Perception is interpretive, thus apprehension of reality is "in some measure" (a qualifier he will soon drop) indeterminate. The perceiving subject employs persuasions to interpret and make determinate what he sees. Jost then interprets Newman in a way that casts his ideas in oddly contemporary terms: "It should be evident that Newman's epistemology is thoroughly interpretive, predicated on the indeterminacy of the concrete and the mediatorial role of mind and language."[17] "Newman's purpose here is to enable his reader to recognize . . . that their own thinking is *fundamentally interpretive*, [emphasis his] at least in the great range of matters he calls the concrete." "[L]anguage that facilitates our contact with the real . . . is inventive since the nature of the real is relatively indeterminate. . . ." "In the *Grammar of Assent* . . . which is in the first instance a philosophical and not a theological analysis, man's nature is, first, a self-justifying fact to be taken as such and an *indeterminacy in itself* [emphasis his]. . . ."[18] In view of the emphases and the incessant reiteration of truth's subjectivity, reality's inaccessibility, and the personal interpretive determination of perception and knowledge, ("*indeterminacy in itself*," "the nature of the real is . . . indeterminate," "thinking is *fundamentally interpretive*,") the occasional qualifiers such as "relatively," or "in the concrete," lose their force. The context of the entire study does not allow much latitude in interpreting these assertions; truth is hollowed out. There is little, if anything, not covered by the "interpretive" and the "indeterminate"; they constitute the whole of reality, our nature, our language.

In view of the crucial impact of this idea of indeterminacy, does Newman really "suggest," as Jost says, that our very perception of reality is interpretive and indeterminate? Does Newman actually embrace such a position in Chapter III of the *Grammar*? Since the essence of Jost's study unfolds from this initial predication, the passages cited (though not quoted) become extremely important. In fact, the passages Jost cites suggest exactly the opposite. In the first, it appears that a misunderstood pronoun might have suggested a misreading. Newman is speaking of real apprehension, and its retention in the faculty of memory:

> Memory consists in a present imagination of things that are past; memory retains the impressions and likenesses of what they were when before us; and when we make use of the proposition which refers to them, *it supplies us with objects by which to interpret it* [emphasis mine]. They are things still, as being the reflections of things in a mental mirror.[19]

There is nothing else on this page that could apply to Jost's reference, the text being a series of examples of memory in action. So what does Newman say here? Is our perception of reality *interpretive*? "Fundamentally?" "Thoroughly?"

Newman says that memory brings back to us past perceptions, memory gives us those perceptions to refer to. This is straightforward enough, but the next clause has two identical pronouns, "it," which refer, however, to different antecedents. "[I]t," says Newman, meaning memory, "supplies us with the objects [the images] by which to interpret it." The second "it" clearly refers to the *proposition*, the thing for which the images are the object. Whereas Jost apparently read this to mean that the memory is interpretive, in fact the memory--which is the "record" of the perceptions--supplies the things *used* to interpret or understand the proposition. In either case, the "perceiving subject" does not perform an ongoing interpretation of perception such that what is perceived is indeterminate. The perceived is determinate (Newman says, "By means of sense we gain knowledge directly"[20]); it has its universal. In fact, a few sentences later, speaking of the memory, Newman says, "I create nothing; I see the facsimiles of facts. . . ."[21]

Newman holds that memory supplies us with the means to interpret propositions, to understand statements about things, precisely because the memory has for its object objectively existent things, "I create nothing. . . ." He creates nothing because of the genuinely cognitive character of sense-data. Newman's position is hardly what Jost makes of it here; one does not find Newman embracing the idea that perception itself is interpretive (constitutive) because it is indeterminate.

The other citation meant to support Jost's view is at the end of the same chapter of the *Grammar*, where Newman is comparing real and notional apprehension. Again, there is little here to suggest "ongoing interpretation" and "fundamental indeterminacy." Newman's only possible statement related to the idea is that real apprehension "has the precedence, as being the scope and end and the test of the notional; and the fuller is the mind's hold upon things or what it considers such, the more fertile is it in its aspects of them, and the more practical in its definitions."[22] The rest of the page simply deals with the appearance of "degree" in assents being due to vividness of apprehension. Newman is saying here that the more complete a mind's "hold" upon real things, the more capable it will be in understanding the various aspects of those already held real things ("of them"). Again, this citation does not seem to justify the heavy burden Jost places upon it. It is henceforth assumed that for Newman, perception is interpretive, and the slant this assumption allows Jost to place on subsequent passages profoundly alters Newman's meaning. Newman has to be essentially recast in this manner, though, for Jost's idea of truth or knowledge is radically at odds with Newman's.

The intersubjectivity of thought posited in the study creates the necessity for a "method"--a word frequently used by Jost. A "method" is necessary to explain the inward-focused cognition of the trapped intellect. The dreaded "metaphysics of presence" has been "exploded," so something must replace it to account for the rationality of thought. For Jost (as he posits in Newman) that "method" becomes a topical dialecticism.

METHOD–AGAIN

The appearance of "method" as a rescue of intelligibility should itself make us suspicious that the "common sky" has been eliminated, and the exposition of Newman's "topics" confirms the suspicion. Certainly, Jost pays much-needed attention to a profound and important manifestation of Newman's rhetorical habit: the common use of paired or opposing terms. An important strength of the study is its determination that in Newman, "special topics are omnipresent, usually appearing as paired terms that structure his inquiries."[23] But he pulls the rhetorical rug from beneath topics by turning them into an architectonic feature of reasoning *per se*. According to Jost, topics are nothing short of "enabling ideas and dispositions by which we live and in which we move and have our being, providing what the hermeneutic tradition calls our 'horizon of understanding,' and what Newman calls a 'view'."[24] Topics become, then, "the very means by which the concrete is known" and are "world-constitutive."[25] In this light, "topics" begin to resemble Kant's categories, or an unusual set of a-priori innate ideas. Indeed, they appear to precede perception somehow, since they are necessary components in the interpretive process through which one perceives.

It is not difficult to see a profound solipsism behind the description of "topics" in this study, which is why Aristotle, not to mention Newman, would very probably be surprised at what had become of topicality.[26] But here the solipsism is not surprising; it is merely the product of a crippled sense of "truth." As being does not "ground" the intellect in truth, the arrival at truth becomes a methodical--albeit solipsistic--dialectic using topics as the opposing terms. Though Jost denies making Newman a Hegelian, he posits that "truth is neither fixed nor determinate *simpliciter*, but emerges from conflict 'with many swayings to the right and to the left'."[27] This last reference to Newman himself highlights the difference between Newman's approach and Jost's: while Newman speaks of the history of a mind's recognition of a truth, Jost speaks of the nature of truth itself, as a mental by-product of method.

Over and over again, Jost refers to or excerpts a passage from Newman and paraphrases it in just such a way as to profoundly alter its meaning. Despite attempts at moderation, Jost has encountered the slippery slope of relativism, and the philosophical consequences Gilson traces in philosophical history are traced out in miniature here. The "value of an inquiry" comes to reside largely "in the performance itself." Knowledge becomes "historical," for which "there is no ahistorical place to stand to grasp the whole." Thus, grasping the whole "is not an achievable aim but a pragmatic posture and direction."[28] Aside from the incipient contradiction (the assertion that "there is no ahistorical place to stand to grasp the whole," presents itself as a grasped whole, not a pragmatic posture) such ideas of truth and knowledge posit an efficient cause as a final cause: the motion of thought is its own end. As such, objective truth is impossible to us and we are trapped in an endless circle of mediated perceptions,[29] interpreted apprehensions, and "realizations" that, instead of being recognitions, are "transformations."

> [T]ruth is a matter of discerning patterns within complex sets of interpreted structures, and real *assent* is less a matter of achieving resolution through a demonstration (whether certain or probable) than it is a matter of *transformation* through the evocation of facts and probabilities--what Newman calls "realization."[30]

AN UNREAL NEWMAN

Many are the consequences of the relativistic, solipsistic principles operative in Jost's study. Although Jost often will hedge his assertions, employ qualifiers, and disclaim the radical consequences of these principles (a procedure required by his attempt to establish a "middle ground"), the principles do exert an inexorable pressure upon the study. There is, for example, the distinct collapse of all sciences into rhetoric which results directly from the indeterminable nature of reason itself. Since Newman "approached the problem of reason . . . as one that was itself indeterminate . . ." Jost asserts that for Newman, "philosophizing is itself preeminently a rhetorical activity," and that "theology" also "is rhetoric--a rhetorical inquiry and a rhetorical argument and judgment."[31] We are not speaking of aspects or qualities here, but things in their essence.[32] The sciences have collapsed again into rhetoric.

Perhaps feeling the need to "shore up" the rational claims of rhetoric, Jost grasps the verificationist straw of post-Kantian "criticism," claiming that Newman's rhetorical theory is "critical to the full enterprise of philosophy."[33] This is exactly the same procedure we have seen before; turn rhetoric into philosophy (by collapsing philosophy) and claim for it philosophical prerogatives. The distinctness of the sciences that Newman so strenuously establishes (after Aristotle) in his *Idea* is here swept away before the architectonic broom of rhetoric. Language itself is essentially rhetorical--regardless of modes of discourse--because for Burke (like Newman), "Wherever there is persuasion, there is rhetoric. And wherever there is meaning, there is 'persuasion'."[34] Like a voracious predator, rhetoric consumes all the sciences, all reason, all language, all thought. Everything collapses into rhetoric, and even rhetoric, as we have seen, makes no pretense of being grounded in an accessible reality. It is lost in an interpretive cosmos of metaphysically absent contingencies, essenceless non-beings, or at best, beings whose essence and existence is bracketed outside intellectual access.

In such a cosmos, it comes as no surprise that Jamesian pragmatism is all that is left. Without any real knowledge, "theory" is a kind of intellectual luxury to be permitted as long as it is subservient to "practice." In an interesting twist, Jost frequently substitutes the word "practice" (as in "In Newman's view, theory must be bonded to practice . . . with the 'practical' as the ultimate court of appeal"[35]) where Newman employs the word *fact*. This substitution demonstrates, paradoxically, the most debilitating feature of this study: its unreal "abstractizing" of Newman's thought. Though Jost attempts to wrest Newman from the clutches of theorizers who either condemn him or claim him for their own, he has largely performed the same appropriation. He has etherealized Newman's words and rhetorical habit entirely out of scope and proportion, with the bizarre consequence that the Newman we are left with is virtually unrecognizable.

Nowhere is this consequence more evident than in Jost's reading of Newman regarding dogma, the development of doctrine, and the Church. Doctrine is "an idea . . . known only in time . . . wholly mediated by the probable and changing."[36] As such, the development of the idea must conform to the "practice" (again) and "understanding" of each time period. Newman's notes for distinguishing valid development, such as the critical note of "continuity," are seen as merely "suggestive topoi" that "run just as much risk of being irrelevant or misused as any other topics. . . ."[37] The development, moreover, is controlled by theologians involved in dialectical antagonism. Whereas, for Newman, the medieval schools were valuable as the testing grounds for theological discernments which were subsequently approved or condemned (if necessary) by Rome, Jost asserts that Newman's idea is one of dialectical wars, school vs. school, and theologians vs. hierarchy. Thus "Newman accordingly stressed *freedom* for theologians . . . and *pluralism* of methods since each school or individual spoke from a unique perspective . . . ."[38] In this way, "a relatively indeterminate Revelation" is developed, and Newman "would have little difficulty agreeing with Hans Kung" that the Church is not "a uniform, single-shaped ecclesiastical 'diakonia' ["ministry"]" but a "multiplicity of disciples, witnesses and ministers."[39] What Newman might have difficulty with, in statements such as this, is the assumptions they make about highly delicate and important matters. Newman certainly embraced the ideal of the medieval schools and the contribution of the laity in the face of contemporary Ultramontanism. But he was no modernist in ecclesiastical structure. After all, he was delighted that the actual definition of papal infallibility corresponded so precisely with his own conception of the matter.[40] In fact, Jost's principle of topical dialecticism so reads Newman as to require him to embrace a plurality of *religions* (not just schools): "Anything less than such a pluralism (which, inadvertently, applies fully as much to Newman's views on the diversity of religions) risks predetermining man's nature, and as such would be theoretical and unreal."[41]

Through a misinterpretation of Newman on first-principles, apprehension and assent, ideas and development, Jost identifies Newman's thought with a surprising array of contemporary theorists: "Michael Polanyi, Hans-Georg Gadamer, Raphael Demos, Kenneth Burke, Chaim Perelman . . ." as well as Hans Kung, "Feyerabend, Rorty, Toulmin, Habermas, Foucault, in the sciences and philosophy; Gadamer [again], Ricoeur, Tracy, and Kaufman in hermeneutics and theology; Burke, Booth, Perelman, Grassi, Valesio, and Fisher in rhetoric. . . ."[42] Undoubtedly, many connections and comparisons can be made between Newman's thought and the figures cited, but connections are not at issue. The fundamental question is whether Jost's reading of Newman is warranted, and the answer, despite many strengths and insights in the work, seems to be negative. Regardless of how Newman may be similar to various contemporary thinkers, the fact remains that the intellect's grasp of a truly existent reality is the starting point for rhetorical thought (as well as any other kind of thought) for Newman, while Jost's starting point is the immersion of the intellect in a sea of indeterminacy.[43] From that essential divergence of principles all else follows; secure "truth" as he may, Jost's Newman remains imprisoned inside a skull that has become a cell.[44] Echoing Nuttall, one begins to think that this kind of rhetoricism, as opposed to rhetorical realism, is little more than a technique for losing the world. The outspoken Stanley Jaki, quick to notice any philosophical skepticism or subjectivism, treats the subject of Newman and reality in detail, pointing out that Newman anchors "indefectibility [of certitude] not in some intangible subjective disposition but in objective truth insofar as the human mind has an affinity for it. . . ."[45] As Frost says, it "has made all the difference."

Joseph Pieper's insightful study *Prudence* can provide a partial corrective to Jost as it delineates some features of practical thought in a fashion harmonious with Newman. Newman's idea of informal reasoning intersects with the concept of prudence at the juncture of "judgment." Ever since Bacchus underscored the connection between judgment and the illative sense,[46] critics have known that there is a strong foundation in the idea of "practical wisdom" for Newman's thought. Though Pieper's Thomistic study focuses more upon action in its external form than the interior action (assent) Newman is primarily concerned with, there is much in *Prudence* Newman would approve, and this precisely because of the nuanced, non-mechanical conception of practical wisdom offered there.

Not surprisingly, Pieper emphasizes the way in which the mind becomes adequated to reality in practical matters. While insisting that the province of practical wisdom is the concrete and particular, he does not mistake a philosophical indeterminacy for an indeterminacy *per se*. The particular, being real, can be known: "Certainly prudence is the standard of volition and action; but the standard of prudence, on the other hand, is the *ipsa res*, the 'thing itself,' the objective reality of being."[47] Since prudence is the virtue by which the good is realized or enacted, it "presupposes that our actions are appropriate to the real situation, that is to the concrete realities which form the 'environment' of a concrete human action."[48]

Like Newman, Pieper observes that making "actions" appropriate to real situations is not automatic or instantaneous. Though the mind does know concrete reality in an immediate way (through the senses), action in accordance with that reality requires another kind of knowledge. However, this other knowledge requires not just perception but the proper alignment of the will and intellect. Clearly, this is where the disorder of the Fall enters the picture, for we can by will or habit delude ourselves about reality in such a way as to inhibit this secondary knowledge. In this sense we can be unreal, we can not "apprehend" what is really true, and thus the necessity of finding a means of enhancing apprehension of the real where it is not (or only partially) apprehended becomes evident.

Concrete situations have a reality to which we must adequate our minds in order to pursue the good in action. "The goodness of concrete human action rests upon the transformation of the truth of real things; of the truth which *must be won and perceived by regarding the ipsa res, reality itself* [emphasis added]."[49] The "transformation" here is not Jost's "transformation" which is a purely internal process whereby subjective phenomena are "crowned" with "realization." Here it means the "winning" of reality itself. Pieper repeatedly stresses the need for openness to reality in order for practical wisdom to exist, precisely because it is easy to isolate ourselves and attempt to act in textbook fashion regardless of the status of real situations. Such an openness in turn assists in rectifying and purifying man's will and intellect: "reason perfected in the cognition of truth shall inwardly shape and imprint his volition and action."[50]

Not surprisingly, the emphasis in Pieper's study (like Newman's) is how this adequation of mind to concrete things is accomplished. While Newman generally confines himself to the influence of things and habits upon concrete judgments, Pieper goes further and explains what can be done to correctly form such judgments. The requirements he sketches out are not, however, unfamiliar to Newman. A three-fold process occurs in facilitating the "transformation of true knowledge into prudent decisions": deliberation, judgment, decision.[51] The first two, deliberation and judgment, are called "receptive-perceptive" and represent "the cognitive character of prudence." The last, decision, "represents the imperative character" of prudence, "*secundum quod est praeceptiva.*"[52] This exposition of Aquinas' thought is surprisingly similar to Newman's ideas about concrete reasoning. In the receptive-perceptive we have a corollary to the illative sense, especially as it operates upon real apprehensions, while in "decision" we have a parallel to the act of assent. If any of these three processes are deficient, the result is imprudence of one sort or another, whether in impulsive thoughtlessness or futile irresoluteness.[53]

This process creative of prudent action requires in turn three faculties or dispositions which also sound familiar to a Newman reader. In order for the receptive-perceptive and imperative components of prudence to do their work properly, the prudent person must employ *Memoria, Docilitas*, and *Solertia*. Because prudence is only possible when "the truth of real things shall become determinative" of an action, memory is essential as "true-to-being."[54] Just as Newman says "I create nothing" (speaking of course of the proper operation of memory), Pieper and Aquinas note that the faculty must "contain" events and things "as they really are and were."[55] *Memoria* is especially sensitive to being corrupted by the will, through "slight retouches, displacements, discolorations, omissions, shifts of accent."[56] This explains in part how the Fall affects practical wisdom, for action often requires knowledge provided by memory to the judgment. Skew or even falsify what the memory brings to judgment, and the trueness-to-being required for prudent action will be amiss. The memory will not be true to being, and the action will be deficient in pursuit of the good.

Docilitas, on the other hand, is "open-mindedness which recognizes the true variety of things and situations to be experienced and does not cage itself in any presumption of deceptive knowledge." This is docility before reality or "facts" as Newman would say, which when lacking, results in a "closed mind and know-it-allness" equally destructive of the "perception of reality."[57] Finally, *Solertia* is similar to *Docilitas* in being open-minded, but its special sense is "objectivity in unexpected situations."[58] A deficiency here results in blind, reflex action not tailored to the peculiarities of the circumstance. Each of these dispositions or faculties, *Memoria, Docilitas, Solertia,* are required for prudent action and illustrative of the perceptive-cognitive character of practical wisdom.

Newman's concern with the possibility of one's intellectual and moral habits detracting from the ability to see realities can be understood as a concern for the proper ordering of the practical intelligence through "memory" of, and "docility" before, concrete reality. It is evident that perception of realities past, present, and future is what Newman desires, and he employs rhetorical thought and discourse to sensitize people to those realities, "things and situations which are 'just so and no different' and which in their actuality bear the seal of a certain necessariness."[59] This last is the corrective to Jost's misapplied indeterminacy. The concrete and the contingent, by means of their actuality, their being itself, "bear the seal of a certain necessariness." They can be comprehended and are determinate not by a "transformation" in the intellect but by the transformation *of* the intellect due to perception of real things and circumstances.

Pieper's text provides a number of avenues for further study, notably the reciprocal influence of volition and judgment, and the manner in which realization of the good "realizes" the person as well--both ideas reminiscent of Newman. For present purposes, however, the key idea is the connection of contingent knowledge to an actually intelligible reality. It should be clear that, though no Thomist, Newman draws a picture of thought that resembles Pieper's study of prudence more than it does Jost's study of Newman. Pieper, like Newman, roots the virtue under discussion in a just perception of reality and the dangers to that perception in a fallen creature. Prudence is

> the circumspect and resolute shaping power of our minds which transforms knowledge of reality into realization of the good. It holds within itself the humility of silent, that is to say, of unbiased perception; the trueness-to-being of memory, the act of receiving counsel; alert, composed readiness for the unexpected. . . . Prudence is, as Paul Claudel says, the "intelligent prow" of our nature which steers through the multiplicity of the finite world towards perfection.[60]

The image of a ship's prow is a good one, for it clearly suggests the changing, shifting surface upon which the ship sails, and the changeless, steady course the ship keeps. Throughout the treacherous changes and fluctuations of the sea, the art of sailing and navigation remains the same and is exactly suited to that shifting element. Thus it is with prudence, and thus with the illative sense and certainty. But as Newman would be quick to point out, the ship may be poorly built or ineptly sailed. The mind's work in practical matters must be governed by right reason and not swayed by prejudice, habit, or sloth. Moreover, this kind of thought is not a mechanical, automatic process. No sailor, however experienced, can tell in advance exactly what exercises of his art will be necessary, and in what order, so as to achieve his end. Practical wisdom, as a whole, as well as prudence, rhetorical reasoning, or any other subset of the practical intelligence, does not "know" anything in some kind of simplistic, naive way. As we have seen, even the knowledge of material realities involves an act of intellectual appropriation. The "absolutism" "exploded" by Burke, and the "impossible metaphysical presences," may or may not be exploded and impossible. For Newman, Aquinas, and Aristotle, at least the things known are truly known because they exist as realities and are apprehended as such by the intellect. Yet this does not mean that intelligible things are wholly appropriated and can thus be presumed upon. Pieper has already pointed out that, greatly intelligible as something might be, it is even more immersed in a darkness of existential mystery. Newman would quite agree, as his life-long resistance to mere mechanistic thinking demonstrates. Such thinking leaves much of a man behind, where it also leaves much of reality. At least the cognition Newman and Aquinas speak of here truly knows without pretense of exhausting the intelligibility of the thing known. Such an "epistemology" seems far more moderate, possessed of a real middle ground, and more realistic than either the "absolute" of the rationalist or the relativism of the "rhetorical" irrationalist.

NEWMAN'S RHETORICAL REALISM

If, then, one wishes to launch a term of classification into a world already ponderously burdened by such terms, perhaps it should be "rhetorical realist." The utility of the epithet is in its definition of scope--rhetoric--while securing that scope from any irrational or sub-rational characteristics predicated of it. This term might be preferable to others used here (say, "rhetorical personalism,") because by this point the personalistic aspect should be well incorporated conceptually within rhetoric itself. In a sense Newman's rhetorical realism was indeed "architectonic." As Jost also asserts, Newman's rhetorical habit of mind is the keystone to the arch of his thoughts and writings upon virtually any subject. The habit integrates the sundry features of his thought which many critics have noticed but which have resisted integration into a comprehensive picture. Newman's personalism, his personal, even "individual-addressed" quality of prose and his strong intellectual preference for personal institutions, education, and discourse has been often noticed by critics, but it is usually either left there--with notice--or elevated into a phenomenological philosophy.

His personalism in fact becomes a cogent, intelligible habit and theme (rather than merely a "quality") when it is seen in the light of rhetorical thought. The life-long sensitivity and even advocacy of "the whole man" in every matter--intellectual, spiritual, even physical--is a manifestation of his almost instinctive perception of how people think and "move" in concrete matters. This perception is why his defense of the Catholic priesthood becomes one of the most famous autobiographies since St. Augustine's *Confessions*. Though many traits of his personality--his affability and serenity, his loyalty to friends, his punctiliousness, etc.--are attributable to independent virtues (and vices), they become ordered or marshalled beneath his overriding sense of purpose and "Christian utilitarianism." They had their own "seat" in his personality, but his vision and rhetorical habit employed them, so to speak, in pursuit of personal, intellectual, and moral good. He may have had a novelist's gift for seeing into other's minds, but he did not "sit back" and enjoy the spectacle. The gift was *used*--with delicacy and discretion--to assist him in understanding the views and motives of associates and contemporaries, to write and address minds as they were, not as he wished they were, to preach with depth and effect. A common observation of Newman's St. Mary's auditors is that he somehow seemed (without the least ingratiation) to address them personally, to plumb their thoughts and feelings.

Likewise, "rhetorical realism" should highlight those aspects of Newman's thought that too often attract systematic studies which result in "Newman the Philosopher" or "Theologian" or "Skeptic." In accordance with his rhetorical mode of thought and his sensitivity to the personal, Newman's conceptions and treatment of knowledge are not properly philosophical at all. Most people know most things through complex, illative, non-demonstrative and non-scientific modes of cognition. The various faculties of a person--intellect, passions, and will--are invaluable in such concrete reasonings, and "science" does not always touch or move them.

In harmony with his sense of purpose, Newman knew that if people are to be brought to knowledge, especially that of Revelation, the mode of knowledge of greatest affinity to them must be cultivated. Thus he asked--and answered--the question, "Can one really know the way we seem to know most things?" That is, is there a kind of real knowledge, a kind of genuine adequation of the mind to reality, available from amassed probabilities, testimony, and participated in by the whole of the knower? In a sense, Newman's "method" (in so far as he has one) in answering this question is to answer with another question: "Why not?" It appears unreasonable and unreal to suppose that knowledge was confined to the few who could systematically demonstrate a thing. The faculty of mind Newman looks to in appropriating knowledge for the "common man" is largely rhetorical; it treats concrete matters and probabilities in order to arrive at truth. That truth, when grasped, is an indefectible certainty because it is a "seeing" of a real thing, a truly existent actuality. Not surprisingly, the fact that rhetoric draws upon *anything* for its material is also suited to Newman, for his "whole man" predisposition would be loath to divide man's nature into an assemblage of unintegrated parts in Gradgrind fashion. Hence, the rhetorical intellect can draw even upon abstract, demonstrative reasonings in the evaluation of particular things and the disposition or estimation of various probabilities.

This is why education is so central to Newman's thought and his life-long work. Clearly, education (specifically of the liberal variety) is best suited to molding the mind so that it can duly and accurately weigh probabilities, claims, and antecedent considerations. This formation is not accomplished in a course of logic, nor through a text of history. It is best fostered by both, together with a number of other subjects, all learned under the aspect of a living voice, a tutor, mentor, a "whole man."

For Newman, then, discourse itself is the central manifestation of knowing or "intellectual" man. Language figures forth the whole man in his intellectual and affective nature. In its highest, most human form, language is oral, for the vocal/aural aspect of language not only includes "more" of the person in the doing, but it evokes the participation of the will in cognition: speech has more of the character of an act than print. Orality is also important because "voices melt us, looks subdue us". There abides in personal, verbal communication variables (and persuasives) such as tone, timbre, and appearance, that are generally unavailable to print. Moreover, from a cultural standpoint, the metaphysical spatialization of "knowledge" encouraged by print contributes to the very conceptions of knowledge Newman felt he must combat. Not, indeed, that Newman denounced or avoided "print." As a man of books, this was impossible. Nevertheless, orality is a component in Newman's preference for personal, rather than purely textual instruction and learning. Paradoxical is the fact that in controversy, Newman preferred print rather than personal debate. This is understandable, however, in light of the famously personal tone he distilled into his controversial writings. Many have commented that Newman seems to rise from the page and address the reader personally. Newman may well prefer this mode for his controversial labors precisely because it allows him to tailor and craft the personal evocations of his prose to a highly exact and specific extent. In this sense, he might be more effectively "personal" by laboring over the subtleties of style that allow a highly crafted voice to penetrate the prose.

I have tried to show that Newman was both "in his age" and "not in his age" at once. He was in his age just as any good rhetorician should be, since he must address concrete persons in contemporary circumstances and be comprehensible to them. He was out of his age in employing and seeking to restore a mode of thought and discourse once respectable but in his time increasingly marginalized. Newman affirmed and appreciated the division of the sciences especially as considered formally, but his predilection was toward the unity of the knowing subject. That is, he allowed philosophy to be ruled by real first principles, but he would not allow philosophy (or material science for that matter) to claim or comprise the entire domain of "knowledge."

Newman was a kind of "throwback" in trying to recover the ground necessary for a mode of thought and discourse not confined to mechanistic, unreal conceptions of knowledge. Obviously, the greatest body of precedent for such an integrated, rhetorical mode was patristic writing, with its "jumble" of logic, passion, philosophy, history, probability, poetry. Yet there are times and circumstances in which being a "throwback" may well be the most radically progressive thing possible. Newman may be thought of not as seeking a backwards return to integrated knowledge and discourse but a forward progression past the stage of disintegration and error, into a rediscovered personalist, rhetorical mode. A scholar once suggested in this connection that as the history of philosophy has moved from the ancient and medieval focus on things, to the "modern" focus on thought, and currently to the post-modern focus on words, it might be reasonable to suppose philosophy had gone full circle and could again concentrate on things. Newman may be radically progressive in looking toward the complete disintegration of human faculties and discourse as the best occasion for the return to integration and personal communication.

While this study has tried to establish the character and depth in Newman of his rhetorical realism, much work in connection to this realism is yet to be done. The return to a personalist mode of discourse was largely intensified in Newman by his sense of man's Fall and his own pastoral purpose, but to what extent did such a return motivate nineteenth-century "Romantic" movements as a whole?[61] How do poetic and connatural perceptions inform Newman's thought and his approach to his rhetoric? How does Newman's rhetorical realism, as here established, exactly fit into the Aristotelian/Thomistic schema of practical wisdom and judgment? We have seen the close interrelation here, but the exact nature of the relation requires further study. In fact, establishing such an exact relation may be impossible; it may require a formalizing of Newman's thought (especially in the *Grammar*) alien to it. We already see many such attempts at formalizing his thought, despite its rhetorical intransigence. This opens up a question also suggestive of study: Why has Newman so consistently been "formalized" despite his clear resistance to such a process? Another way of putting the question, is simply to ask to what extent Newman succeeded in clearing the ground for a culturally "respectable" rhetorical realism, a personal mode of knowing and discourse. The very fact that he has been so frequently "abstracted" and systematized--even by the most sympathetic of readers--suggests that he may have failed. We still seem largely dichotomized into the strictly "logical/scientific," and the "affective."

In related areas his rhetorical ideal of mind as embraced in the *Idea* appears to be repudiated; the words on liberal education are sometimes trolleyed out for a commencement address but they are rarely accepted in essence or acted upon. Specialization has won the day. Of late, a new rhetoricism has arisen with a strong curricular architectonic impetus, but it is largely "rhetoric" *sans* "realism." As Jost demonstrates, at its best it is often all too relativistic. Newman's other great opponent, religious liberalism, has also captured the moral high ground, such that any suggestion of a universal supernatural truth is regarded as naive and embarassing--and probably even dangerous.

Doubtless, the question of Newman's "success" or "failure" will depend on the kind of success looked for. Even in his own day, especially his latter years, Newman felt that his efforts were not adequate to reverse the perils he had fought. But his belief as to the nature of these perils and the best means to combat them never changed. Certainly, his personalism even in manner persisted undimmed by years. Nearly fifty years after the amusing meeting between Thomas Arnold and Newman, a much older Newman, recently elevated to the College of Cardinals, met Thomas Arnold's son, Matthew Arnold. Newman had specifically asked the Duke of Norfolk to include Arnold in an invitation list for a reception to be held in London. Arnold's account of the meeting evokes the same impression of Newman's profound personal integrity and warmth as impressed the senior Arnold years before. Though there is a sense of Arnold's condescension (and feeling out of place) towards the pious people surrounding Newman, the account reveals Arnold's reverence and deep affection for one he seemed to know so well despite their lack of personal contact.

> Newman stood in costume, in a reserved part of the drawing room, supported by a chaplain and by the D. of Norfolk. Devotees, chiefly women, kept pressing up to him; they were named to him, knelt, kissed his hand, got a word or two and passed on. I don't know that I should have had the courage to cleave the press, but Lady Portsmouth took charge of me and conveyed me safe to the chaplain who whispered my name to Newman. I made the most deferential of bows, he took my hand in both of his and held it there during our interview, which of course was very short. He said: "I ventured to tell the Duchess I should like to see you," and I said I was glad of the opportunity to tell him how much I owed him. He asked me a question or two about myself, and then about Tom and his troubles; nothing of any interest passed, but I am glad to have spoken to him and shaken hands with him. The sentiment of him, of his sermons, of his position in the Church and in English religion, filled Oxford when I was there; it suited the place, and I am glad, and always shall be glad, to have been there at that moment, and grateful to Newman for the atmosphere of feeling he then created for me.[62]

If Newman did fail in convincing the world of a more fully human mode of knowledge and discourse, then perhaps the failure is attenuated by his being so effective an example of them. The "feeling" Newman created at Oxford is not so much a feeling as a successful embodiment of his own ideal of mind and manner. His prose is possessed of this embodiment as well. What Arnold tries to render "safe" by calling a "feeling" is in fact the whole man, Newman himself, his intellect, personality and grasp of the truth. Thus there is a peculiar attraction felt even by those who do not agree with Newman about the most fundamental matters. Like the elder Arnold who shook his hand, and the younger Arnold who grasped it years later, Newman's readers are often drawn in reading him despite disagreement. Readers are not allowed to rest. By affection and instruction they are brought to a glimpse of Newman's own vision. Perhaps, paradoxically, this accounts for the strange lack of readership Newman has currently. In a world that has largely repudiated the things held most important by Newman, many who do read him respond as did the elder Arnold: it would not do to meet Newman often. The desire to avoid stems from *attraction*, not repulsion, for the glimpse of things Newman engenders can be "dangerous" to contemplate. Newman will not allow readers to merely "appreciate" him; as DeLaura has noted, he will *move* them.[63] He will move them by guiding them in person through experience after experience. They learn to see as he sees, not simply because he is persuasive, but because he has mastered the art of engendering apprehension and assent to realities. They learn not by way of abstract infusion, but by way of a person, a man, taking them in person to the proper vision of the thing known. He does not "convince" so much as he instructs one in the means of seeing for oneself. Or, as the "Soul" says to the Angel in Newman's "Dream of Gerontius":

> I would have nothing but to speak with thee
> For speaking's sake. I wish to hold with thee
> Conscious communion. . . .

Notes

I. NEWMAN: PHILOSOPHER OR RHETORICIAN?

[1] Trevor, *Light in Winter*, 264.

[2] Ibid., 265.

[3] Ibid.

[4] Ibid.

[5] For a brief comparison of the standard biographies including Ian Ker's one-volume work, see Phillip D. Attenbury, "New Perspectives on Newman and The Oxford Movement." Certainly there were numerous significant events in Newman's life, though most of these were the result of evolutions in thought and personal associations.

[6] See Vincent Blehl, "Early Criticism of the *Apologia*," for an account of the reception of the *Apologia*.

[7] Murray, *Oratorian*, 62.

[8] Trevor, *Light in Winter*, 4-5.

[9] Sometimes he is called all of these at once. In what used to be the dining-hall for the old Oratory school are many plaques presented to Newman from various groups in honor of his elevation to the College of Cardinals. Most of these certificates mention Newman's accomplishments, and the lists read like a litany of every kind of intellectual activity.

[10] DeLaura, *Hebrew and Hellene*, xii.

[11] Svaglic, "*Man and Humanist*," 153.

[12] See page 153 in *Victorian Prose: A Guide to Research* (1973) where Martin Svaglic notes that no general study of Newman as a rhetorician has been written. Despite the passage of twenty years, the remark is still largely true. Though he says Holloway treats many large issues and Houghton takes a broad literary approach to the *Apologia* specifically, it remains that a comprehensive study of what "rhetoric" is in Newman is lacking. See also Robin C. Selby's *The Principle of Reserve in the Writings of John Henry Cardinal Newman*, (1975) which takes a comprehensive look at Newman by studying his "reserve." The study is highly useful in identifying Newman's reserve with the concern for tailoring truths to the adequacy of the minds receiving them.

[13] Svaglic, "*Man and Humanist*," 154.

[14] Ker, *Achievement*, ix-x.

[15] Jost, *Rhetorical Thought*, ix.

[16] Ibid, x.

[17] A phrase Jost also employs frequently.

[18] Jost, *Rhetorical Thought*, 25-26.

[19] Aristotle, *Rhetoric*, 1356a, 20-25.

[20] See Jost, 12. See also J. H. Walgrave's *Newman the Theologian*, 8-9, where Walgrave expressly affirms the primarily literary nature of Newman's work and the difficulties of extracting a system from that work. Thomas Vargish (*Newman the Contemplation of Mind*) opens his study of Newman's epistemology by warning that it is not technical in a philosophical or scientific sense (vii). Yet, because of the philosophical nature of Vargish's study, Newman's thought ends up looking far more "subjective" than it seems to warrant in its own context.

[21] Sillem, *Philosophical Notebook*, 1: 21.

[22] Walgrave, *Newman the Theologian*, 13.

[23] Sillem, *Philosophical Notebook*, 1: 1.

[24] Ibid., 17.

[25] Ibid., 3.

[26] Jost, *Rhetorical Thought*, xi.

[27] Weatherby, *Newman in His Age*, 1.

28 Ibid., 287.

29 Boekraad, *Conquest of Truth,* 139.

30 Nuttall, *Common Sky,* 164.

31 Though Culler demonstrates that Newman uses the word "philosophy" in different ways in the *Idea* (*Imperial Intellect* 182-188), Newman fully understood the classical idea of philosophy as the study of causes.

32 Culler, *Imperial Intellect,* 182-210.

33 Sillem, *Philosophical Notebook,* 1: 149.

34 Quoted in Ward, *Life of Newman,* 1: 64-65.

35 Jost, *Rhetorical Thought,* 123.

36 This was a phrase used repeatedly by Professor Fish in his debates at the Conference on the Core Curriculum in Denton, Texas, spring 1990.

37 Hilary Fraser (*Beauty and Belief,* 21), speaking of Newman's "theology," says it is a fusion of the personal and polemical, and that "Such a rhetorical mode is a necessary philosophical consequence of his theory of the nature of literature." Stephen Prickett (*Romanticism and Religion,* 7) also notes that theologians frequently miss the "literary premises" of Newman and others.

38 Aristotle, *Rhetoric,* 1354a, 1-5; 1355b, 5-10.

39 Sillem, *Philosophical Notebook,* 1: 238.

40 Quoted in Ward, *Life of Newman,* 2: 256.

41 Ibid., 257.

42 Ward, *Life of Newman,* 2: 260.

43 Newman, *Idea of a University,* 109-110.

44 Title page: *Aristotelis Ethicorum Nichomacheorum*; Libri Decem; codicum MSS. Collatione Recogniti et Notis Illustrati; A Gulielmo Wilkinson, AM; E Coll. Reginae; Editio Quarta; Oxonii; E Typographeo Clarendoniano; MDCCCXVIII. Page 453.

45 Ibid., 380.

46 Sillem (1: 151) traces Newman's idea of the "illative sense" to his study of these works.

47 Sillem, *Philosophical Notebook,* 1: 149; Culler, *Imperial Intellect,* 199.

48 Sillem, *Philosophical Notebook,* 1: 149; 1: 235-240.

49 Ibid., 236.

50 Trevor, *Light in Winter,* 402.

51 Sillem, *Philosophical Notebook,* 1: 239-240.

52 Trevor, *Light in Winter,* 402.

53 They were not, of course, all that "balmy." The resulting neo-Thomism was largely corrupted by Kantian rationalism. See Gilson, *Thomist Realism and the Critique of Knowledge.*

54 Newman, *Letters and Diaries,* 11: 279.

55 *Divi Thomae Aaquinatis Doctoris Angelici Ordonis Praedicatorum Opera Editio Altera Veneta* MDCCLXXV. For a discussion of Newman relative to nineteenth-century "medievalism," see Kevin L Morris, *The Image of the Middle Ages in Romantic and Victorian Literature,* 136-142.

56 Sillem. *Philosophical Notebook.* 1: 238.

57 Ward, *Life of Newman,* 2: 501.

II. RHETORICAL KNOWLEDGE AND ARISTOTLE

1 There are two texts of particular interest, regarding the *Rhetoric,* in the Oratory archives. One is a manuscript, title page reading: "E Libris Joan. Henr. Newman, Coll. Trin. Oxon, 1819, An Analysis of The Rhetoric of Aristotle." This is a simple summary of the *Rhetoric.* Newman's heavily marked tutorial text is the *Aristotelis De Rhetorica*; Libri Tres; ad Fidem Manuscriptorum Recogniti; in usum academicae Juventutis Oxonii; e typographeo Clarendoniano; MDCCCXXVI. This text is signed and dated "John Henry Newman Oriel College 1827."

2 Jost, *Rhetorical Thought,* 12. For a concise estimate of the place of classical rhetoric in the nineteenth century, see Martin J. Svaglic's "Classical Rhetoric and Victorian Prose."

3 Chesterton, *Victorian Age,* 26.

4 Newman, *Letters and Diaries,* 5: 225.

5 McKeon, *Introduction to Aristotle,* 716.

6 Ibid.

7 Aristotle, *Rhetoric,* 1355b, 25-35.

8 Ibid., 1358a, 5-10.

9 Aristotle, *Nicomachean Ethics,* 1094b, 25-30.

10 Idem., *Rhetoric,* 1355b, 25-26.

11 Ibid., 1356a, 25.

12 Ibid., 1355a, 31.

13 Cicero, *De Inventione,* 3-5.

14 Roberts, "Introduction," v.

15 Aristotle, *Rhetoric,* 1355a, 35-40.

16 Ibid., 1355a, 14-17.

17 Culler alludes to the truth-finding potential of rhetoric in his criticism of Holloway's *Victorian Sage,* citing the work's anti-metaphysical and nominalist thrust. See A. Dwight Culler, "Method in the Study of Victorian Prose," *The Victorian Newsletter* 9 (Spring 1956): 1-4. See also his reply to a reader's comment "A Rejoinder," *The Victorian Newsletter* 10 (Autumn 1956): 16.

18 McKeon, *Introduction to Aristotle,* xxxv.

19 Aristotle, *Rhetoric,* 1357a, 35-40.

20 Ibid., 1355a, 13-17.

21 Ibid., 1402b, 22-40.

22 Ibid., 1356b, 5-10.

23 Ibid., 1358a, 35-40.

24 Ibid., 1356a, 21-25.

25 Ibid., 1356a, 1-5.

26 Ibid., 1356a, 14.

27 Ibid., 1356a, 15.

28 Ibid., 1356a, 20.

29 Ibid., 1356b, 26.

30 Ibid., 1378a, 9.

31 Idem., *Metaphysics,* 980a, 20; 981b, 28.

32 McKeon, *Introduction to Aristotle,* xxxv.

33 Ibid., xxv.

34 Ibid.

35 Ibid.

36 Aistotle, *Posterior Analytics,* 88b, 33-35.

37 Idem., *On the Soul,* 427a, 20.

38 Ibid., *Nicomachean Ethics,* 1098b, 1-5.

39 Ibid., 1095b, 1-8.

40 Ibid., 1139a, 31.

41 Ibid., 1179b, 20-30.

42 Ibid., 1143a, 5-8.

43 Ibid., 1143a, 9-15.

III. Newman's Purposive Rhetoric

1 Holloway, *Victorian Sage*, 1-3.

2 Newman, *Apologia*, 40.

3 In Newman's own words, "Do not stirring times bring out poets? Do they not give opportunity for the rhetoric of poetry, and the persuasion?" Quoted in Tillotson, *A View of Victorian Literature*, 44.

4 Murray, *Oratorian*, 121.

5 Newman, *Autobiographical Writings*, 201.

6 Murray, *Oratorian*, 10.

7 "His exploration of the mind of man was directed by a concern, religious in origin, for the destiny of Christianity and the Church, involved in the vicissitudes of an unstable world." Walgrave, *Newman the Theologian*, 5.

8 See also Selby, *The Principle of Reserve*, 102, for a discussion of the importance of the Fall to Newman.

9 Weatherby, *Newman in His Age*, 20-21.

10 Quoted in Weatherby, *Newman In His Age*, 18.

11 See my article "John Henry Newman: The Rhetoric of the Real" for further discussion of Newman, the Fall, and rhetoric. Some of the material on the following two pages is taken directly from that article.

12 Aquinas, *Summa Theologica*, 1, II, 85, 3.

13 Ibid.

14 Garrigou-Lagrange, *Tinity and God*, 659.

15 Newman, *Parochial and Plain Sermons*, 1022; emphasis added.

16 Trevor, *Light in Winter*, 100.

17 Newman, *Parochial and Plain Sermons*, 1023.

18 Culler, *Imperial Intellect*, 238. Culler criticizes Newman's *University Discourses* for first arguing that a liberal education is pursued for its own sake, then turning around to discuss the practical advantages of such an education (222-223). If Newman's rhetorical purpose is kept in mind, however, one sees that he has established a balanced and comprehensive view of education. While a liberal education (and gentlemanliness) in and of itself may be above utility, there is no denying that certain practical advantages are attached to it. The rhetorical Newman is free to emphasize both essential and accidental aspects of education in bringing his audience to embrace it.

19 Quoted in Murray, *Oratorian*, 189-191.

20 Owens, *Future of Metaphysics*, 21-22.

21 Murray, *Oratorian*, 84-85.

22 Quoted in Murray, *Oratorian*, 37.

23 Trevor, *Light in Winter*, 67-68, 207.

24 Quoted in Trevor, *Light in Winter*, 207.

25 Quoted in Ward, *Life of Newman*, 1:62-63.

26 Ibid., 63. For Newman's affability, see also R. W. Church's *Oxford Movement*, 161-162.

27 Quoted in Trevor, *Pillar of the Cloud*, 391.

28 "Newman penetrated the hidden recesses of every human heart" with the same "calm but inexorable scrutiny which we have seen him bring to bear when probing his own conscience. . . ." Bouyer, *Newman: His Life and Spirituality*, 180.

29 Ward, *Life of Newman*, 1:16.

30 Houghton, *Victorian Frame of Mind*, 161.

31 Ward, *Life of Newman*, 1:15.

32 Trevor, *Light in Winter*, 203.

33 Trevor, *The Pillar of the Cloud*, 58-59. It is difficult to understand how someone who organizes such activities as the Tracts, the *Library of the Fathers* translations, the founding of an

Oratory, the design and building of the Oratory Church and residence, the founding of a University, etc. etc. can be called *not* a man of action.

34 Ward, *Life of Newman*, 1:16. Such de-inidivualizing receptivity is displayed by Walker Percy in his novel *The Last Gentleman*.

35 Chesterton, *Victorian Age*, 31.

36 Trevor, *Light in Winter*, 401.

37 Ibid., 202.

38 Ibid.

39 Ward, *Life of Newman*, 1:233.

40 For additional description of Newman's manner of oratory, see Church's *Oxford Movement* 121-126.

41 Trevor, *Light in Winter*, 401.

42 Quoted in Culler, *Imperial Intellect*, 140.

43 Quoted in Ward, *Life of Newman*, 1:316.

44 Quoted in Culler, *Imperial ntellect*, 148.

45 Quoted in Trevor, *Light in Winter*, 591.

46 Newman, *Present Position*, 288-289. These discourses make up a psychologically acute study of prejudice and misinformation, and a "rhetoric" for meeting the dispositions of such a time. Indeed, were it titled *The Development, Psychology and Eradication of Prejudice*, the book would certainly attract more attention today than it does.

47 Sillem, *Philosophical Notebook*, 1:59-60.

48 Ibid., 60-62.

49 Altick, *Victorian People and Ideas*, 204.

50 Newman, *Theological Papers, Faith and Certainty*, 156.

51 Quoted in Ward, *Life of Newman*, 1:247.

52 Ward, *Life of Newman*, 1:247.

53 Newman, *Theological Papers, Faith and Certainty*, 8-9.

54 Newman's sensitivity was a source of frustration to him in another respect. His keen perception of mental processes made him sharply aware of contradiction in the thought of contemporary skeptics and rationalists. While fashionable nineteenth-century rationalism, agnosticism, and even the new social science were content to consider reasoning and knowledge entirely demonstrative, empirical in origin, and "concrete," Newman reminded them that their everyday lives gave the lie to such narrow conceptions of reason. A hundred times a day, Newman protested, these intellectuals were acting with unshakable certainty upon truths known to them by no such demonstrative means. His argument was largely disregarded by these intellectuals who accused him of novelty and mere word-play. This struck Newman as unfair, for just as he insisted that Christians meet the arguments of the age fairly and with due awareness of the arguments' strengths, he expected the progressive secular thinkers of the age to treat his arguments in the same way. It seems that no amount of rhetorical sensitivity is enough to protect one from being misunderstood or disregarded.

55 Newman, *Theological Papers, Faith and Certainty*, 150.

56 Ibid., 151.

57 Quoted in Ward, *Life of Newman*, 2:393.

58 Ibid.

IV. RHETORICAL PERSONALISM

1 Quoted in Ward, *Life of Newman*, 2:44.

2 Garrigou-Lagrange, *Trinity and God*, 147.

3 Aquinas, *Summa Theologica*, I, 29, 1.

4 Garrigou-Lagrange, *Trinity and God*, 173.

5

> . . . [P]ersonality, metaphysically considered, being the subsistence of the
> spiritual soul communicated to the human composite, and enabling the latter to
> possess its existence, to perfect itself and to give itself freely, bears witness in
> us to the generosity or expansivity of being which, in an incarnate spirit,
> proceeds from the spirit and which constitutes, in the secret springs of our
> ontological structure, a source of dynamic unity and unification from within.

Maritain, *Challenges*, 73. See cited page for the idea of subjectivity of persons and objectivity of conceptualized knowledge. Another study will have to explore how Newman's personalistic ideas could be drawn out or filled in along Thomistic lines using the idea of the incommunicability of the *suppositum* and the non-conceptual means of "knowing" selves through connaturality.

6 Newman's personalism is only partially at home among the various "personalist" philosophies of the nineteenth and twentieth centuries. Often deistic and moral in emphasis, personalism is largely a reaction to the materialistic or mechanistic philosophies of the eighteenth and nineteenth centuries which "dehumanized" man and left his place in the world wholly devoid of significance (Mann). The personalists of the last two centuries seek to rectify this through the deliberate focus on the person as the center and source of all meaning, value, and even reality. In a very broad sense, any philosophy that speaks to "person" or "personhood" is called personalism--a breadth nearly anarchic in "uniting" such disparate philosophers as Sartre, Jacques Maritain, Thomas Aquinas, and B. P. Bowne. While Newman may be a philosophical personalist in the broad sense, many personalist philosophers (often found in journals like *Esprit* and *The Personalist*) are idealistic and even solipsistic. Attempting to recover man's spiritual dignity, personalism tends to "denigrate material things and treat them as mere appearances or flux without any substantial character" (Mann). It also treats God as "finite" due to the predication of "person" to the Divine Being (Mann). E. S. Brightman, in describing idealistic personalism, defines all being as "personal consciousness," while the American personalist B. P. Bowne takes this idealism to its solipsistic extreme by postulating an internal "principle of order" which gives meaning to all experience (Mann). As J. A. Mann notes, "How can such a personally structured process ever achieve an authentic grasp of extramental reality? Here Bowne joins many others in his implicit assumption that the laws of thought are identical with the laws of the real." "Personalism,"173.

7 Nuttall, *A Common Sky*, 131-132.

8 Murray, *Oratorian*, 119-120.

9 Quoted in Ward, *Life of Newman*, 2:439.

10 Quoted in Murray, *Oratorian*, 211-212.

11 Newman, *Present Position of Catholics*, 272-273.

12 Ibid., 298.

13 Ibid. Of course, Newman does not suggest that personal influence can eliminate that fundamental spiritual warfare between the world (as in "the world, the flesh and the devil") and the Kingdom of Christ. In that warfare, Christians can always expect to be reviled in one way or another. Rather, Newman is probably thinking of the history of the Roman persecutions which slowly abated (despite resurgences) as familiarity with Christians increased.

14 Idem., *Historical Sketches*, 2:217.

15 Quoted in Murray, *Oratorian*, 257.

16 Newman, *Historical Sketches*, 2:218.

17 Ibid., 223. "It is not surprising that [Newman's] unsystematic, richly varied work has often suggested that he belongs more to the world of patristic than to that of modern theology. [Now quoting C. Stephen Dessain] 'St. Bernard is called the last of the fathers because in him dogma and piety and literature are still one. . . . Newman, who leaves later developments on one side, took over where St. Bernard left off, and perhaps should be allowed to succeed to his title'" Ker, *Achievement*, 151.

18 Ibid., 220-221.

19 Deen, "Rhetoric of Newman's *Apologia*," 480.

20 Newman, *Historical Sketches*, 3.

21 Ibid., 2:223.

22 Newman, *Theological Papers, Inspiration and Infallibility*, 119.

23 Fraser, *Beauty and Belief*, 57.

24 Newman, *Theological Papers, Faith and Certainty*, 84.

25 Aquinas, *Summa Theologica*, I, 14, 1.

26 Newman, *Theological Papers, Faith and Certainty*, 81.

27 Idem., *Mixed Congregations*, 175.

28 Ibid.

29 Newman, *Essays Critical and Historical*, 1:286.

30 Idem., *Mixed Congregations*, 367.

31 Quoted in Murray, *Oratorian*, 18.

32 Culler *Imperial Intellect*, 222.

33 Ibid., 45.

34 Ibid.

35 Newman, *Historical Sketches*, 3:16.

36 Culler, *Imperial Intellect*, 72.

37 Newman, *Historical Sketches*, 3:6.

38 Interestingly enough, Gerard Manley Hopkins said that, because Newman thought out loud, his prose was rhetorically rather poor and ineloquent. See Jude V. Nixon, "The Kindly Light," 108.

39 Newman, *Historical Sketches*, 3:8.

40 Ibid., 8-9.

41 Ibid., 9.

42 Ibid., 14.

43 Ibid.

44 Ibid., 14-15.

45 Quoted in Newman, *Historical Sketches*, 3:225.

46 Newman, *Historical Sketches*, 3:185.

47 Ibid., 186-187.

48 Ibid., 73.

49 Ibid., 72.

50 Ibid., 74.

V. INTELLECTUAL ANTECEDENTS: RHETORICAL DISCOURSE IN THE PATRISTIC AND MEDIEVAL ERAS

1 Of course, much nineteenth-century thought was in good measure a reaction against this narrow conception of knowledge. From the Romantics through the Victorians, many writers chaffed at the confines such conceptions imposed.

2 This chapter is heavily indebted to James J. Murphy's *Rhetoric in the Middle Ages*, 1974. The historical data and rhetorical terminology are derived from this seminal work, and unless otherwise noted, all references are to that text.

3 Murphy, *Rhetoric in the Middle Ages*, 49.

4 Ibid., 50.

5 Ibid., 53.

6 Ibid., 35.

7 Ibid., 49.

8 Ibid., 38.

9 Ibid., 60.

10 Ibid., 23.

11 Ibid., 26.

12 See also Aristophanes' *The Clouds* for a dispute between old and new, personalist and mechanistic, musical and sophistical education.

13 Murphy, *Rhetoric in the Middle Ages,* 32.

14 Ibid.

15 Ibid., 63.

16 Ibid.

17 Ibid.

18 Ibid.

19 Ibid.

20 Culler, *Imperial Intellect,* 189.

21 Murphy, *Rhetoric in the Middle Ages,* 287.

22 Augustine, *Christian Doctrine,* 23.

23 Ibid., 36.

24 Murphy, *Rhetoric in the Middle Ages,* 288.

25 Ibid.

26 Ibid.

27 Ibid.

28 Ibid., 290.

29 Ibid.

30 Ibid., 291.

31 Ibid.

32 Ibid.

33 Ibid., 195.

34 Ibid., 106.

35 Ibid., 71-74.

36 Ibid., 74.

37 Ibid., 195.

38 Ibid., 82-87.

39 Ibid., 161.

40 Ibid., 102.

41 Ibid., 103.

42 Ibid., 105.

43 Ibid., 271.

44 Ibid., 272.

45 Ibid., 273.

46 Ibid., 277.

47 Ibid., 276-277.

48 Ibid., 282.

49 Ibid., 274-275.

50 Ibid., 270.

51 Ibid., 279.

52 Ibid., 293.

53 Ibid.

54 Ibid.

VI. INTELLECTUAL ANTECEDENTS: RHETORICAL LOGIC AND DE-PERSONALIZED THOUGHT

[1] Ong, *Ramus,* vi. Most of the data in this chapter are taken from Ong's text, and unless otherwise noted, all references are to that text. Ong's study is particularly important as its analysis and historical scope contribute largely to this present study.

[2] Ibid., 55.

[3] Ibid., 57.

[4] Ibid.

[5] Ibid., 59.

[6] Ibid., 56.

[7] Ibid.

[8] Ibid., 101.

[9] Ibid., 60.

[10] Ibid., 95.

[11] Ibid., 93.

[12] Ibid.

[13] Ibid., 100.

[14] Ibid., 100-101.

[15] Ibid., 102.

[16] Ibid., 103-106.

[17] Ibid., 102-103.

[18] Ibid., 106-107.

[19] Ibid., 107.

[20] Ibid., 108.

[21] Ibid., 109.

[22] Ibid., 107-108.

[23] Ibid., 109-110.

[24] Ibid., 111.

[25] Ibid.

[26] Ibid., 112.

[27] Ibid.

[28] Ibid., 115.

[29] Ibid., 121.

[30] Ibid., 122-123.

[31] Ibid., 152.

[32] Ibid., 30.

[33] Ibid., 307.

[34] Ibid., 311.

[35] Ibid., 311, 313.

[36] Ibid, 311-313.

[37] Ibid., 268.

[38] Ibid.

[39] Ibid., 253.

[40] Ibid.

[41] Ibid., 211.

[42] Ibid.

[43] Ibid.

[44] Ibid., 212.

[45] Ibid.

46 Ibid., 212-213.

47 Ibid., 213.

48 Ibid.

49 Ibid., 295.

50 Ibid., 297.

51 Ibid., 203.

52 Ibid., 128.

53 Ibid., 73-74.

54 Ibid., 74.

55 Ibid.

VII. INTELLECTUAL ANTECEDENTS: PHILOSOPHICAL ROOTS, MECHANISTIC BRANCHES

1 Jaki, *Cosmos and Creator*, 100.

2 Ibid.

3 Owens, *Future of Metaphysics*, 29-30.

4 Ibid., 30.

5 Aquinas, *Summa Theologica*, I, I, 75, 2.

6 Nuttall, *A Common Sky*, 150.

7 Ibid., 151. Of course, form is not "imposed" like an impression on clay. It is the inherent "whatness" of a thing, without which no matter could exist at all. The difficulty in such spatial metaphors as "imposition" is that they suggest movement; the only ultimate "imposer" of forms, of course, is God, who determines the essence of any created thing.

8 For a discussion of individuation, see Owens, *Christian Metaphysics*, 230.

9 Maritain, *Introduction to Philosophy*, 166-167.

10 Ibid., 167.

11 Ibid., 167-168.

12 Nuttall, *A Common Sky*, 150.

13 Aquinas, *Summa Theologica*, I, I, 76, 5.

14 Maritain, *Introduction to philosophy*, 167-168.

15 Aquinas, *Summa Theologica*, I, I, 76, 1.

16 Ibid., I, I, 76, 5.

17 Ibid., I, I, 75, 5.

18 Ibid., I, I, 79, 3.

19 Ibid.

20 Ibid., I, I, 84, 6.

21 Aquinas makes an important distinction between "common" and "signate matter," saying that common matter is included in the species. Though an important detail, it does not essentially alter the immateriality of "form." *Summa Ttheologica*, I, I, 85, 1.

22 Gilson, *Philosophical Experience*, 145.

23 Weatherby, *Keen Delight*, 33.

24 Ibid.

25 Aquinas, *Summa Theologica*, I, I, 79, 3.

26 Maritain, *Introduction to Philosophy*, 172.

27 Aquinas, *Summa Theologica*, I, I, 86, 1.

28 Ibid., I, I, 85, 2.

29 Gilson, *Philosophical Experience*, 125.

30 Jaki, *Cosmos and Creator*, 92.

31 Gilson, *Philosophical Experience*, 31-60.

32 Ibid., 200-201.

33 Ibid., 132.

34 Quoted in Gilson, *Philosophical Experience*, 132.

35 Gilson, *Philosophical Experience*, 141.

36 Ong, *Ramus*, 73-74.

37 Maritain, "Descartes or the Incarnation of the Angel," 53-89.

38 Gilson, *Philosophical Experience*, 164-165.

39 Jaki, *Cosmos and Creator*, 92.

40 Ibid., 93.

41 Ibid.

42 Quoted in Jaki, *Cosmos and Creator*, 94.

43 Gilson, *Philosophical Experience*, 235.

44 Owens, *Future of Metaphysics*, 9.

45 Nuttall, *A Common Sky*, 164.

46 Ibid., 15.

47 Newman, *Grammar*, 107.

48 Sillem, *Philosophical Notebook*, 1: 193.

49 Nuttall, *A Common Sky*, 16.

50 Ibid., 92.

51 Ibid.

52 Quoted in Nuttall, *A Common Sky*, 40.

53 Nuttall, *A Common Sky*, 15.

54 Jaki, *Cosmos and Creator*, 94.

55 Gilson, *Philosophical Experience*, 174-175.

56 Nuttall, *A Common Sky*, 28.

57 Ibid.

58 Ibid., 19.

59 Nuttall, *A Common Sky*, 60.

60 Jaki, *Cosmos and Creator*, 105.

61 Nuttall, *A Common Sky*, 257.

62 Ibid., 100.

VIII. NEWMAN'S *PHILOSOPHICAL NOTEBOOK*

1 Burtt, *Metaphysical Foundations*, 236-237. Quoted in Nuttall 23.

2 Weatherby, *Newman in His Age*, 8-9.

3 Ibid., 287.

4 Ibid., 1.

5 Though they cannot be entered into here, there are similar fundamental difficulties in Weatherby's *The Keen Delight*; there--again despite disclaimers--the final position appears to be that one cannot write good Christian poetry without having a Thomist metaphysics.

6 cf. Hilary Fraser's *Beauty and Belief*, 47 for a good statement of this balance in Newman's view of reason. The idea that reason was both capable yet limited, especially as regards religion, is noted by Stephen Prickett in *Romanticism and Religion*, 69:

> [T]o preserve the possibility of rational belief in a God who was both supernatural and transcendent, and, on the other, to subject such a belief to the full investigation of the educated mind. . . . has a name. That name, as Chesterton, in the same tradition, was to reassert . . . is "Orthodoxy."

This kind of balance, applied to Newman's social thought, provides the corrective to Weatherby's charge that Newman abandoned the Thomistic hierarchical social polity of European tradition, in favor of political liberalism. Keeping in mind Newman's sensitivity to man's fallen state (a state limiting the good attainable by *any* social polity) and his pastoral motivation to find ways of pursuing the good in concrete circumstances, he was hardly able to pretend the world was otherwise than nineteenth-century political reality made it. Newman did not embrace the new social order, but his prudence dictated that, since this order obtained, he had best find ways of obtaining the good in a world of flawed and liberal social polity.

[7] Maritain, *Introduction to Philosophy*, 142.

[8] Pieper, *Silence of St. Thomas*, 74.

[9] Ibid., 71.

[10] Ibid., 65.

[11] Ibid., 98.

[12] See Gilson, *Philosophical Experience*, 109-110.

[13] See Harrold's "Newman and the Alexandrian Platonists," 290, for a discussion of Newman's interest in the economical and mysterious aspect of the material universe.

[14] Pieper, *Silence of St. Thomas*, 95.

[15] McGowan, *Representation and Revelation*, 17.

[16] Owens, *Elementary Metaphysics*, vii.

[17] Pieper, *Silence of St. Thomas*, 87.

[18] It is worth remembering that the *Summa Theologica* was written for beginners. See Aquinas' preface.

[19] Pieper, *Silence of St, Thomas*, 30.

[20] Sillem, *Philosophical Notebook*, 1:1, 5, 76.

[21] Ibid., 59-60.

[22] Ibid., 97.

[23] Ibid., 50-51.

[24] Ibid., 85.

[25] Quoted in Sillem, *Philosophical Notebook*, 1:100.

[26] Sillem, *Philosophical Notebook*, 1:73.

[27] Ibid., 13

[28] Ibid., 8.

[29] In fact, it is noteworthy that the history of rhetoric and the history of education are largely identical for vast periods in the West. Moreover, education became data-transfer at the same time as the acquisition of knowledge was thought to follow mathematical [Cartesian] or mechanical models.

[30] There seems to be an historically persistent tendency to be dissatisfied with anything less than "philosophy." In this light, one almost begins to sympathize with the anti-philosophical rhetoric of Stanley Fish. The operative word, of course, is "almost." One does not correct one error with another.

[31] Quoted in Sillem, *Philosophical Notebook*, 1:245.

[32] Thus the variety of material in the *Notebook* is great almost to the point of being amusing. See vol. 2: 24, 113, 165.

[33] Sillem, *Philosophical Notebook*, 2:200.

[34] Ibid., 201.

[35] Ibid., 200.

[36] Ibid., 203.

[37] Ibid.

[38] Ibid., 204.

[39] Ibid.

[40] See Gilson's *Thomist Realism*, 24-25.

[41] Nuttall, *A Common Sky*, 100.

42 The paradox of skepticism encouraging scientific rationalism is not as unusual as it may appear. David J. DeLaura notes a similar paradox in *Hebrew and Hellene* (xi) regarding religious matters. As faith ebbs, the secular culture becomes "religionized." Richard D. Altick (*Victorian People and Ideas*, 236) mentions another Victorian religious paradox similar in form. He observes that the Victorian need for faith was intensified because the "grounds of faith now had become so elusive."

43 Sillem, *Philosophical Notebook*, 2:205.

44 Ibid., 208.

45 cf. C. F. Harrold's "Newman and the Alexandrian Platonists," 285-286, for a discussion of the idea that angels are involved in the administration of an economical creation.

46 Sillem, *Philosophical Notebook*, 2:211.

47 Aquinas, *Summa Theologica*, I, 78, 3.

48 Sillem, *Philosophical Notebook*, 2:208.

49 Ibid., 202.

50 Ibid.

51 Ibid., 30.

52 Ibid., 8.

53 Ibid.

54 Ibid., 189.

55 Ibid.

56 Ibid.

57 Weatherby does not consider this, perhaps because the mode of discourse of the argument is still properly rhetorical, not philosophical. He is careful not to assert that Newman would deny the Thomistic proof; instead, he says it is not a matter of denial but philosophical "emphasis." Newman's "philosophical emphasis" was essentially modernist because Newman felt such old proofs "do not warm or enlighten" him, and offer no support to his "moral being." Weatherby misses the strong rhetorical thrust of these comments. It is hardly the principle task of philosophy to "warm" someone or "enlighten" them in the sense Newman intends. The rhetorician is concerned with arguments that are *effective* and that produce assent. This is why rhetoric is an operation of the practical intellect. The fact that Newman is interested not in arguments objectively valid but arguments that are appealing, that "warm" and make the "moral being rejoice" should be indication enough that his interest is rhetorical. *Newman in His Age*, 18-19.

58 It is possible, however, to overstate the importance of this pre-conditioning. The pendulum has swung from the mechanistic extreme of Newman's day to the "associative" extreme of our own. As will be seen in Jost's text, pre-conditioning can be considered so important that it is thought to virtually necessitate rational assent. This extreme becomes a kind of mirror-image mechanism to the one Newman fought, for it has an automatic quality all its own. Freedom in assent is brought into question, as is the objective truth-value of a proposition assented to; all is a product of pre-conditioning

59 Sillem, *Philosophical Notebook*, 2: 167.

60 Ibid., 169.

61 Ibid., 37.

62 Ibid., 43.

63 Ibid.,47.

64 Ibid.

65 Ibid., 49.

66 Ibid., 51.

67 Ibid., 52-53.

68 Ibid., 67.

69 Ibid., 87.

IX. NEWMAN'S *GRAMMAR OF ASSENT*

1 Newman, *Letters and Diaries*, 25:199.

2 Ibid., 84.

3 Ibid., 59.

4 Corbett, "Rhetorical Lessons," 403-403. Corbett also refers to Charles Frederick Harrold as saying the same thing of the *Grammar* (402). Corbett goes on to pinpoint the text's study of probability and the observation that persuasion results from a combination of strategies, but he does not discuss these at all, especially as related to epistemology or rhetorical knowledge.

5 Walgrave, *Newman the Theologian*, 62-63.

6 Verdeke, "Aristotelian Roots," 177.

7 Several works should be mentioned here. John Coulson's *Religion and Imagination* (1981) draws attention to the relation of imagination and religious faith/assent, and highlights the conceptual gap suffered by a culture when religious faith is weakened due to lack of imaginative reinforcement (secularization). However, his work too readily identifies imagination with "real assent" and disregards, in practice, Newman's repeated cautions and endorsements as to the power and value of the notional. In fact, Coulson performs a modern version of Agricola's fusion of dialectic and philosophy; though the importance of imagination in thought needs to be given due recognition, Coulson excessively rhetoricizes (or poeticizes) theology, in which case, as we have seen, one loses both.

M. Jamie Ferreira's *Doubt and Religious Commitment* (1980) argues that, in the *Grammar*, Newman's affirmation of the indefectibility of certitude, and the incompatibility of doubt to faith, does not mean violence is done to reason in order to have religious belief. Ferreira's later book, *Scepticism and Reasonable Doubt* (1986), studies the tradition of English skepticism and the reaction it inspired, called "naturalism," i.e., the appeal to human nature, mental laws, or the general testimony of mankind. Newman's is this last answer to skepticism, according to Ferreira, and the appeal to certainty and knowledge entails more than a mere assertion of the unavoidability of natural beliefs.

Finally, one of the most oft-cited and generally useful works on the *Grammar* needs mention. A.J. Boekraad's *The Personal Conquest of Truth* (1955) provides an excellent discussion of Newman's personalism and its effect on his thought: his sympathy for the workings of others' minds, his emphasis on the role of will on formal and informal reasonings. He notes the highly purposive character of the *Grammar* and its non-philosophical manner. Nevertheless, Boekraad reads the text as essentially philosophical and specifically phenomenological.

8 Bacchus, "How to Read the *Grammar of Assent*," 107.

9 Jaki, "Newman's Assent to Reality," 193.

10 Gilson, Introduction to *Grammar of Assent*, 10.

11 Jaki, "Newman's Assent to Reality," 193.

12 Bacchus, "How to Read the *Grammar of Assent*," 109.

13 Vargish, *Newman: The Contemplation of Mind*, vii.

14 Newman, *Letters and Diaries*, 19:294.

15 Idem., *Grammar of Assent*, 11-12.

16 Ibid., 185.

17 Ibid., 228.

18 Ibid.

19 Ibid., 19.

20 Ibid., 22.

21 Ibid.

22 Ibid.

23 Ibid., 27.

24 Ibid.

25 Ibid., 28.

26 Ibid., 14.

27 Ibid.

28 Ibid., 29-30.

29 Ibid., 31.

30 Ibid., 16.

31 Gilson, Introduction to *Grammar of Assent*, 11.

32 Newman, *Grammar of Assent,* 105.

33 Ibid., 32.

34 Ibid., 122.

35 Ibid., 116.

36 Ibid., 125-126.

37 Gilson, Introduction to *Grammar of Assent*, 14.

38 Newman, *Grammar of Assent,* 63.

39 Ibid.

40 Ibid., 59-60.

41 Ibid., 62.

42 Ibid., 58.

43 Ibid., 69.

44 Ibid.

45 Ibid., 42-43.

46 Ibid., 90.

47 Ibid., 71.

48 Ibid., 72.

49 Ibid., 72-73.

50 Ibid., 129.

51 Ibid., 130.

52 Ibid., 144-145.

53 Ibid., 151.

54 Ibid., 149-150.

55 Ibid., 152.

56 G. R. Evans, "Newman and Aquinas on Assent" 202-211. This article is very useful in pointing out Newman's indebtedness in the *Grammar* to Aquinas. He notes that Newman expresses confidence that the *Grammar* is essentially in agreement with Aquinas, and that Newman was inspired and confirmed by Aquinas' "*cogitare cum assensu*"--thought with assent. This idea is contrary to the Protestant idea of inquiry into faith, which presupposes reasoning first followed by faith. The will goes with the intellect for Newman and Aquinas (205). This *cogitare cum assensu* is what Newman means when he speaks of "the one complex act both of inference and assent." Holloway misconstrues this to mean exposition becomes proof (Holloway, *The Victorian Sage,* 8).

57 Newman, *Grammar of Assent,* 159.

58 See p. 160-161. It is here that Newman makes an error in practice, though not, I think, in his theory. He postulates the transformation of three Protestants, one who becomes Catholic, another who becomes Unitarian, and the third who slides into infidelity. Each, he says, changes the sundry assents of religious association without changing his fundamental certitude--to that certitude each remains committed. The first's certitude was Christ's Divinity, the second's was Scripture as the rule of faith and private judgment as its interpreter, the third's was that the "priesthood was a corruption of the simplicity of the Gospel." Now, Newman has affirmed that certitude is indefectible because it exists in reference to a truth. He likewise says these three Protestants "started with just one certitude" apiece, and that the subsequent stages of their religious development remained true to these original commitments or certitudes. But surely Newman would not hold that the second and third Protestants' certitudes were in fact true. He believes such propositions wholly false, so how can these be certitudes? I believe this is not an inconsistency in Newman's theory, but rather an error in its exposition. The example could be rescued, however, in accordance with the old adage that every error contains a truth. The second Protestant could well be

certain that Scripture is inspired and that it requires interpretation. The third could well be certain that the contemporary institution of the priesthood is not detailed in its trappings and accidents in the original Gospels. Both of these could, according to Newman's theory, be certitudes because they are truths. They could abide in the respective persons while their other assents regarding doctrines and religious affiliations change. Newman also does not limit certitude and its indefectibility to the supernatural sphere; it is equally operative in the natural.

59 Newman, *Grammar of Assent*, 172.

60 Ibid., 174. It is interesting that Newman uses the word "connatural" with reference to the poetry and rhetoric of words, for "connatural" is a scholastic term of profound significance. It has to do with the way poetic knowledge is gained and communicated, referring to the experiential and personal. Jacques Maritain says that connatural knowledge is known

> no longer through inclination, by looking at and consulting what we are and the inner bents or propensities of our own being. . . . In this knowledge through union or inclination, connaturality or congeniality, *the intellect is at play not alone, but together with affective inclinations and the dispositions of the will, and as guided and shaped by them.*

Maritain, *Challenges*, 262, emphasis added. This connatural knowledge is "immanent and *consubstantial*" with poetry, one with its very essence" (247; emphasis his). In view of these and other explanations of poetic or connatural knowledge, its incorporation of the intellect, will, and passions, could Newman's rhetorical habit of mind in fact be a "rhetorico-poetic" one?

61 Ibid., 175.

62 In fact, Aquinas makes exactly this same distinction. See *S. T.* II-I, 94, 2.

63 Thus, Newman's famous statement that logic's "chain of conclusions hangs loose at both ends," that it misses first principles and concrete issues, refers to its practical effect, not its essence. First principles will always be questioned by someone, and there will always be someone who does not assent to a valid conclusion.

64 Newman, *Grammar of Assent*, 174-175.

65 Ibid., 185-186.

66 Ibid., 186.

67 Newman distinguishes between informal and natural inference. The first deals with probabilities, the second with things perceived almost instinctively. In fact, the relation between the two is one of set/subset. Natural inference is a species of informal inference. The grounds of distinction are by no means clear, both proceeding from probability, *per modum unius*. Thus Francis Bacchus' strong separation of the two inferences seems excessive--a minor blot on an otherwise excellent and useful introduction to the *Grammar*, "How to Read the *Grammar of Assent*."

68 Newman, *Grammar of Assent*, 187.

69 Ibid., 189-190.

70 Ibid., 190.

71 Ibid.

72 Ibid., 196.

73 Evans, "Newman and Aquinas on Assent," 202-211.

74 Newman, *Grammar of Assent*, 196.

75 Ibid., 206.

76 Ibid., 202.

77 Ibid., 214.

78 Ibid.

79 Church, *The Oxford Movement*, 317.

80 Nixon, "The KIndly Light," 128.

81 Verdeke, "Aristotelian Roots," 180-181.

82 Newman, *Grammar of Assent*, 232.

83 Ibid., 223.

84 Ibid.

85 Ibid., 241-242.

X. THE *GRAMMAR* AND RHETORICAL KNOWLEDGE

[1] Thus Robin C. Selby's *The Principle of Reserve in the Writings of John Henry Newman* (1975) makes too much of Newman's "skepticism." A conviction that this world is insufficient and a deep sensitivity to unseen or spiritual realities is not necessarily skepticism. See p. 98.

[2] Newman, *Grammar of Assent*, 169-170.

[3] Ibid., 181.

[4] Ibid., 145.

[5] Ibid., 243.

[6] Ibid., 46.

[7] Ibid., 224.

[8] Jaki, "Newman's Assent to Reality," 201-205.

[9] c.f. Newman, *Grammar of Assent*, 184.

[10] Quoted in Ker, "Newman on Truth," 67.

[11] Newman, *Grammar of Assent*, 109.

[12] Ibid., 118.

[13] Ibid., 222.

[14] Ibid.

[15] Ibid., 222-223.

[16] Ibid., 264.

[17] H. Francis Davis agrees. Though his "Newman and Thomism" is a partial study of the relation--and seems to cast Newman in an excessively Thomistic light at times--it does attest to the fact that "reality" was Newman's basic principle.

[18] Newman, *Grammar of Assent*, 29.

[19] Gilson, Introduction to *Grammar of Assent*, 15.

[20] Newman, *Grammar of Asent*, 114.

[21] Ibid., 16.

[22] Ibid., 128.

[23] Ibid., 117.

[24] Ibid., 265.

[25] Ibid., 106.

[26] Ibid., 117-118.

[27] Ibid., 118.

[28] Ibid., 266.

[29] To be sure, Newman is non-systematic enough not to confine himself even to these two senses of "probable." Largely due to his desire to shatter the blind confidence and presumption in the adherents of "demonstration" (from philosophers to scientists), Newman will occasionally use "probable" to mean the conventional "uncertain." He will accuse theoretical sciences of being probable in this way too, an inconsistent accusation in light of his other statements about the truth-value and object of notional and formal reasoning.

[30] Newman, *Grammar of Assent*, 166-167. In his "Editor's Introduction" to the *Grammar of Assent* (1985) Ian Ker highlights a passage which would seem to contradict my description of certitude as resting in a truth. He quotes Newman as saying "I will not urge . . . that certitude is a conviction of what is true, and that these so called certitudes [abandoned certitudes--my note] have come to naught, because, their objects being errors, not truths, they were not certitudes at all." (lxix) Likewise, Ker's earlier summary of the *Grammar* refers to indefectibility thus: "It would be quibbling to say that certitude is a conviction of what is true and that a false certitude is not a certitude at all." (xvii) At the risk of quibbling about quibbling, it should be noted that Newman does not say that defending indefectibility in this way would be to quibble. He simply says that he will not defend it in this fashion so as to sidestep the possible objection that he quibbles. The passage reads: "Now, in meeting this difficulty, I will not urge (lest I should be accused of quibbling), that certitude is a conviction of what is true, and that these so-called certitudes have come to nought, because, their objects being errors, not truths, they really were not certitudes at

all; . . ." (165) As the rest of the sentence makes clear, the implication is that this is indeed a point he could urge it he chose to do so: ". . .nor will I insist, as I might, that they ought to be proved first to be something more than mere prejudices, assents without reason and judgement, before they can fairly be taken as instances of the defectibility of certitude; . . . (Ibid)

The indefectibility of certitude has been a stumbling block for many critics, but Newman's position appears quite definite. While Ker justly notes that indefectibility is a general rule, capable of exceptions, the limited and narrow allowance for exceptions must be weighed against the many and emphatic assertions of the rule. Newman's explanation of indefectibility is in fact something very like "certitude is a conviction of what is true" and so-called certitudes come to nought because they "were not certitudes at all." The very first sentences of Newman's section on indefectibility state that "It is the characteristic of certitude that its object is a truth, a truth as such, a proposition as true. There are right and wrong convictions, and certitude is a right conviction; if it is not a right with the consciousness of being a right, it is not a certitude." (145) Moreover (and as Ker points out [lxix]), Newman does actually insist that the only test of certitude is a negative one: a conviction that fails is not in fact a certitude. Thus it would seem that Newman does indeed meet the difficulty of discarded certitudes by denying their claim to certitude. It is telling that Newman likes to refer to these as "so-called" or "supposed" certitudes.

It should also be remembered that Newman does not claim all unchanged convictions are, properly speaking, certitudes; he merely asserts that as the object of certitude is truth, a proper certitude cannot ordinarily fail. Exceptions are possible; corrupted or debased faculties (self-deception, cowardice) can work mischief on a certitude, but as always the abuse cannot mitigate against proper use.

[31] Ibid., 268.

[32] Ibid., 196.

[33] Ibid., 297.

[34] Newman does hold that knowledge of God is attained by means of nature, contrary to Weatherby's assertion, and the proposition is not held merely out of obedience to the religious doctrine concerning it. See *Grammar*, 156.

[35] Holloway, *Victorian Sage,* 9. The acuity of this observation is vitiated somewhat by Holloway's next "points." By overemphasizing the texture of language and dismissing content, Holloway advocates a nominalistic or prose aesthetic of surface textures and emotional reactions.

[36] Ibid., 188.

[37] Newman, *Grammar of Assent,* 200.

[38] Ibid., 14, 63-64.

[39] Ibid., 63.

[40] Ibid.

[41] Ibid., 64.

[42] Ibid., 56.

[43] Ibid., 205.

[44] Ibid., 225.

[45] Ibid., 298.

[46] Ibid., 65-66.

[47] Ibid., 66-67. These last two passages Newman included in the *Grammar*, though they first appeared in the Tamworth Reading Room letters.

[48] Ibid., 83.

[49] Ibid., 273.

[50] Ibid., 274.

[51] Ibid., 225.

XI. NEWMAN AND RHETORICAL REALISM

[1] Bouyer, "Great Preachers," 88.

[2] Jost, *Rhetorical Thought,* x.

3 Ibid., 5.

4 Ibid., 7.

5 Ibid., 38.

6 Ibid., 70, 120.

7 Ibid., xi.

8 Ibid.

9 Ibid., 211, 89.

10 Ibid., 25.

11 Ibid.

12 Ibid., 25-26.

13 Ibid., 26.

14 For a comprehensive look at Newman and reality, see Jaki's "Newman's Assents to Reality, Natural and Supernatural," especially in footnote 59 on page 217 where Jaki comments on similar contemporary theories of Nicholas Lash and T.S. Kuhn.

15 Jost, *Rhetorical Thought,* 37.

16 Ibid., 21.

17 Ibid., 54.

18 Ibid., 71, 151, 215.

19 Newman, *Grammar of Assent,* 22-23.

20 Ibid., 169.

21 Ibid., 23.

22 Ibid., 30.

23 Jost, *Rhetorical Thought,* 19.

24 Ibid., 17.

25 Ibid., 156, 157.

26 See Jost, *Rhetorical Thought,* 184-185.

27 Jost, *Rhetorical Thought,* 53.

28 Ibid., 62, 193.

29 Ibid., 210.

30 Ibid., 97.

31 Ibid., 57, 139, 123.

32 See also pages 39, 201.

33 Jost, *Rhetorical Thought,* 122.

34 Ibid., 24.

35 Ibid., 23.

36 Ibid., 130.

37 Ibid., 136-137. See also page 128. In the light of these statements, the anti-modernist disclaimer lodged in a footnote is difficult to understand (271). Jost indicates he does not mean to suggest that doctrine has "no integrity as knowledge." But when the epistemology does not accord integrity to *any* kind of knowledge, how tenable is the disclaimer?

38 Ibid., 137.

39 Ibid.

40 Trevor, *The Pillar of the Cloud,* 441.

41 Jost, *Rhetorical Thought,* 216.

42 Jost, *Rhetorical Thought,* 89, 194. For Jost vs Newman on first principles, see Jost page 53, then compare Newman's *Grammar,* 192-193.

43 Corbett ("Some Rhetorical Lessons," 411) also links Newman to Perelman and Toulmin, noting that they each seek a "realistic paradigm" for how the mind thinks.

44 The image is from Nuttall's *A Common Sky,* which features a frontispiece depicting a cut-away view of a man's head, inside of which is a little switchboard operator "receiving" all the sense data.

45 Jaki, "Newman's Assent to Reality," 204.

46 Bacchus, "How to Read the *Grammar of Assent*," 115.

47 Pieper, *Prudence,* 17-18.

48 Ibid., 19.

49 Ibid., 41.

50 Ibid., 16.

51 Ibid., 22-23.

52 Ibid., 23.

53 Ibid., 23-24.

54 Ibid., 26.

55 Ibid.

56 Ibid., 27.

57 Ibid., 28.

58 Ibid., 29.

59 Ibid., 30.

60 Ibid., 36.

61 Cf. Tillotson's *A View of Victorian Literature* 40-41, where Victorian authors are said to attempt to recover "physical voice" in their writings.

62 DeLaura, *Hebrew and Hellene,* 5-6.

63 DeLaura, "Newman's *Apologia* as Prophecy," 492-503.

Altick, Richard D. *Victorian People and Ideas*. New York: W. W. Norton & Company, 1973.

Aquinas, St. Thomas. *The "Summa Theologica" of St. Thomas Aquinas*. Translated by the Fathers of the English Dominican Province. 2d rev. ed. London: Burns Oates & Washbourne, 1920.

Aristotle. *The Works of Aristotle Translated into English*. Edited by W. D. Ross. Oxford: Clarendon Press, 1908-1952.

Atteberry, Phillip. "New Perspectives on Newman and the Oxford Movement." *Nineteenth Century Prose* 18 (Summer 1991): 84-94.

Augustine, St. *On Christian Doctrine*. Translated by D. W. Robertson, Jr. Indianapolis: Bobbs-Merrill, 1958.

Bacchus, Francis Joseph. "How to Read the 'Grammar of Assent.'" In *The Month*, 106-115. London: Simpkin, Marshall, and Co., 1924.

Boekraad, A. J. *The Personal Conquest of Truth According to John Henry Newman*. Louvain: Nauwelaerts Publishing House, 1955.

Blehl, Vincent Ferrer. "Early Criticism of the *Apologia*." In *Newman's "Apologia": A Classic Reconsidered*, edited by Vincent Blehl and F. X. Connally, 47-63. New York: Harcourt, Brace & World, 1964.

Bouyer, Louis. "Great Preachers--XIII. John Henry Newman." *Theology* 55 (March 1952): 87-91.

---. *Newman: His Life and Spirituality*. London: Burns & Oates, 1958.

Burtt, Edwin A. *The Metaphysical Foundations of Modern Physical Science*. 2d ed. 1954. Reprint. Garden City, New York: Doubleday, 1959.

Chesterton, G. K. *The Victorian Age in Literature*. The Home University of Modern Knowledge. 1913. Reprint. London, New York: Oxford University Press, 1946.

Church, Richard William. *The Oxford Movement: Twelve Years 1833-1845*. London, New York: Macmillan and Co., 1891.

Cicero. *De Inventione*. Loeb Classical Library. 1949.

Corbett, Edward P. J. "Some Rhetorical Lessons from John Henry Newman." *College Composition and Communication* 4 (December 1980): 402-412.

Coulson, John. *Religion and Imagination*. Oxford: Clarendon Press, 1981.

Culler, A. Dwight. "Method in the Study of Victorian Prose." *The Victorian Newsletter* 9 (Spring 1956): 1-4.

---. *The Imperial Intellect*. New Haven: Yale University Press, 1955.

Davis, H. Francis. "Newman and Thomism." In *Newman: Studien Dritte Folge*, Hrsg. Heinrich Fries und Werner Becker, 157-169. Nürnberg: Glock und Lutz, 1957.

Deen, Leonard W. "The Rhetoric of Newman's *Apologia*." In *Apologia Pro Vita Sua*. Norton Critical Editions. 1st ed. Edited by David J. DeLaura, 480-492. New York: 1968.

DeLaura, David J. *Hebrew and Hellene in Victorian England*. Austin & London: University of Texas Press, 1969.

---. "Newman's *Apologia* as Prophecy." In *Apologia Pro Vita Sua*. Norton Critical Editions. 1st ed. Edited by David J. DeLaura, 492-503. New York: 1968.

Dessain, Charles Stephen. "Newman's Philosophy and Theology." In *Victorian Prose*. Edited by David J. DeLaura, 166-184. New York: The Modern Language Association of America, 1973.

Evans, G. R. "Newman and Aquinas on Assent." *Theological Studies* 30 (1979): 202-211.

Ferreira, M. Jamie. *Doubt and Religious Commitment*. Oxford: Clarendon Press, 1980.
---. *Scepticism and Reasonable Doubt*. Oxford: Clarendon Press, 1986.
Fraser, Hilary. *Beauty and Belief: Aesthetics and Religion in Victorian Literature*. Cambridge: University Press, 1986.
Garrigou-Lagrange, Reginald. *The Trinity and God the Creator*. Translated by Frederic Eckhoff. St. Louis: Herder Book Co., 1952.
Gilson, Etienne. Introduction to *A Grammar of Assent*, by John Henry Cardinal Newman. New York: Doubleday & Company, 1955.
---. *Thomist Realism and the Critique of Knowledge*. Translated by Mark A. Wauck. San Francisco: Ignatius Press, 1986.
---. *The Unity of Philosophical Experience* 1938. Reprint. London: Sheed and Ward, 1955.
Harrold, Charles F. "Newman and the Alexandrian Platonists." *Modern Philology* 37 (February 1940): 279-291.
Holloway, John. *The Victorian Sage*. London: Macmillan & Co., 1953.
Houghton, Walter. *The Art of Newman's Apologia*. New Haven: Yale University Press. 1945. Reprint. Archon Books, 1966.
---. *The Victorian Frame of Mind 1830-1870*. New Haven: Yale University Press, 1957.
Jaki, Stanley. *Cosmos and Creator*. Edinburgh: Scottish Academic Press, 1980.
---. "Newman's Assent to Reality, Natural and Supernatural." In *Newman Today*. Edited by Stanley Jaki. San Francisco: Ignatius Press, 1989.
Jost, Walter. *Rhetorical Thought in John Henry Newman*. Columbia, South Carolina: University of South Carolina Press, 1989.
Ker, Ian. *The Achievement of John Henry Newman*. Notre Dame, Indiana: University of Notre Dame Press, 1990.
---. "Newman on Truth." *The Irish Theological Quarterly* 44 (1977): 67-68.
Mann, J. A. "Personalism." *New Catholic Encyclopedia*. Washington, D.C.: The Catholic University of America, 1967.
Maritain, Jacques. *Challenges and Renewals*. Edited by Joseph W. Evans and Leo R. Ward. Notre Dame & London: University of Notre Dame Press, 1966.
---. *An Introduction to Philosophy*. Translated by E. I. Watkin. New York: Sheed & Ward, 1937.
---. "Descartes or The Incarnation of the Angel." In *Three Reformers*. New York: Charles Scribner's Sons, n.d.
McGowan, John P. *Representation and Revelation: Victorian Realism from Carlyle to Yeats*. Columbia, Missouri: University of Missouri Press, 1986.
McKeon, Richard. *Introduction to Aristotle*. 2d, rev. ed. Chicago and London: The University of Chicago Press, 1973.
Morris, Kevin L. *The Image of the Middle Ages in Romantic and Victorian Literature*. Kent, England: Croom Helm Ltd., 1984.
Murphy, James J. *Rhetoric in the Middle Ages*. Berkeley, Calif.: University of California Press, 1974.
Murray, Placid. *Newman The Oratorian*. Leominster, Herefordshire, England: Fowler Wright Books, 1980.
Newman, John Henry Cardinal. *Apologia Pro Vita Sua*. Norton Critical Editions. 1st ed. Eited by David J. DeLaura. New York: 1968.
---. *Autobiographical Writings*. Edited by Henry Tristram. London: Sheed and Ward, 1956.
---. *Discourses Addressed to Mixed Congregations*. London, New York: Longmans, Green, and Co., 1906.

Newman, John Henry Cardinal. *An Essay in Aid of a Grammar of Assent.* New York: Doubleday & Company, Inc., 1955.

---. *An Essay in Aid of a Grammar of Assent.* Edited by Ian Ker. New York: University Press; Oxford: Clarendon Press, 1985.

---. *Essays Critical and Historical.* 2 vols. London: Longmans, Green and Co., 1897.

---. *Historical Sketches.* 3 vols. London: Longmans, Green, and Co., 1888-1889.

---. *The Idea of a University.* London: Longmans, Green, and Co., 1896.

---. *Lectures on the Present Position of Catholics in England.* Edited by Daniel M. O'Connell. Chicago: Loyola University Press, 1925.

---. *Letters and Diaries.* Edited by Charles Dessain, Ian Ker, and Thomas Gornall. Oxford: Clarendon; London: T. Nelson, 1961-.

---. *Parochial and Plain Sermons.* San Francisco: Ignatius Press, 1987.

---. *The Philosophical Notebook.* 2 vols. Edited by Edward J. Sillem. Louvain: Nauwelaerts Publishing House, 1970.

---. *The Theological Papers of John Henry Newman on Faith and Certainty.* Edited by J. Derek Holmes. Oxford: Clarendon Press, 1976.

---. *The Theological Papers on Biblical Inspiration and on Infallibility.* Edited by J. Derek Holmes. New York: Oxford University Press, 1979.

Nixon, Jude V. "The Kindly Light. A Reappraisal of the Influence of Newman on Hopkins." *Texas Studies in Literature and Language* 31 (Spring 1989): 105-142.

Nuttall, A. D. *A Common Sky.* London: Chatto & Windus, 1974.

Ong, Walter J. *Ramus: Method, and the Decay of Dialogue.* 1958. Reprint. Cambridge: Harvard University Press, 1983.

Owens, Joseph. *An Elementary Christian Metaphysics.* 1963. Reprint. Houston, Texas: Center for Thomistic Studies, 1985.

---. *St. Thomas and the Future of Metaphysics.* Milwaukee: Marquette University Press, 1957.

Pieper, Josef. *Prudence.* Translated by Richard and Clara Winston. London: Faber and Faber, 1959.

---. *The Silence of St. Thomas: Three Essays.* Translated by Daniel O'Connor. London: Faber and Faber, 1957.

Prickett, Stephen. *Romanticism and Religion: The Tradition of Coleridge and Wordsworth in the Victorian Church.* Cambridge: Cambridge University Press, 1976.

Roberts, W. Rhys, Introduction to *Rhetorica.* In *The Works of Aristotle Translated into English.* Oxford: Clarendon Press, 1908-1952.

Selby, Robin. *The Principle of Reserve in the Writings of John Henry Cardinal Newman.* London: Oxford University Press, 1975.

Sillem, Edward, ed. *The Philosophical Notebook of John Henry Newman.* 2 vols. Louvain: Nauwelaerts Publishing House, 1969.

Svaglic, Martin J. "Classical Rhetoric and Victorian Prose." In *The Art of Victorian Prose.* Edited by George Levine and E. William Madden, 268-288. New York: Oxford University Press, 1968.

---. "Man and Humanist." In *Victorian Prose.* Edited by David J. DeLaura. 115-165. New York: The Modern Language Association, 1973.

Tillotson, Geoffrey. *A View of Victorian Literature.* Oxford: Oxford University Press. 1978.

Trevor, Meriol. *Newman: Light in Winter.* London: Macmillan & Co., 1962.

---. *Newman: The Pillar of the Cloud.* London: Macmillan & Co., 1962.

Vargish, Thomas. *Newman: The Contemplation of Mind.* Oxford: Clarendon Press, 1970.

Verdeke, Gérard. "Aristotelian Roots of Newman's Illative Sense." In *Newman and Gladstone Centennial Essays*. Edited by James Bastable, 177-195. Dublin: Veritas Publications, 1978.

Walgrave, J. H. *Newman the Theologian*. Translated by A. V. Littledale. New York: Sheed & Ward, 1960.

Ward, Wilfrid. *The Life of John Henry Cardinal Newman*. 2 vols. London: Longmans, Green, and Co., 1913.

Weatherby, Harold L. *Cardinal Newman in His Age*. Nashville: Vanderbilt University Press, 1973.

---. *The Keen Delight*. Athens: University of Georgia Press, 1975.

Whalen, David M. "John Henry Newman: The Rhetoric of the Real." *Nineteenth Century Prose* 18.2 (1991): 1-9.

INDEX

Abelard, Peter, 147—148
Aeterni Patris, 15
Agent intellect, 81, 124, 144. *See also under*
   Aquinas
Agnostics, 62
Agricola, Rudolph, 90—92, 95, 96, 99,
   100, 207
   Dialectical Invention, 90
Albertus Magnus, 88
Alexander of Ashby
   On the Mode of Preaching, 85
Altick, Richard D., 46, 239n. 42
Ambrose, St., 75
Analogies, visual, 93—95, 96, 103
Angels, 52, 53
Aquinas, St. Thomas. *See also*
       Metaphysics: Thomistic;
       Newman: Aquinas
   abstraction, 112—113
   agent intellect, 111, 112
   angelic intellect, 118
   form, 109—114
   matter, 109, 236n. 21
   particulars, 165
   preaching, 84
   the Fall, 34
   the soul, 108, 110
   truth, 19
   cogitare cum assensu, 184
   epistemology, 106—114, 208, 219, 123
   formal theology, 10
   intelligible species, 114—115
   person, definition of, 52—54
   priority of reality, 115
   theological shift from, 90—91
   summary of opponents, 48
   Summa Contra Gentiles, 176
   Summa Theologica, 53, 82, 108, 114
Argument, 22—23, 28, 29, 127
Aristophanes, 234n. 12
Aristotle. *See also under* Newman
   catagories, 92, 93, 95
   common sense, 113
   dialectic, 91
   differentia among sciences, 5, 214
   form, 109
   idealsim, 115
   in the Middle Ages, 90
   in the 19th century, 73
   matter, 109
   practical knowledge, 25—28, 54

truth, 19—23, 28—29, 80, 81, 208,
   209, 219. *See also* Truth
De Interpretatione, 81
Metaphysics, 13, 18, 26, 95, 106
Nichomachean Ethics, 12, 165, 184, 187
On the Soul, 18, 27
Organon, 88
Poetics, 12
Posterior Analytics, 12, 18, 26
Rhetoric, 10, 12, 17—19, 23—25, 79,
   184
Topics, 18, 81, 89
Arnold, Matthew, 224—225
Arnold, Dr. Thomas, 1—2, 37, 224, 225
Assent. *See under* Newman
Athanasius, St., 8, 15
Attenbury, Phillip D., 227n. 5
Augustine. St., 8, 76
   imitation, 78—79
   language, 80—81
   Pagan letters, 75
   preaching, 84
   Confessions, 220
   De catechizandis rudibus, 79, 81
   De Doctrina Christiana, 76, 79
   De Magistro, 79
Bacchus, Francis, 163, 216, 242n. 67
Bacon, Francis, 6, 8
Basil, St., 8, 75
Bellarmine, St. Robert, 90
Bentham, Jeremy, 38
Benthamism, 98
Berkeley, Bishop, 110, 124, 125, 140, 141,
   145, 146
Bernard, St., 14
Bible, 97
Blehl, Vincent, 227n. 6
Boekraad, A. J., 7, 240n. 7
Boethius, 52, 53, 90, 91
Bonaventure, St., 88, 115
Booth, Wayne C., 215
Bouyer, Louis, 205, 230n. 28
British Empiricism. *See* Empiricism; Locke
Burke, Kenneth, 5, 6, 207, 208, 214, 215,
   219
Campbell, George, 5
Cano, Melchior, 90
Cantor of Paris, Peter, 82
Carlyle, Thomas, 17
Categories, 92—96, 104
Catholics, 58

Certainty, 16, 106. *See also* Newman:
    certitude; Newman: Grammar of Assent;
    Newman: indefectibility of certitude
Character, 24, 25, 27, 28
Chesterton, G. K., 17, 42
Christian utilitarianism, 38
Chrysostom, St. John, 8, 61
Church Fathers, 8, 9, 10, 15, 74, 75, 76,
    83. *See also under* Newman
Church, R. W.
    The Oxford Movement, 187, 231n. 40
Cicero, 19, 73, 78, 79, 81, 91, 100, 106
    Plea for Rabirius, 100
Claudel, Paul, 219
Clement of Alexandria, 74
Coleridge, Samuel Taylor, 11, 13, 76
Communication, 73, 75—76, 80—81, 85,
    87, 95, 126. *See also* Language
Comte, Auguste, 17, 125
Contingency, 21, 28, 29, 218
Copia, 102
Coplestone, Edward, 66
Corbett, Edward P. J., 162, 240n. 4, 245n.
    43
Coulson, John, 240n. 7
Creed, the, 62
Culler, A. Dwight, 8, 13, 36, 66, 67, 79,
    228n. 31, 229n. 17, 230n. 18
Cyprian, 74
Cyril of Jerusalem, 8
Dalgairns, J. D., 14, 42
Deconstruction, 97
Decorum, 102
Deen, Leanard, 60
DeLaura, David J., 3, 225, 239n. 42
Demonstration. *See also* Newman:
                Demonstration; Reason
    Aristotle, 104
    first principles, 20
    in literature, 101
    Liberalism, 46
    rhetorical, 154
    scientific, 29, 54, 71, 89, 91—92, 126,
        127, 163—164, 165, 170, 198
Demos, Raphael, 215
Depersonalization, 129
Descartes. *See also* Epistemology
    and Newman, 106
    and Ramus, 103
    doubt, 46, 192
    idealism, 115
    ideas, 115
    knowledge, 118
    method, 99
    the senses, 110, 116
Dessain, C. S., 3

Dialectic, 82, 88—89, 91—92, 96, 99, 103.
    See also Agricola
Doubt, 46, 170, 192
Duke of Norfolk, 224
Edinburgh Review, 66
Educational subjectivism, 98
Empiricism, 105, 122, 123, 124, 162.
    see also Locke
Enthymeme, 22
Epistemology, 46, 125, 219. *See also under*
    Aquinas; Locke; Newman
    Descartes, 107, 108, 116—118
Evans, G. R., 178, 241n. 56
Example, 22
Fall, the, 216, 218, 223. *See also under*
    Aquinas; Newman
Felix, Minicius, 74
Ferreira, M. Jamie, 240n. 7
Feyerabend, Paul, 215
Fish, Stanley, 5, 10, 238n. 30
Fisher, Walter, 215
Foucault, Michel, 215
Fraser, Hilary, 62, 228n. 37, 237n. 6
Froude, Hurrell, 17
Froude, J. A., 40
Froude, William, 2, 163, 187
Gadamer, Hans-Georg, 215
Garrigou-Lagrange, R. M., 34, 53
Gibbon, Edward, 200, 202
Gilson, Etienne, 14, 125, 131, 158, 213,
        228
    on Descartes, 116, 117
    on Locke, 123
    on Newman, 169, 171
    on Thomistic epistemology, 112, 113,
        133
Grassi, Ernesto, 215
Gregory the Great, St.
    Cura Pastoralis, 85
Habermas, Jurgen, 215
Harrold, C. F. 239n. 45
Hawkins, Edward, 1
Hegel, G. W. F., 120
Holloway, John, 3, 200, 227n. 12, 229n.
    17, 241n. 56, 244n. 35
Homer, 78
Hopkins, Gerard Manley, 187, 233n. 38
Horace,
    Ars Poetica, 77—78
Houghton, Walter, 3, 41, 227n. 12
Hume, David, 46, 76, 119, 124, 141, 173
Husserl, Edmund, 7, 120
Huxley, T. H., 17, 41, 52
Idealism, 105. *See also* Descartes
Illative sense, 106, 136. *See also under*
    Newman
Imitation. *See* St. Augustine

Intersubjectivity, 5, 138, 139. *See also* Jost
Isidore of Seville,
    Etymologia, 81
Isocrates, 81
Jaki, Stanley, 116, 119, 125, 163, 164,
    193, 215, 245n. 14
James, William, 38
Jerome, St., 75
Jost, Walter, 4—5, 6, 17, 156—157, 205,
        217, 224
    dogma, 214
    indeterminacy, 114, 138, 208, 209, 210,
        211, 215, 218
    interpretive thought, 210, 211
    intersubjectivity, 208, 211
    knowledge, 207—208, 213
    method, 211, 212
    Newman and rhetorical thought, 206,
        220
    reduction of sciences to rhetoric, 10, 92,
        214
    topics, 15, 212, 215
    truth, 208, 210, 212, 213
Justin, Martyr, 74
Kant, 46, 116, 119, 163, 212
Kaufman, Gordon, 215
Keble, John, 17
Ker, Ian, 193, 243n. 30
Knowledge. *See also* Agricola; Aquinas;
        Aristotle; Descartes: knowledge;
        Epistemology; Newman:
        knowledge; Ramus; Truth
    and Newman, 104, 185
    and the senses, 110
    connatural, 242n. 60
    education, 66—67
    ennunciation (orality), 92—95
    in Aquinas, 109—114, 133, 138, 219
    in Aristotle, 20—21, 137
        practical, 25—27
        rhetorical, 29
    in books, 67—69
    in Descartes, 117
    in the Church Fathers and Middle Ages,
        75—76, 78, 83, 85
    in the 19th century, 125—126
    of particulars, 113, 114
    personal, 65
    Renaissance shift, 87, 92, 97—98, 99,
        103, 105
    scientific, 73—74
Kung, Hans, 215
Lactantius, 74
Language, 80, 81, 222. *See also* Augustine,
    St.; Communication; Newman: language
Lash, Nicholas, 5

Learning, 79, 80, 81, 83, 85, 94. *See also*
    Communication; Language; Newman:
    education
Leibniz, Gottfried Wilhelm, 118, 119
Leo XIII, Pope, 14, 106
Liberal education, 32, 38
Liberalism, 32, 45—46, 161, 224, 273n. 6
Locke, John. *See also* Empiricism
    and assent, 169—170
    and Descsartes, 121
    empiricism, 114, 115, 122, 162
    epistemology, 121, 123
    Newman's interest in, 6, 8, 14, 46, 76,
        121
    reflexivity, 138
    the senses, 110
    Essay Concerning Human Understanding,
        120
Logic. *See also* Newman: formal inference
    and method, 99
    Aristotle, 92—93
    Newman, 12, 23, 59
    Peter of Spain, 88—90
    topical, 96
Lombard, Peter, 14
Malebranche, N., 118, 119
Manning, Cardinal, 52
Maritain, Jacques, 14, 109, 125, 131, 132,
    133, 158, 232n. 5, 242n. 60
Marston, Roger, 115
Material science, 125—126
Maurus, Rabanus,
    De institutione clericorum, 82
McGowan, James P., 133
McKeon, Richard, 5, 6, 17, 207—209
Mechanistic thought, 105, 126, 131, 143,
    187
Medieval schools, 10, 134. *See also under*
    Newman
Medieval education, 88, 90
Melancthon, Philipp, 90
Metaphysics, 46, 93, 120, 125. *See also*
        Aristotle; Newman
    Thomistic, 106—108, 110, 123, 132
Method, 99—100, 103, 108, 129, 202. *See*
    also under Jost; Ramus
    scholastic, 134
Meynell, Dr. Charles, 11
Mill, John Stuart, 38, 98
Mitford, Mary Russell, 40
More, St. Thomas, 88
Murphy, James J., 75, 79, 80, 82, 84
Murray, Placid, 2, 32
Newman, John Henry,
    abstraction, 166—167
    analogy, 149

Newman (*continued*)
  and education, 65—70, 134, 135, 221.
    See also Learning
  and gentlemanliness, 31-32, 36—37, 56
  apologetics, 47—48
  apprehension, 166—168, 173, 195,
    210—211
  Aquinas, 8, 10, 12, 13—14, 134, 120,
    156, 189, 200, 207, 241n. 56,
    243n. 17
  argument, 231n. 54. *See also* Newman:
    apologetics
  Aristotle, 6, 7—8, 12,13, 63, 165, 198
  Arnold, Dr. Thomas, 1—2. *See also*
    Arnold, Dr. Thomas
  as a modernist, 215
  as a philosopher, 3, 11, 15, 130, 131,
    193
  as a rhetorician, 157—158, 239n. 57
  as a theologian, 3, 15, 232n. 17
  assent, 85, 164, 165, 169—176, 195,
    197, 201
  being, 147
  biographies of saints, 59—60
  certitude, 176—179, 185, 188, 195, 196,
    198, 202, 203, 207
  certitude, indefectibility of, 177—179,
    199, 241n. 58, 243n. 30
  Church Fathers, 8, 30, 59, 60, 61, 64.
    See also Church Fathers
  conscience, 175—176
  demonstration, 28, 146
  depersonalization, 126—127, 193
  "Discipline and Influence," 61
  dogma, 175
  doubt, 46, 170, 192
  epistemology, 14, 128, 142. *See also*
    Newman: knowledge; Newman:
    truth
  Fall, the, 33—34, 54, 64
  first principles, 142, 181, 242n. 63
  idea of perfection, 55
  illative sense, 20, 188—189, 203, 216,
    217, 219
  inference, 165, 242n. 67
    formal, 179—182, 202—203
    informal, 182—184, 186,
      189, 190
  intellectual sympathy, 41—42, 44
  knowledge, 26, 133, 153, 164, 196,
    202, 206, 221. *See also*
    Newman: truth
  language, 68, 222
  liberalism, 237n. 6. *See also*
    Liberalism
  Locke. *See* Locke
  manner of speaking, 43

  matter, 140—141
  medieval schools, 66, 214, 215
  memory, 210—211
  metaphysics, 11, 14—15, 49, 107
  modernism, 130
  nominalism, 147—148
  orality, 70. *See also* Newman:
    education
  pastoral purpose, 31—32, 34—35, 67
  personal influence, 49, 57—59, 71
  personalism, 51, 54, 59, 65, 67, 71,
    74, 95, 96, 98, 135, 138, 193,
    220, 224
  personalism in theology, 61—63
  persuasion, 35, 38, 167
  philosophy of rhetoric, 4
  practical, the, 33, 49, 155
  practical orientation, 33
  probability, 23, 146, 156—157, 164,
    170, 183, 186, 190, 196, 198,
    243n. 29. *See also* Probability
  proof from conscience, 151—154
  reason, 144, 150. *See also* Newman:
    knowledge
  rhetorical art, 201, 233n. 38
  rhetorical knowledge, 128, 138, 184—
    185, 189, 191, 196—199
  rhetorical mode of thought, 3, 5, 6, 7,
    15, 16, 31, 74, 85, 105, 137,
    140, 153—155, 183, 188, 190,
    203, 220, 221—223
  rhetorical personalism, 151, 161, 220
  rhetorical purpose, 143, 146
  rhetorical realism, 201, 206, 220—223
  rhetoric of conduct, 37—39, 56, 72
  sense perception, 141, 144—145, 149,
    195
  sermons, 9
  skepticism, 8, 47—48, 49, 131, 141,
    180, 191—193, 243n. 1. *See also*
    under Weatherby
  solipsism, 127
  spirit, 140
  students, 40
  "Tamworth Reading Room," 136
  truth, 15, 150, 191—192, 195,
    196—199, 207, 221. *See also*
    Truth; Newman: knowledge
  university discourses, 44—45
  will, the, 63—64
  Apologia, 2, 31, 33, 51, 60, 161
  Callista, 61
  Development of Christian Doctrine, 13
  Devotions and Meditations, 55
  Discourses Before Mixed Congregations,
    9
  Dream of Gerontius, 225

Grammar of Assent, 4, 11, 13, 16, 27, 30, 105, 135, 140, 157, 161—190, 223
  its purpose, 162—164
  religious assent, 174—175
  as a rhetorical text, 162, 164—165, 168, 175—176, 179, 194, 203, 205
Historical Sketches, 59
Idea of a University, 9, 13, 36, 168, 214, 223
Oxford University Sermons, 136, 161
Philosophical Notebook, 6, 16, 36, 105, 131, 139, 140-157, 161, 164, 206
Present Position of Catholics in England, 9, 45, 57
Rise and Progress of Universities, 67
Neri, St. Phillip, 32, 38, 56
Nuttall A. D., 7, 55, 122, 123, 124, 125, 127, 138, 155, 172, 215, 245n. 44
O'Donoghue, N. D., 193
Ong, Walter J., 89, 90, 92, 93, 94, 95, 97, 101, 102, 104, 105, 118
  Ramus and Talon Inventory, 103
  Ramus, Method, and the Decay of Dialogue, 87
Orality, 80, 81, 82, 83, 85, 222. *See also* Communication; Newman
Oratory, 32, 37, 42, 55—57
Owens, Joseph, 38, 107, 108, 131, 134, 158
Oxford
  education in, 13, 65, 66, 67
  Newman at, 1, 35, 39—40, 224—225
Oxford Movement, 1, 17, 31, 32
Oxford Noetics, 8
Paley, William, 8
Passions, the, 24
Paul, St. 76
Pedagogy, 98
Pembroke, Berkeley of, 39
Percy, Walker, 231n. 34
Perelman, Chaim, 5, 207, 215
Perrone, Giovanni, 8, 155
Person, the, 52—54
Personalism, 20th century, 232n. 6. *See also under* Newman
Persuasion, 18, 48, 84, 85, 137
Peter of Spain, 88—91, 139
  Summulae logicales, 88—90
Phenomenology, 7, 120, 220, 240n. 7
Philosophy, 7—8, 10, 18, 20, 36, 49, 120, 209. *See also* Aquinas, Aristotle, Newman
Pieper, Josef, 14, 131, 133, 134, 135, 158
  docilitas, 217, 218

memoria, 217, 218
prudence, 216—219
solertia, 217
Prudence, 216
The Silence of St. Thomas: Three Essays, 132
Pius IX, Pope, 44
Plato, 10, 74, 111, 115, 122, 123
  Phaedrus, 79
Poetic reasoning, 101
Polanyi, Michael, 207, 215
Practical wisdom, 54, 216—219. *See also* Aristotle: practical knowledge
Pragmatism, 214
Preaching, 39, 83—85
Predicable, 93
Prejudice, 2, 57—58, 231n. 46
Prickett, Stephen, 228n. 37, 237n. 6
Priscian
  Institutiones grammaticae, 81
Probability. *See also under* Newman
  province of rhetoric, 21—23, 29
  and Newman, 86, 146, 154
  in Peter of Spain, 89—91
  and Descartes, 117
Probable reasoning, 18, 28—29, 90, 91, 100
Proof, 163
Prudence, 219
Psychology, 7, 9, 19
  psychologism, 127
Quintilian, 78, 79, 81, 91, 100
  Institutio oratoria, 77
Rambler, 31
Ramus, Peter. *See also* Agricola
  and rhetoric, 100, 102
  as a humanist, 87, 90
  confusion of probable logic, 91—92
  dialectic, 96
  mechanistic reasoning, 97, 117, 118
  method, 99—100, 101, 202
  pedagogy, 99
  predication, 95
  Ramist logic, 88
  topical logic, 99
  Remarks on Aristotle, 99
  Structure of Dialectic, 99
Rationalism, 136, 163—164. *See also* Kant
Realism, metaphyical, 113, 115. *See also* Aquinas; Aristotle; Newman: rhetorical realism
Reality, accessibility of, 143
Reason, 5, 33, 34, 35—36, 96, 143, 179. *See also* Knowledge
Reid, Thomas, 6, 8, 113
Relativism, 7
Renaissance. *See also* Ramus; Agricola

Renaissance (*continued*)
  and logic, 90
  and method, 103
  antischolasticism, 106
  humanism, 87
  idea of discourse, 73, 92
  idea of knowledge, 16, 92, 97—98
  oratory, 100
Reynolds, Sir Joshua, 11
Rhetoric, 5, 10, 17—30, 206
  intellectual potential of, 6, 7, 15, 30
  proper use of, 19
  rhetorical art, 18, 23—24, 27, 84—85.
      See also Newman: rhetorical art
  rhetorical education, 74, 77—79, 82,
      238n. 29
  rhetorical faculty, 18, 19
  rhetorical forma, 76
  rhetorical knowledge, 128, 156, 240n. 4.
      See also under Newman
  rhetorical personalism, 78, 83, 85, 101,
      102. *See also under* Newman
Ricoeur, Paul, 215
Robert of Basevorn, 84
Roberts, W. Rhys, 19
Romantic Movement, 127, 223
Rorty, Richard, 208, 215
Ruskin, John, 17
Salisbury, John of
  Metalogicon, 82,
Scientism, 66, 74, 159, 161, 173
Scott, Sir Walter, 42
Scotus, Duns, 115
"Second Sophistic," 75—76
Selby, Robin C., 227n. 12, 230n. 8, 243n.
  1
Shairp, Principle, 9
Sidney, Sir Phillip, 101
Sillem, Edward
  on Newman and ideology, 137
  on Newman and philosophy, 6—7, 10,
      13, 14, 121, 138—139
  The Philosophical Notebook, 135
Skepticism. *See also under* Newman
  and impossibility of certitude, 178
  and Richard McKeon, 209
  and scientific rationalism, 239n. 42
  growth of philosophical, 126, 133
  intersubjectivity and, 139
  Newman and, 7, 163
  19th-century, 161
Solipsism, 7, 120, 122, 124, 126, 127, 212
Sophistry, 7. *See also* "Second Sophistic"
Spinoza, B., 118, 119
St. John, Ambrose, 42
Stephen, Leslie, 122
Structuralism, 97

Suarez, Francis, 90
Subjectivism, 7. *See also* Skepticism
Summa Theologica, see Aquinas, St.
  Thomas
Svaglic, Martin, 3, 227n. 12, 229n. 2
Synesius of Cyrene, 74
Talbot, Monsignor, 55
Talon, Omer,
  Training in Oratory, 100
Tertullian, 74
Theology, 10, 13, 214—215. *See also under*
  Newman
Therese, St., of Lisieux, 55
Thomistic epistemology. *See* Metaphysics:
  Thomistic
Thought
  mechanistic, 96, 107—108, 117. *See*
      also Method; Rationalism
  schematic, 107
Tillotson, Geoffrey, 246n. 61
Topics, 89, 104. *See also* Agricola
Toulmin, Steven, 5, 215
Tracy, David, 215
Tractarian Movement, 36, 40
Trevor, Meriol, 2, 39
Trivium, 74
Truth, 16, 63—65, 66, 69, 98, 136, 164,
      168, 185. *See also* Aquinas; Aristotle;
          Knowledge; Newman
  and rhetoric, 72, 84, 139
  as demonstrable, 67, 117
  Augustine, St., 80
  in Aristotle, 19—20s, 28—29
      rhetorical truth, 20—23
  intersubjective agreement, 208
  knowing subjects
Tucker, Abraham, 135
Ullathorne, Bishop, 41
Understanding, 28
Universals, 21, 113
Utilitarianism, 73
Valesio, Paolo, 215
Vargish, Thomas, 164, 227n. 20
Verdeke, Gerard, 162, 187
Virgil, 42
Voltaire, 121
Walgrave, J. H., 6, 7, 227n. 20
  Newman the Theologian, 162, 230n. 7
Ward, Wilfrid, 41, 42,
Ward, W. D., 52, 155
  On Nature and God, 151
Weatherby, Harold
  Christian poetry, 237n. 5
  epistemology, 112—113
  God's image in creation, 33, 244n. 34
  Newman's philosophical modernism,
      129—132

Newman's skepticism, 7, 35, 156, 158,
        180, 191, 198, 206, 207
    rhetorical argument, 239n. 57
    Cardinal Newman in His Age, 129
    The Keen Delight, 129, 237n. 5
Whately, Richard, 12, 22
William of Champeaux,147-148
William of Ockham, 115

DATE DUE

			Printed in USA